THE BAKER BOOK OF
BIBLE
CHARTS, MAPS,
AND TIME LINES

JOHN A. BECK

BakerBooks

a division of Baker Publishing Group
Grand Rapids, Michigan

© 2016 by Baker Publishing Group

Published by Baker Books
a division of Baker Publishing Group
P.O. Box 6287, Grand Rapids, MI 49516-6287
www.bakerbooks.com

Printed in the United States of America

Library of Congress Cataloging-in-Publication Data
Names: Beck, John A., 1956–
Title: The Baker Book of Bible charts, maps, and time lines / John A. Beck.
Description: Grand Rapids, MI : Baker Books, 2016. | Includes index.
Identifiers: LCCN 2015045545 | ISBN 9780801017124 (pbk.)
Subjects: LCSH: Bible—Handbooks, manuals, etc. | Bible—Charts, diagrams, etc. | Bible—Geography—Maps. | Bible—Chronology—Charts, diagrams, etc.
Classification: LCC BS417 .B43 2016 | DDC 220.9/1022—dc23
LC record available at http://lccn.loc.gov/2015045545

Interior design by William Overbeeke

16 17 18 19 20 21 22   7 6 5 4 3 2 1

Contents

Charts

Archaeology of the Old Testament   126

Illustrations or Reconstructions

Part Three New Testament

New Testament Time Line   153

New Testament Maps

Charts

Archaeology of the New Testament   208

Illustrations or Reconstructions

PART ONE

GENERAL BIBLE

General Time Line

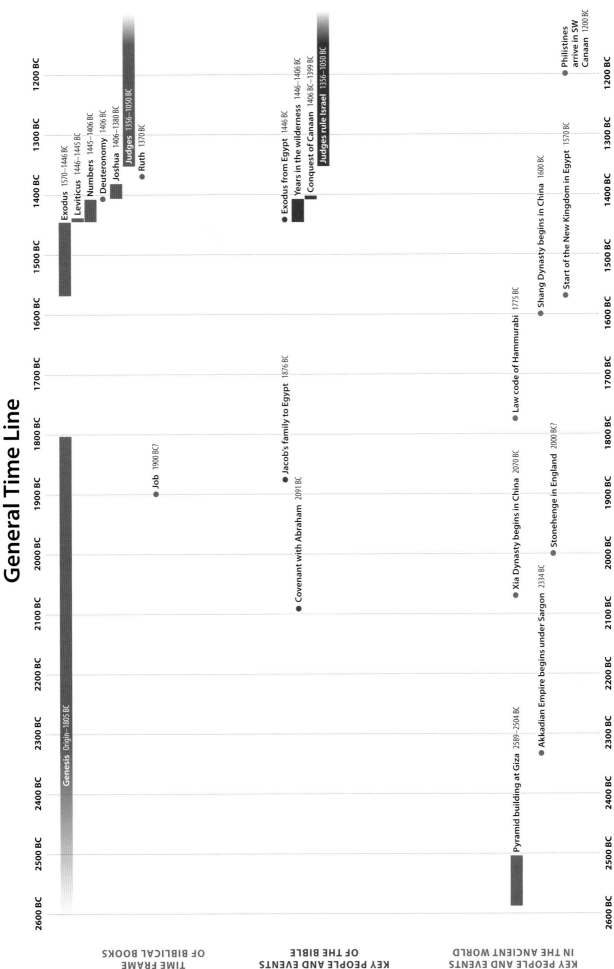

TIME FRAME OF BIBLICAL BOOKS

Genesis Origin–1805 BC

Exodus 1570–1446 BC
Leviticus 1446–1445 BC
Numbers 1445–1406 BC
Deuteronomy 1406 BC
Joshua 1406–1380 BC
Judges 1356–1050 BC
Ruth 1370 BC

Job 1900 BC?

KEY PEOPLE AND EVENTS OF THE BIBLE

Covenant with Abraham 2091 BC
Jacob's family to Egypt 1876 BC
Exodus from Egypt 1446 BC
Years in the wilderness 1446–1406 BC
Conquest of Canaan 1406 BC–1399 BC
Judges rule Israel 1356–1050 BC

KEY PEOPLE AND EVENTS IN THE ANCIENT WORLD

Pyramid building at Giza 2589–2504 BC
Akkadian Empire begins under Sargon 2334 BC
Xia Dynasty begins in China 2070 BC
Stonehenge in England 2000 BC?
Law code of Hammurabi 1775 BC
Shang Dynasty begins in China 1600 BC
Start of the New Kingdom in Egypt 1570 BC
Philistines arrive in SW Canaan 1200 BC

2600 BC 2500 BC 2400 BC 2300 BC 2200 BC 2100 BC 2000 BC 1900 BC 1800 BC 1700 BC 1600 BC 1500 BC 1400 BC 1300 BC 1200 BC

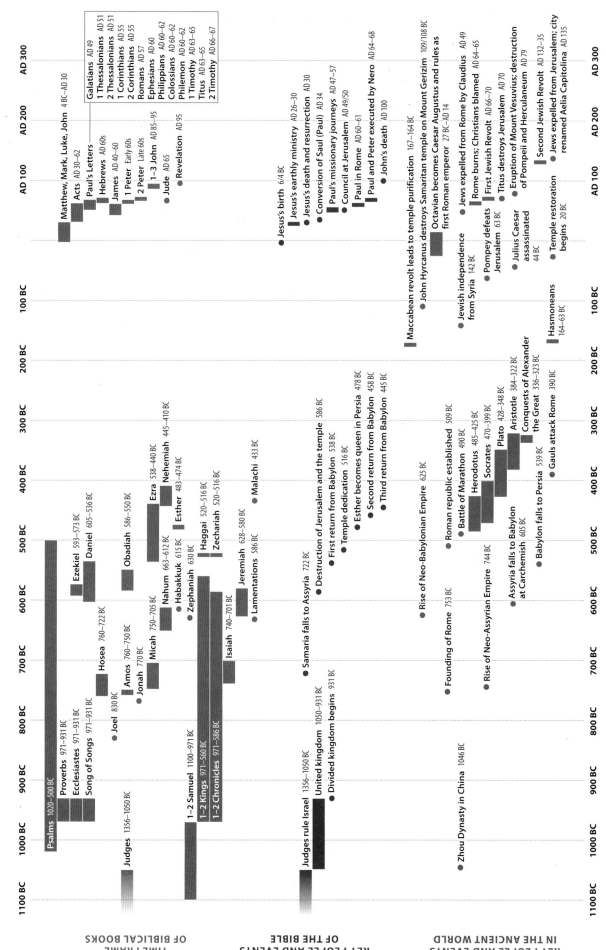

TIME FRAME OF BIBLICAL BOOKS

Psalms 1020–500 BC
Proverbs 971–931 BC
Ecclesiastes 971–931 BC
Song of Songs 971–931 BC
Judges 1356–1050 BC
Joel 830 BC
Jonah 770 BC
Amos 760–750 BC
Hosea 760–722 BC
Micah 750–705 BC
Nahum 663–612 BC
Habakkuk 615 BC
Zephaniah 630 BC
Obadiah 586–550 BC
Isaiah 740–701 BC
Jeremiah 628–580 BC
Lamentations 586 BC
Ezekiel 593–573 BC
Daniel 605–931 BC
Ezra 538–440 BC
Nehemiah 445–410 BC
Esther 483–474 BC
Haggai 520–516 BC
Zechariah 520–516 BC
Malachi 433 BC
1–2 Samuel 1100–971 BC
1–2 Kings 971–560 BC
1–2 Chronicles 971–586 BC
Matthew, Mark, Luke, John 4 BC–AD 30
Acts AD 30–62
Paul's Letters AD 60s
Hebrews AD 60s
James AD 40–60
1 Peter Early 60s
2 Peter Late 60s
Jude AD 65
1–3 John AD 85–95
Revelation AD 95

Galatians AD 49
1 Thessalonians AD 51
2 Thessalonians AD 51
1 Corinthians AD 55
2 Corinthians AD 55
Romans AD 57
Ephesians AD 60
Philippians AD 60–62
Colossians AD 60–62
Philemon AD 60–62
1 Timothy AD 63–65
Titus AD 63–65
2 Timothy AD 66–67

KEY PEOPLE AND EVENTS OF THE BIBLE

United kingdom 1050–931 BC
Divided kingdom begins 931 BC
Samaria falls to Assyria 722 BC
Destruction of Jerusalem and the temple 586 BC
First return from Babylon 538 BC
Temple dedication 516 BC
Esther becomes queen in Persia 478 BC
Second return from Babylon 458 BC
Third return from Babylon 445 BC
Jesus's birth 6/4 BC
Jesus's earthly ministry AD 26–30
Jesus's death and resurrection AD 30
Conversion of Saul (Paul) AD 34
Paul's missionary journeys AD 47–57
Council at Jerusalem AD 49/50
Paul in Rome AD 60–61
Paul and Peter executed by Nero AD 64–68
John's death AD 100

KEY PEOPLE AND EVENTS IN THE ANCIENT WORLD

Zhou Dynasty in China 1046 BC
Judges rule Israel 1356–1050 BC
Founding of Rome 753 BC
Rise of Neo-Assyrian Empire 744 BC
Assyria falls to Babylon at Carchemish 605 BC
Babylon falls to Persia 539 BC
Rise of Neo-Babylonian Empire 625 BC
Roman republic established 509 BC
Battle of Marathon 490 BC
Herodotus 485–425 BC
Socrates 470–399 BC
Plato 428–348 BC
Aristotle 384–322 BC
Conquests of Alexander the Great 336–323 BC
Gauls attack Rome 390 BC
Maccabean revolt leads to temple purification 167–164 BC
John Hyrcanus destroys Samaritan temple on Mount Gerizim 109/108 BC
Octavian becomes Caesar Augustus and rules as first Roman emperor 27 BC–AD 14
Jewish independence from Syria 142 BC
Pompey defeats Jerusalem 63 BC
Julius Caesar assassinated 44 BC
Temple restoration begins 20 BC
Hasmoneans 164–63 BC
Jews expelled from Rome by Claudius AD 49
Rome burns; Christians blamed AD 64–65
First Jewish Revolt AD 66–70
Titus destroys Jerusalem AD 70
Eruption of Mount Vesuvius; destruction of Pompeii and Herculaneum AD 79
Second Jewish Revolt AD 132–35
Jews expelled from Jerusalem; city renamed Aelia Capitolina AD 135

1100 BC   1000 BC   900 BC   800 BC   700 BC   600 BC   500 BC   400 BC   300 BC   200 BC   100 BC   AD 100   AD 200   AD 300

Ancient Near East and Its Road Systems

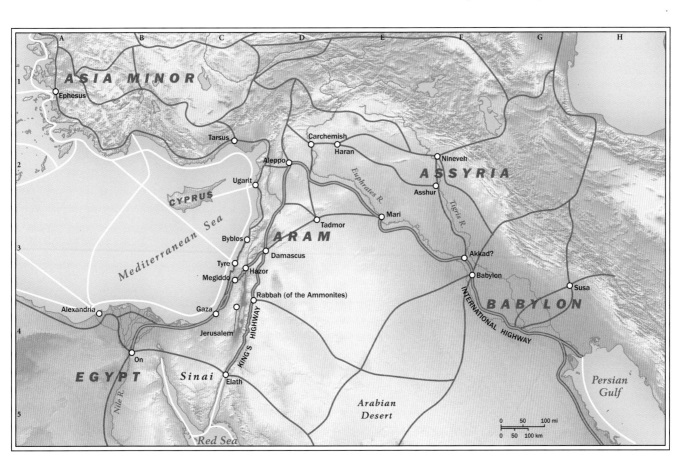

Modern Mediterranean World

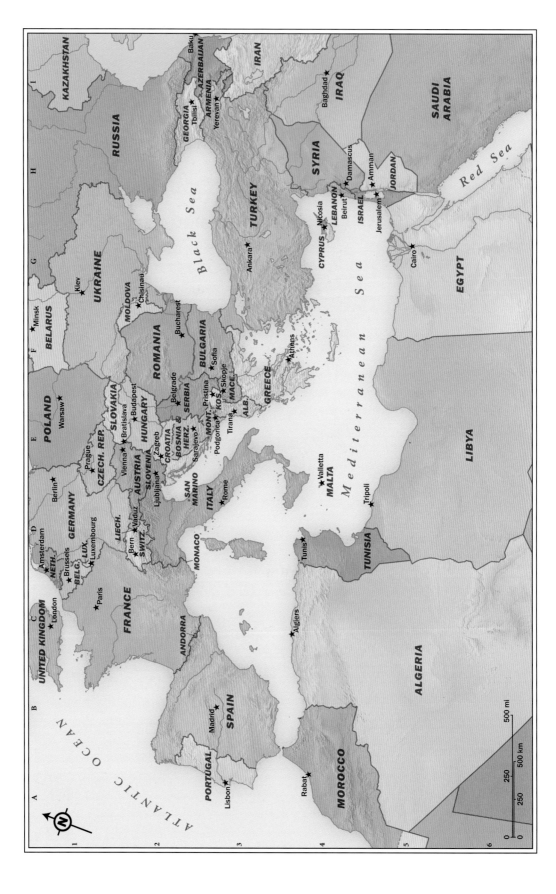

Old and New Testament Cities in the Promised Land

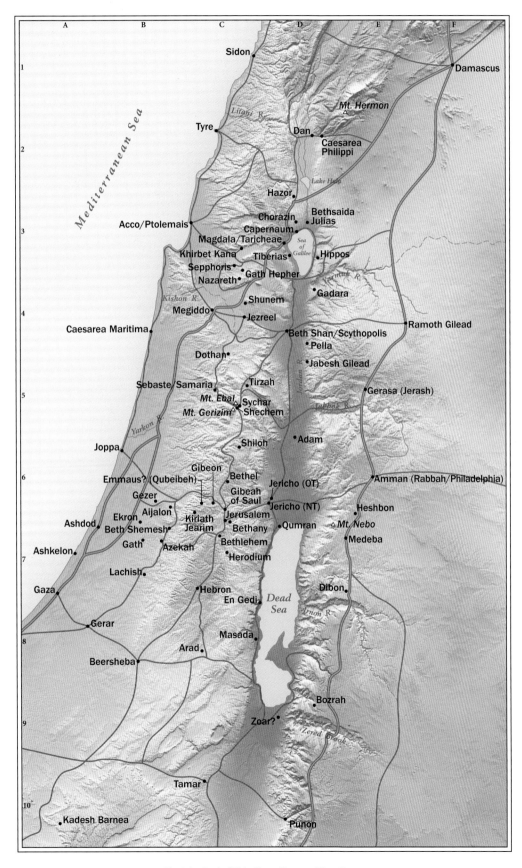

Geographical Zones of the Promised Land

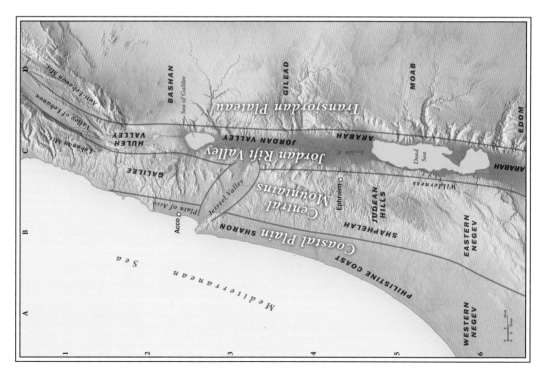

Rainfall in the Promised Land

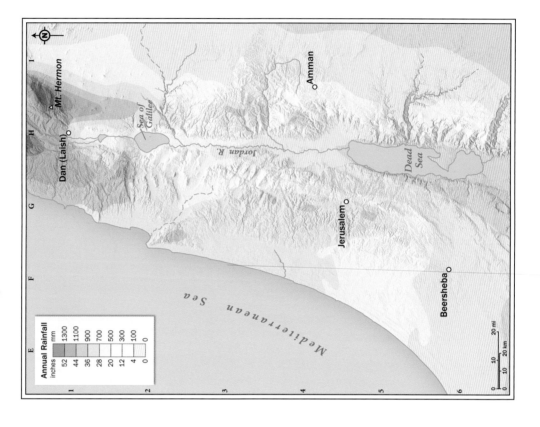

Road Systems in the Promised Land

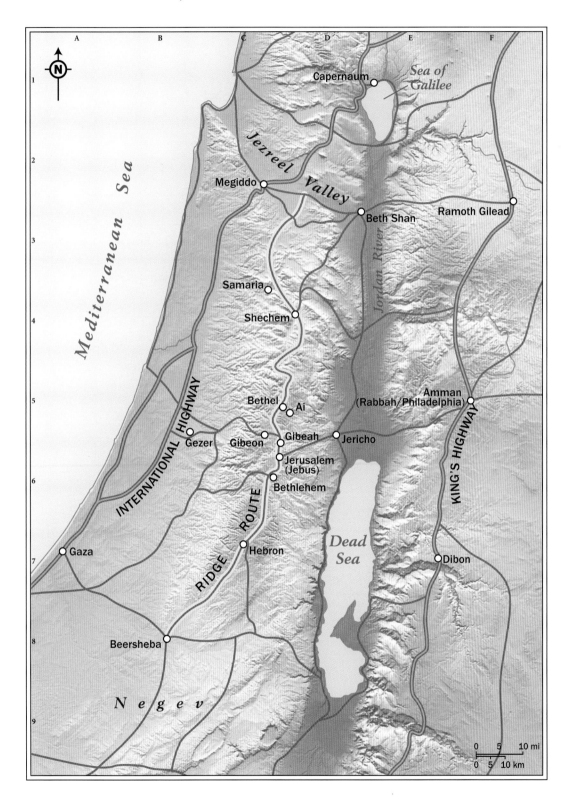

The Bible's Human Side

The Bible is a collection of books with a human side.

Key Bible Passage

2 Peter 1:21

Facts

- The Bible was written by about forty individuals who came from a wide variety of backgrounds, including politics, medicine, shepherding, fishing, and tax collecting.
- The Bible was written from the fifteenth century BC to the first century AD.
- The Bible was written in various places, including Africa, the Middle East, and Europe.
- The Bible was written in known languages: Hebrew, Aramaic, and Greek.

Impact

- Bible books differ from one another in writing style.
- Bible books include references to the geography and culture of the people who wrote them.
- Bible books will present the world using the scientific perspective of the author's era.
- Bible books may present the same thoughts of God from differing perspectives.
- Bible books sound real and relevant because they flow from the lives of real people who have experienced the same issues in life we face.

The Bible's Divine Side

The Bible is a collection of books that present the thoughts of God.

Key Bible Passages

John 17:17
1 Corinthians 2:13
2 Timothy 3:16–17
2 Peter 1:20–21

Facts

- The Bible came to be through a supernatural process called divine inspiration.
- The Holy Spirit moved the thoughts of God into writing through human hands without extinguishing each writer's unique background, vocabulary, and writing style.
- The Holy Spirit prevented the writers from introducing errors in what they wrote.
- The Bible presents insights into life and living unavailable in any other source.

Impact

- The Bible is true in all that it asserts as truth.
- The Bible is worthy of our attention and trust.
- The Bible provides life-changing answers to the big questions in life.

Bible Book Overview

Genesis

This book of beginnings presents the origin of the world and its ruin by sin before revealing God's plan to redeem the world through a Savior who is linked to the chosen people, Israel, a nation descended from Abraham's family.

Organization

1. Our world created and ruined—Genesis 1–11
2. God's rescue plan and Abraham's family—Genesis 12–50

Key Content

The fall into sin—Genesis 3:1–24
First promise of a Savior—Genesis 3:15
Covenant with Noah—Genesis 9:8–17
Covenant with Abraham's family—Genesis 12:1–7; 15:1–21; 17:1–16

Exodus

With Moses in the lead, the Lord brings Israel out of slavery in Egypt to Mount Sinai, where he organizes them as his covenant people.

Organization

1. Israel in Egypt—Exodus 1–11
2. From Egypt to Sinai—Exodus 12–18
3. The Mosaic covenant and law code—Exodus 19–40

Key Content

God calls Moses to lead Israel—Exodus 3:1–4:17
The ten plagues—Exodus 7:14–12:30
Red Sea crossing—Exodus 13:17–14:31
Ten Commandments—Exodus 20:1–17
Golden calf—Exodus 32:1–35

Leviticus

God gives detailed instructions on how Israel is to think, live, and worship as his holy nation set apart from all others as his covenant people.

Organization

1. Instructions on becoming holy—Leviticus 1–16
2. Instructions on maintaining holiness (Holiness Code)—Leviticus 17–27

Key Content

Call to be holy—Leviticus 11:45; 19:2; 20:26

Kosher food laws—Leviticus 11:1–47; 17:1–16
Day of Atonement—Leviticus 16:1–34

Numbers

Although Israel had developed into a sizable nation, its faith has not grown with their numbers. This record of Israel's thirty-eight years in the wilderness is marked by repeated rebellion and divine punishment as Israel edges closer but fails to enter the promised land.

Organization

1. Census and preparation to leave Mount Sinai—Numbers 1–9
2. Rebellion and wilderness wandering—Numbers 10–25
3. Preparations to enter the promised land—Numbers 26–36

Key Content

Rebellion against Moses's leadership—Numbers 12:1–16
Rebellion of people following promised-land report—Numbers 13:1–14:45
Rebellion against Aaron—Numbers 16:1–50
Rebellion of Moses—Numbers 20:1–13
Rebellion of Balaam—Numbers 22:1–35

Deuteronomy

This book presents a series of addresses given by Moses to the Israelites as he is about to die and as they are about to enter the promised land. These addresses contain a mix of history and law designed to encourage Israel's absolute allegiance to the covenant and their obligations defined within it.

Organization

1. Historical overview—Deuteronomy 1–4
2. Terms of the covenant—Deuteronomy 5–26
3. Final warning and encouragement—Deuteronomy 27–34

Key Content

Ten Commandments—Deuteronomy 5:1–21
Shema—Deuteronomy 6:4–9
Blessing and curses—Deuteronomy 28:1–68
Death of Moses—Deuteronomy 34:1–12

Joshua

Israel defeats the major Canaanite urban centers in multiple battles, thereby fulfilling the land promise the Lord made to Abraham. The conquered land is then divided proportionally among the twelve tribes of Israel.

Organization

1. Conquest of the promised land—Joshua 1–12
2. Division of the promised land—Joshua 13–21
3. The witness altar and Joshua's final word—Joshua 22–24

Key Content

Rahab hides the spies—Joshua 2
Crossing the Jordan River—Joshua 3–4
The fall of Jericho—Joshua 6
Covenant renewal at Shechem—Joshua 8:30–35; 24:1–27

Judges

Israel's failure to complete the conquest left Canaanites in the land, which has fostered Israel's assimilation to pagan worship and ideology. Judges presents a series of individual stories organized into a pattern that shows the people of God trapped in a deteriorating cycle of apostasy and punishment caused by their covenant infidelity.

Organization

1. The final conquest fails—Judges 1–2
2. Six episodes of apostasy, oppression, and deliverance—Judges 3–16
3. Chaos reigns—Judges 17–21

Key Content

Ehud—Judges 3:12–30
Deborah—Judges 4–5
Gideon—Judges 6–8
Samson—Judges 13–16

Ruth

During the troubled time of the Judges, Ruth the Moabite and Boaz the Israelite illustrate the faithfulness and kindness that flow from a healthy relationship with the Lord; in turn the Lord shows the blessings he is eager to shower on those who live this faith-filled life. Ruth becomes the great-grandmother of David and an ancestor of Jesus.

Organization

1. Ruth connects with Israel and the Lord—Ruth 1
2. Ruth meets Boaz—Ruth 2
3. Ruth and Boaz become a family—Ruth 3–4

Key Content

Your God is my God—Ruth 1:16–17
Genealogy of David—Ruth 4:13–22

1–2 Samuel

This pair of books tells the story of Israel's transition from the moral and political uncertainty of the time of the judges to the nation's greater stability and success under the monarchy. Israel's king is to rule as a champion of the Mosaic covenant and as a model of David's greater son, the Messiah, who will rule an eternal kingdom.

Organization

1. The days of Samuel—1 Samuel 1–7
2. The days of Samuel and Saul—1 Samuel 8–15
3. The days of Saul and David—1 Samuel 16–21
4. The days of David—2 Samuel 1–24

Key Content

The call of Samuel—1 Samuel 3
Ark narratives—1 Samuel 4–6
Israel asks for a king—1 Samuel 8:6, 20
David and Goliath—1 Samuel 17
Saul's death—1 Samuel 31
Jerusalem becomes the capital city—2 Samuel 5:6–12
The ark of the covenant to Jerusalem—2 Samuel 6
The Davidic covenant—2 Samuel 7:8–16
David and Bathsheba—2 Samuel 11

1–2 Kings

This pair of books presents the rule of Solomon, the division of his kingdom, and the spiritual decline of both Israel and Judah, which culminates in their exile from the promised land. They illustrate that the rising and falling fortunes of these kings and their subjects are related to their wavering dedication to the Mosaic covenant.

Organization

1. Solomon—1 Kings 1–11
2. The divided kingdom of Israel and Judah—1 Kings 12–2 Kings 17
3. Judah—2 Kings 18–25

Key Content

Solomon's wisdom—1 Kings 3
Temple construction and dedication—1 Kings 5–8
Queen of Sheba visits—1 Kings 10:1–13
Kingdom divides—1 Kings 12:1–24
Golden calf worship—1 Kings 12:25–33
Elijah and the prophets of Baal—1 Kings 18
Naboth's vineyard—1 Kings 21
Elijah taken into heaven—2 Kings 2:1–18
Elisha raises the Shunammite's son—2 Kings 4:8–37
Exile of Israel—2 Kings 17
Hezekiah's reforms—2 Kings 18:1–8

Josiah's reforms—2 Kings 22:1–23:25

Exile of Judah—2 Kings 25:1–21

1–2 Chronicles

This pair of books retells the history of God's people with special emphasis on the time of David, Solomon, and the kings of Judah. While it presents the exile as the price of Israel's sins, the tone is more positive, looking ahead to the future success that obedience to the Mosaic covenant will bring.

Organization

1. Genealogies from Adam to the return from exile—1 Chronicles 1–9
2. David's reign—1 Chronicles 10–29
3. Solomon's reign—2 Chronicles 1–9
4. Kings of Judah—2 Chronicles 10–36

Key Content

Death of Saul—1 Chronicles 10

David captures Jerusalem—1 Chronicles 11:4–9

Davidic covenant—1 Chronicles 17

Solomon's wisdom—2 Chronicles 1:1–12

Temple construction—2 Chronicles 3–4

Kingdom divides—2 Chronicles 10

Hezekiah's reforms—2 Chronicles 29

Josiah's reforms—2 Chronicles 34

Exile and return of Judah—2 Chronicles 36:15–23

Ezra

Judah returns to the promised land from exile and reestablishes temple worship in Jerusalem. But these joy-filled days are complicated with challenges that accompany the temple's reconstruction and with spiritual repair work that needs to occur in the lives of the returning exiles so that they might become the faithful people of God they were called to be.

Organization

1. First return under Zerubbabel—Ezra 1–2
2. Rebuilding the temple and restoration of worship—Ezra 3–6
3. The second return under Ezra and his reforms—Ezra 7–10

Key Content

Decree of Cyrus releasing exiles—Ezra 1:1–4

Temple foundation laid—Ezra 3:7–13

Completion and dedication of the temple—Ezra 6:13–18

The intermarriage problem—Ezra 9:1–10:17

Nehemiah

Nehemiah returns to Jerusalem on a mission to rebuild its defensive walls. However, it is the spiritual rehabilitation of Israel led by Ezra and Nehemiah, not the rebuilt walls, that brings real security for God's people.

Organization

1. Nehemiah rebuilds the walls—Nehemiah 1–7
2. Ezra reads the law and rebuilds the people—Nehemiah 8–12
3. Nehemiah reads the law and rebuilds the people—Nehemiah 13

Key Content

Nehemiah returns from Persia—Nehemiah 2:1–10

Nehemiah's wall inspection—Nehemiah 2:11–18

Dedication of the wall—Nehemiah 12:27–47

Esther

Esther tells the story of a Jewish girl in exile who becomes queen of Persia in order to champion God's plan to rescue his chosen people once again from a government-authorized annihilation. This story forms the basis for the Jewish festival of Purim.

Organization

1. Esther becomes queen—Esther 1:1–2:18
2. Threats revealed—Esther 2:19–3:15
3. Esther counters the critical threat—Esther 4–8
4. The festival of Purim—Esther 9–10

Key Content

Mordecai's passionate appeal to Esther—Esther 4:12–14

Purim established—Esther 9:18–28

Job

This story and extended dialogue explore the cause of the suffering in the life of God's people. Because mortals are unable to rise above the horizon of their own limitations, a satisfactory explanation of every instance of suffering will not be found. Our wearied spirits find rest only in trusting the all-powerful and all-knowing God who loves us.

Organization

1. Job's well-being is taken away—Job 1–2
2. The cause explored via dialogue—Job 3–37
3. God asserts his limitless power and knowledge—Job 38–41
4. Job's well-being is restored—Job 42

Key Content

The Lord gave and the Lord has taken away—Job 1:21

I know my Redeemer lives—Job 19:25

Poem: "Where Can Wisdom Be Found?"—Job 28

Psalms

Psalms is a collection of divinely inspired poetry that puts words to every season of life. Here we find elegantly composed songs of instruction and correction, poems that give voice to our grief and our joy, and refrains to lift our hearts in thanksgiving.

Organization

1. Book one—Psalms 1–41
2. Book two—Psalms 42–72
3. Book three—Psalms 73–89
4. Book four—Psalms 90–106
5. Book five—Psalms 107–150

Key Content

Blessed living—Psalm 1

The Lord is my Shepherd—Psalm 23

God is our refuge and strength—Psalm 46

Have mercy on me—Psalm 51

Praise the Lord—Psalm 103

Songs of ascent—Psalms 120–134

Proverbs

This book is a collection of proverbs or sayings that investigates and teaches the basic knowledge, skills, and attitudes needed to live successfully. Such wise living is grounded in an absolute trust in the Lord.

Organization

1. Introduction to wisdom and its value—Proverbs 1–9
2. Six collections of wise sayings—Proverbs 10–31

Key Content

The fear of the Lord is the beginning of wisdom—Proverbs 1:7

Trust in the Lord with all your heart—Proverbs 3:5

The wife of noble character—Proverbs 31:10–31

Ecclesiastes

Ecclesiastes is a reflection that explores many different pathways that promise a meaningful and satisfying life. The conclusion is that a life lived without God is a life destined for disappointment.

Organization

1. General survey of the paths that promise a meaningful life—Ecclesiastes 1–11
2. Remember your creator—Ecclesiastes 12

Key Content

Everything is meaningless—Ecclesiastes 1:2

There is a time for everything—Ecclesiastes 3:1–8

Fear God and keep his commandments—Ecclesiastes 12:13–14

Song of Songs

This book is a series of lyric poems that celebrate the sexual intimacy and pleasure that the Lord meant for a husband and wife to enjoy.

Organization

1. Anticipation—Song 1–3
2. Wedding—Song 4
3. Pleasure—Song 5–8

Key Content

You have stolen my heart—Song 4:9

Her beauty celebrated in metaphors—Song 4:1–7; 7:1–9

Isaiah

Isaiah urges Judah to repent of its rebellion against God, warning them that it is facing exile from the promised land. When the exile to Babylon comes, Isaiah pours out words of comfort and encouragement, speaking of the forgiveness the messiah will bring and life in an eternal home.

Organization

1. Divine judgment for Judah and the nations—Isaiah 1–39
2. Comfort for Judah and the nations—Isaiah 40–66

Key Content

Song of the vineyard—Isaiah 5:1–7

Isaiah's call to service—Isaiah 6

To us a child is born—Isaiah 9:1–7

Comfort, comfort my people—Isaiah 40:1–8

Suffering Servant—Isaiah 53

Arise, shine, for your light has come—Isaiah 60:1–3

New heavens and a new earth—Isaiah 65:17–25

Jeremiah

Jeremiah lambasts God's people for failing to take personal responsibility in living out their covenant responsibilities and decries the kings who are leading their people toward exile. When his persistent call to repentance fails, the Babylonian exile comes. Then Jeremiah speaks of restoration within seventy years made possible by God's mercy and a return to covenant fidelity.

Organization

1. Call of Jeremiah—Jeremiah 1
2. Vivid words of warning and hope—Jeremiah 2–35

3. Jeremiah suffers and Jerusalem falls—Jeremiah 36–45
4. Judgment on the nations—Jeremiah 46–51
5. Revisiting the destruction of Jerusalem—Jeremiah 52

Key Content

Temple sermon—Jeremiah 7
Righteous branch—Jeremiah 23:5–6
Letter to the exiles—Jeremiah 29
New covenant—Jeremiah 31:31–34
Jeremiah carried to Egypt—Jeremiah 42–43

Lamentations

This collection of poetic laments gives voice to the sorrow and horror caused by the destruction of Jerusalem and the demolition of the temple.

Organization

1. The city weeps—Lamentations 1
2. It's God's doing—Lamentations 2
3. Hope amid the ashes—Lamentations 3
4. Horror—Lamentations 4
5. Plea for forgiveness—Lamentations 5

Key Content

Is it nothing to you, all you who pass by?—Lamentations 1:12
Because of the Lord's great love, we are not consumed—Lamentations 3:22

Ezekiel

As a fellow exile in Babylon, Ezekiel employs highly visual language to hammer home the reason for the exile before delivering the promise of restoration.

Organization

1. Call of Ezekiel—Ezekiel 1–3
2. Prophecies against Judah and Jerusalem—Ezekiel 4–24
3. Prophecies against the nations—Ezekiel 25–32
4. Prophecies of restoration—Ezekiel 33–48

Key Content

Symbolized siege of Jerusalem—Ezekiel 4
God's glory leaves the temple—Ezekiel 10
Shepherds of God's people—Ezekiel 34
Valley of dry bones—Ezekiel 37
Temple vision and the Lord's return—Ezekiel 40–43
A purifying river flows from the temple—Ezekiel 47

Daniel

Using events from the life of Daniel and visions of the future seen by Daniel, God's people in exile are reminded that he alone will determine their destiny. There is hope for those in exile, because the messiah will establish the kingdom of God at the expense of any nation that opposes him.

Organization

1. Events from the life of Daniel and his friends—Daniel 1–6
2. Visions of the future—Daniel 7–12

Key Content

A statue representing four world empires—Daniel 2
Fiery furnace—Daniel 3
Writing on the wall—Daniel 5
Lions' den—Daniel 6
Son of man and the Ancient of Days—Daniel 7:13–14

Hosea

In the days just before the northern kingdom falls to Assyria, the worship of the Lord has deteriorated into empty formalism while the people passionately pursues the worship of Baal. Hosea likens Israel to his unfaithful wife, who, though punished, will be given a second chance.

Organization

1. Unfaithful wife, faithful husband—Hosea 1–3
2. Unfaithful Israel, faithful God—Hosea 4–14

Key Content

Hosea's troubled marriage—Hosea 1:2–9
Come, let us return to the Lord—Hosea 6:1
Mercy not sacrifice—Hosea 6:6
Reaping the whirlwind—Hosea 8:7

Joel

A horrible locust plague affecting Judah becomes a symbol of the impending judgment on the day of the Lord. Only those who repent and rely on God's mercy will be spared.

Organization

1. The day of the Lord and the locust plague—Joel 1:1–2:17
2. God's mercy prevails—Joel 2:18–3:21

Key Content

Rend your heart not your garments—Joel 2:13
Pouring out of the Holy Spirit—Joel 2:28–32
Valley of Jehoshaphat (judgment)—Joel 3:2

Amos

As the wealthy in the northern kingdom enjoy a more prosperous economic season, they join worship of Baal with acts of social injustice, ignoring the needs of the poor and the demands of God. Amos declares these matters will be addressed on the coming day of the Lord.

Organization

1. Judgment on the nations—Amos 1:1–2:5
2. Judgment on Israel—Amos 2:6–6:14
3. Visions of judgment and restoration—Amos 7–9

Key Content

Let justice roll like a river—Amos 5:24

The divine plumb line—Amos 7:7–9

Restoration of David's fallen tent—Amos 9:11

Obadiah

Although related to Israel and obligated to support them in accomplishing their mission, the Edomites have gloated over their misfortunes and even joined in harming God's people during the Babylonian invasion of the promised land. The day of the Lord is coming for them.

Organization

1. Edom's sin—Obadiah 1–14
2. Edom's punishment—Obadiah 15–21

Key Content

The eagle will soar no more—Obadiah 4

Jonah

The life of Jonah becomes the message. As God corrects Jonah's narrow view of who deserves divine mercy, he is correcting our own. God's mercy extends beyond the boundaries we erect, even to those who seem least deserving of it.

Organization

1. Jonah flees the mission—Jonah 1–2
2. Mission accomplished in spite of Jonah—Jonah 3–4

Key Content

Jonah's call—Jonah 1:1–2

Great fish—Jonah 1:17

Should I not be concerned?—Jonah 4:11

Micah

As Assyria prepares to invade Israel and Judah, Micah links this invasion with a lack of social justice and pervasive worship of pagan gods, which are a product of Israel's broken relationship with the Lord. Words of judgment alternate with words of hope.

Organization

1. Judgment on Israel and Judah—Micah 1–3
2. Hope for Israel and Judah—Micah 4–5
3. The case for Israel's destruction—Micah 6
4. Zion has reason for hope—Micah 7

Key Content

The King from Bethlehem—Micah 5:2

Act justly, love mercy, walk humbly—Micah 6:8

I watch in hope for the Lord—Micah 7:7

Nahum

The Lord had commissioned the Assyrians to punish Israel, but this gentile nation conducted its assigned task with extreme cruelty. Consequently Nahum uses vivid and graphic language to describe the corresponding cruelty that will fall on the Assyrian capital city of Nineveh.

Organization

1. The case against Nineveh—Nahum 1
2. The attack on Nineveh—Nahum 2–3

Key Content

God is a refuge for his troubled people—Nahum 1:7

Habakkuk

Habakkuk is a dialogue between God and this prophet. It addresses two questions the faithful in Israel are asking: Why is God allowing wickedness to prosper in Judah? How could God use pagan Babylon to punish his chosen people?

Organization

1. Why is evil unpunished?—Habakkuk 1:1–11
2. Why punish with unrighteous Babylon?—Habakkuk 1:12–2:20
3. God's answers produce trust and joy—Habakkuk 3

Key Content

Why are you silent, Lord?—Habakkuk 1:13

I will be joyful in God my Savior—Habakkuk 3:18

Zephaniah

The day of the Lord will be a day of judgment for Judah and the nations insofar as they reject the rule of God and remove him from the rightful place in their lives. But it will also be a day of deliverance for the faithful remnant, who will be brought home and honored before all people of the earth.

Organization

1. Judgment on Judah and the nations—Zephaniah 1:1–3:8
2. Redemption of the faithful—Zephaniah 3:9–20

Key Content

The great day of the Lord—Zephaniah 1:14–18

Haggai

The return from exile created the opportunity to rebuild the Lord's temple and live holy lives, but mistaken attitudes and misplaced priorities have caused work on the project to stop and faith life to decline. Haggai calls for a change of heart so that the temple and people can be prepared for the messiah's arrival.

Organization

1. Call to rebuild the temple—Haggai 1:1–2:9
2. Call to holy living—Haggai 2:10–19
3. Call to confidence—Haggai 2:20–23

Key Content

Glory of the new temple—Haggai 2:9
Zerubbabel as signet ring—Haggai 2:23

Zechariah

Words of encouragement to restart the building of the temple in Jerusalem join with visions and language that urge Israel to prepare in all dimensions of living and thinking for the age of the messiah's coming.

Organization

1. Call to repent—Zechariah 1:1–6
2. Eight visions—Zechariah 1:7–6:8
3. Prepare for the messiah's coming—Zechariah 6:9–8:23
4. The age of the messiah's coming—Zechariah 9–14

Key Content

Messiah's entry into Jerusalem—Zechariah 9:9
Look on the one they have pierced—Zechariah 12:10
Strike the shepherd, and the sheep will be scattered—Zechariah 13:7

Malachi

The passage of time has begun to erode confidence in the better days to come promised by the prophets. In six dialogues, Malachi argues the delay is not cause to become careless in living holy lives or cause to doubt that the day of the Lord is near.

Organization

1. God's love confirmed—Malachi 1:1–5
2. Call to repent—Malachi 1:6–2:17
3. Day of the Lord is near—Malachi 3–4

Key Content

The forerunner, a new Elijah—Malachi 3:1; 4:5
Sun of righteousness will rise—Malachi 4:2

Matthew

The story of Jesus is told so as to emphasize his identity as the Messiah, David's royal son, who fulfills the Old Testament promises that anticipated his coming.

Outline

1. Birth and early years—Matthew 1–2
2. Jesus's ministry—Matthew 3–20
3. Jesus's passion and resurrection—Matthew 21–28

Key Content

Jesus the Immanuel—Matthew 1:22
Visit of the Magi—Matthew 2:1–12
Flight to Egypt—Matthew 2:13–18
Sermon on the Mount—Matthew 5–7
You are the Christ—Matthew 16:16
Parable of the ten virgins—Matthew 25:1–13
The sheep and the goats—Matthew 25:31–46
Great Commission—Matthew 28:16–20

Mark

This simpler and shorter presentation of Jesus's life emphasizes the need for the Son of Man to suffer in order to accomplish his mission on earth as its redeemer. Mark pays particular attention to the public recognition of Jesus as one who teaches with authority.

Outline

1. Jesus's ministry—Mark 1–10
2. Jesus's passion and resurrection—Mark 11–16

Key Content

Authority—Mark 1:22, 27; 2:10; 3:15; 6:7; 10:42; 11:27–29, 33
Appointing the Twelve—Mark 3:13–19
Raising Jairus's daughter—Mark 5:21–43
Blind man healed at Bethsaida—Mark 8:22–26
Jesus speaks of his death—Mark 9:30–32; 10:32–34
Widow's mite—Mark 12:41–44

Luke

In this first of his two-part presentation on the historic origins of the Christian church and the unique message it shares (Luke-Acts), Luke offers a more comprehensive account of Jesus's life that emphasizes the human side of the Savior, his compassion for others, and his passion to save Jew and gentile alike.

Outline

1. Jesus's birth and early years—Luke 1–2
2. Jesus's ministry—Luke 3:1–19:27
3. Jesus's passion and resurrection—Luke 19:28–24:53

Key Content

The annunciation to Mary—Luke 1:26–38
Prophecy of Zechariah—Luke 1:67–80
Christmas story—Luke 2:1–20
Jesus as a boy in the temple—Luke 2:41–52
Rejected at Nazareth—Luke 4:14–30
Widow's son raised at Nain—Luke 7:11–17
Good Samaritan—Luke 10:30–37
Mary and Martha—Luke 10:38–42
Rich man and poor Lazarus—Luke 16:19–31
Zacchaeus—Luke 19:1–10
Road-to-Emmaus revelation—Luke 24:13–35

John

This simply written but thought-provoking account of Jesus's life adds information not included in the other Gospels, focusing particularly on the close of Jesus's life in Judea and Jerusalem. John's goal is to convince the members of the early church that Jesus is the promised Christ, the Son of God, who opens the path to eternal life (John 20:31).

Outline

1. Jesus's ministry—John 1–11
2. Jesus's passion and resurrection—John 12–21

Key Content

Word became flesh—John 1:1–18
Water becomes wine—John 2:1–11
The Samaritan woman at Jacob's well—John 4:1–38
Healing at the Bethesda pools—John 5:1–15
Bread of life—John 6:25–59
Healing man born blind—John 9:1–12
Raising of Lazarus—John 11:1–44
Jesus's prayer for all believers—John 17:6–26
Restoration of Peter—John 21:15–25

Acts

In this second of his two-part presentation on the historic origins of the Christian church and the unique message it shares (Luke-Acts), Luke presents the triumphs and challenges of the church as the good news about Jesus expanded from Jerusalem, Judea, Samaria, and Galilee on its way to the ends of the earth (1:8).

Outline

1. The gospel in Judea, Samaria, and Galilee—Acts 1:1–11:18
2. The gospel in Syria and Cyprus—Acts 11:19–13:12
3. The gospel in Asia Minor and Europe—Acts 13:13–28:31

Key Content

Jesus's ascension—Acts 1:1–11
Pentecost—Acts 2:1–47
Death of Stephen—Acts 7:54–60
Philip and the Ethiopian—Acts 8:26–40
Conversion of Saul—Acts 9:1–31
Peter and Cornelius—Acts 10:1–48
Council at Jerusalem—Acts 15:1–35
Paul appeals to Caesar—Acts 25:9–12
Shipwreck of Paul—Acts 27:13–44

Romans

Paul composes this theological essay for the Christians at Rome in order to anchor their understanding of life and forgiveness in the basics of the Christian faith, which are valid for all time and for Jew and gentile alike.

Outline

1. Righteousness from God—Romans 1–8
2. Israel's hope—Romans 9–11
3. Life as a living sacrifice—Romans 12–16

Key Content

Not ashamed of the gospel—Romans 1:16–17
Righteous not by law but faith—Romans 3:19–24
Legacy of Christ and Adam—Romans 5:12–19

Struggle with the sinful nature—Romans 7:18–25
Confidence in the coming glory—Romans 8:18–39

1 Corinthians

Many converts in the church at Corinth have come from a pagan background, which continues to inform their attitudes and lifestyle. This letter of Paul addresses a long list of concerns that, left unaddressed, would compromise the integrity and well-being of the church.

Outline
1. Divisions in the church—1 Corinthians 1–4
2. Cases of immorality—1 Corinthians 5–6
3. Marriage—1 Corinthians 7
4. Meaning of Christian freedom—1 Corinthians 8–10
5. Worship—1 Corinthians 11–14
6. Resurrection—1 Corinthians 15–16

Key Content
Cross as foolishness and power—1 Corinthians 1:18
Lord's Supper—1 Corinthians 11:17–34
Spiritual gifts—1 Corinthians 12:1–31
Essay on love—1 Corinthians 13:1–13
Gift of tongues—1 Corinthians 14:1–25

2 Corinthians

Following his first letter and a delayed return visit to Corinth, a group of individuals began attacking the integrity of Paul's leadership and thus his message. This highly personal and highly spirited letter pushes back against the criticisms.

Outline
1. Overview of Paul's ministry—2 Corinthians 1–7
2. Collection for the poor in Jerusalem—2 Corinthians 8–9
3. Defense of Paul's role as apostle—2 Corinthians 10–13

Key Content
Seen temporary, unseen eternal—2 Corinthians 4:17–18
Ministry of reconciliation—2 Corinthians 5:17–21
Instruction on charitable giving—2 Corinthians 9:6–11
Boast only in the Lord—2 Corinthians 10:17
Sufficiency of God's grace—2 Corinthians 12:8

Galatians

Some Jewish Christians have been insisting that gentiles had to observe the Old Testament ceremonial laws, including the law regarding circumcision. Paul responds with a vigorous and passionate defense of the gospel: salvation by grace alone through faith alone without assistance from observing the law.

Outline
1. Paul's authority established—Galatians 1–2
2. Grace, faith, and freedom—Galatians 3–6

Key Content
Redeemed from the curse of the law—Galatians 3:13–14
One in Jesus—Galatians 3:28
Set free to remain free—Galatians 5:1
Fruits of the Spirit defined—Galatians 5:22–23

Ephesians

Paul sets out the grand and uplifting vision of a unified church intimately bound to Christ and reveals how that vision may become a reality.

Outline
1. God's purpose for the church—Ephesians 1–3
2. God's plan to fulfill that purpose—Ephesians 4–6

Key Content
Grace and faith—Ephesians 2:8–9
Unity in Christ—Ephesians 2:14; 4:3–6
Husbands and wives—Ephesians 5:22–33
Armor of God—Ephesians 6:10–18

Philippians

During the discouraging time of his detention in Rome, Paul is prompted to write a warm note of thanks for the support gift the Christians in Philippi had sent to him. In this note, Paul speaks about what is getting him through this difficult time: a focus on humility, contentment, and his eternal citizenship in heaven.

Outline
1. Greetings and personal news—Philippians 1:1–26
2. Live humbly—Philippians 1:27–2:30
3. Warnings and encouragement—Philippians 3:1–4:23

Key Content
To live is Christ, to die is gain—Philippians 1:21
The model of Christ's humility—Philippians 2:6–8
Heavenly citizenship—Philippians 3:20–21
Achieving contentment—Philippians 4:12–13

Colossians

When the Christians in Colossae begins to blend the good news about Jesus with other pagan and religious ideas, Paul pens this corrective note, which highlights the full adequacy and superiority of Christ.

Outline

1. Greeting—Colossians 1:1–14
2. The adequacy and superiority of Christ—Colossians 1:15–2:23
3. Holy living in Christ—Colossians 3:1–4:18

Key Content

Christ is God—Colossians 2:9–10

Made alive in Christ—Colossians 2:13

Relationship to the ceremonial laws of the Old Testament—Colossians 2:16–17

Set your hearts and minds on things above—Colossians 3:1–2

1–2 Thessalonians

A shorter stay and more abrupt departure from this city make it necessary for Paul to write these two letters. While clarifying his teaching on the second coming of Jesus, Paul uses this anticipated return to encourage and direct the actions of these believers facing persecution. The second letter, written only months after the first, celebrates the growth of this church but reinforces the content of the first.

Outline

1 Thessalonians
1. Greeting—1 Thessalonians 1
2. Paul's character and role—1 Thessalonians 2:1–3:13
3. Live as those awaiting the Lord's return—1 Thessalonians 4:1–5:28

2 Thessalonians
1. Greeting—2 Thessalonians 1
2. Live as those awaiting the Lord's return—2 Thessalonians 2–3

Key Content

1 Thessalonians
Resurrection of those who sleep—1 Thessalonians 4:13–18

Live in the light of the day—1 Thessalonians 5:7–8

2 Thessalonians
Man of lawlessness—2 Thessalonians 2:1–12

Stand firm—2 Thessalonians 2:15

1 Timothy

This letter contains sage advice from the seasoned leader Paul to the younger Timothy, who has been left to lead the church at Ephesus.

Outline

1. Greetings and initial concerns—1 Timothy 1
2. Guidance on worship, leadership, and general management—1 Timothy 2–6

Key Content

Jesus as the sole mediator—1 Timothy 2:5

Men and women in worship—1 Timothy 2:8–15

Your young age is not an issue—1 Timothy 4:12

Contentment and money—1 Timothy 6:6–10

2 Timothy

As Paul comes to the close of his life, he expresses his heartfelt concern for the church at Ephesus and its leader Timothy as these Christians prepare to face more difficult days of persecution.

Outline

1. Endure the difficult days to come—2 Timothy 1:1–3:9
2. Anchor in the trustworthy Word—2 Timothy 3:10–4:22

Key Content

All Scripture is God-breathed—2 Timothy 3:16–17

I have fought the good fight—2 Timothy 4:7–8

Titus

Paul offers guidance and encouragement to his trusted friend Titus, whom he has left on the island of Crete to lead the church there.

Outline

1. Personal instructions for Titus—Titus 1
2. Sound doctrine and doing good—Titus 2–3

Key Content

Washing of rebirth and renewal by the Holy Spirit—Titus 3:5

Philemon

In this personal letter, Paul asks Philemon to welcome back into his household the runaway slave, Onesimus, because he has been of great assistance to Paul and has become a fellow child of God.

Outline

1. Greeting—Philemon 1–7
2. Request—Philemon 8–25

Key Content

"I am sending him—who is my very heart—back to you"—Philemon 12

Hebrews

This letter was written to Jewish Christians who were trying to blend the thought patterns and ritual of the old covenant with the new. This letter argues that the new covenant is superior because it is mediated by Jesus. He is the author of our salvation and the perfecter of our faith who has fulfilled the promise of salvation described in the symbols of the old covenant.

Outline

1. Christ is the premier leader—Hebrews 1–7
2. Christ is the premier high priest and sacrifice—Hebrews 8–10
3. Christ is worthy of our faith—Hebrews 11–12
4. Final encouragements—Hebrews 13

Key Content

God's Word is a living, active, two-edged sword—Hebrews 4:12

Jesus was tempted just like we are, but without sin—Hebrews 4:15

Jesus is the all-sufficient sacrifice—Hebrews 7:27

Faith is being sure of what we hope for—Hebrews 11:1

Jesus is the author and perfecter of our faith—Hebrews 12:2

James

James argues that faith unaccompanied by appropriate deeds is a sham. The writer demonstrates the nature of faith in action by discussing how faith responds in the face of anger, favoritism, wealth, boasting, and hardship.

Outline

1. Trials and temptations—James 1:1–18
2. The lifestyle that faith yields—James 1:19–5:20

Key Content

Every good and perfect gift comes from above—James 1:17

Faith without works is dead—James 2:17

Be patient until the Lord's coming—James 5:7

Prayer is powerful and effective—James 5:16

1 Peter

Anticipating the coming of persecution, Peter writes to believers in five Roman provinces to encourage them to persevere and to focus on living holy lives during these more difficult days.

Outline

1. Greetings and praise—1 Peter 1:1–12
2. Live holy lives in the midst of suffering—1 Peter 1:13–5:14

Key Content

An inheritance that cannot perish or fade—1 Peter 1:4

Called to be holy—1 Peter 1:16

You are a chosen people—1 Peter 2:9

Cast all your worries on God who cares for you—1 Peter 5:7

2 Peter

With his life coming to a close, Peter writes to his beloved church about its secure foundation in the revealed Word of God and its secure future in the return of Jesus.

Outline

1. The source of truth—2 Peter 1
2. False teachers and their fate—2 Peter 2
3. Jesus's certain return—2 Peter 3

Key Content

Truth revealed by the Holy Spirit—2 Peter 1:21

The Lord is not slow in keeping his promises—2 Peter 3:9

1 John

An early form of gnosticism, which perceived spirit as always good and the body as always evil, has led to misperceptions regarding the nature of Jesus and the need for living a moral life. John uses the language of light and love to confirm the righteousness of the God-man, Jesus; and he summons God's people to live in light and love.

Outline

1. God is light; live in the light—1 John 1–2
2. God is love; live in love—1 John 3–5

Key Content

The blood of Jesus purifies from all sin—1 John 1:7

God's love and Jesus's atoning sacrifice—1 John 4:10

Perfect love drives out all fear—1 John 4:18

2–3 John

These two letters have a number of things in common. Both are very short, are addressed to a specific person, and flow from the common practice of inviting visiting teachers into the home in order to provide food and shelter for them. Second John warns about extending this hospitality to false teachers and so expanding the reach of their heresy. Third John commends Gaius and others, who support the teachers sent out by John with the truth to share.

Key Content

Walk in love—2 John 6

Imitate what is good—3 John 11

Jude

The younger brother of Jesus urges the chosen of God to resist the persuasive words of false teachers, who teach that those who are saved by grace are able to sin without restraint or penalty (Jude 4).

Outline

1. Greeting—Jude 1–2
2. False teachers and their fate—Jude 3–16
3. Hold to the truth—Jude 17–25

Key Content

Build yourselves up in faith and prayer—Jude 20

Jesus alone keeps us from falling—Jude 24

Revelation

Through notes written to seven churches and a series of visions, John paints a picture of this world's history culminating in the return of Jesus. The challenges and uncertainty of the last days will only increase as Satan and his allies fight to destroy the people of God. But the victory of Jesus is never in doubt. He will sustain his people, destroy those who oppose his kingdom, and rule in a new heaven and new earth, which will be the eternal home of all believers.

Outline

1. Letters to the seven churches—Revelation 1–3
2. Visions of revolt against Jesus—Revelation 4–16
3. Visions of certain victory by Jesus—Revelation 17–22

Key Content

Jesus is the Alpha and Omega—Revelation 1:8

Worthy is the Lamb who was slain—Revelation 5:12

Blessed are those who die in the Lord—Revelation 14:13

Armageddon—Revelation 16:16

New Jerusalem—Revelation 21:1–2

Bible Translation

Need

Old Testament written in classical Hebrew with a few passages in Aramaic (found in Daniel and Ezra).

New Testament written in Koine (common) Greek.

Goal

To transfer the thought world of the Bible from the Hebrew, Aramaic, and Greek into English while minimizing the possibility of misunderstanding.

Complication

Because each language will naturally communicate an idea using its own vocabulary, grammar, and sentence structure, translators must make a decision to favor either the original language or the receiving language. A discussion of their translating preferences will be found in the preface of the English edition.

Translating Style

Translators will adopt a philosophy that favors either formal or functional equivalence.

Formal Equivalence

This style of translating favors the language patterns of the original language. In word-for-word fashion, the translator wishes to make the vocabulary, grammar, and style of the original language apparent in the translation.

This style of translating makes the relationship of the translation to the original text clearer but results in a translation that is less natural and harder to read in the receiving language.

Functional Equivalence

This style of translating favors the language patterns of the receiving language. In thought-for-thought fashion, the translator works to reproduce the meaning of the original as accurately and naturally as possible in the receiving language.

This form of translation reads more naturally but obscures the relationship of the translation to the language elements of the original.

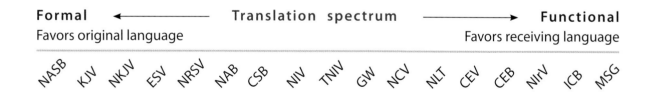

Formal ← Translation spectrum → Functional

Favors original language   Favors receiving language

NASB   KJV   NKJV   ESV   NRSV   NAB   CSB   NIV   TNIV   GW   NCV   NLT   CEV   CEB   NIrV   ICB   MSG

Ancient Texts of the Bible

The Lord did not see fit to preserve the original documents the inspired authors of the Bible wrote (the so-called autographs). However, copies of those originals and translations of copies allow us to confidently reconstruct the content of those original documents. These are the key ancient texts that aid in that process.

Text	Language	Earliest Date
Septuagint	Greek	3rd century BC
Dead Sea Scrolls	Hebrew	3rd century BC
Samaritan Pentateuch	"Early" Hebrew	2nd century BC
Aquila, Symmacus, and Theodotion	Greek	2nd century AD
Old Latin	Latin	2nd century AD
Peshitta	Syriac	2nd century AD
Targum	Aramaic	3rd century AD
Coptic	Coptic	3rd century AD
Vulgate	Latin	4th century AD
Codex Sinaiticus	Greek	4th century AD
Codex Vaticanus	Greek	4th century AD
Codex Alexandrinus	Greek	5th century AD

Fifty-Two-Week Bible Reading Plan

Week	Scripture Reading
1	John 1–21
2	Genesis 1–26
3	Genesis 27–50
4	Exodus 1–24
5	Exodus 25–40
6	Leviticus 1–27
7	Numbers 1–21
8	Numbers 22–36; Deuteronomy 1–9
9	Deuteronomy 10–34
10	Joshua 1–24
11	Judges 1–21
12	Matthew 1–28
13	Ruth 1–4; 1 Samuel 1–15
14	1 Samuel 16–31; 2 Samuel 1–9
15	2 Samuel 10–24; 1 Kings 1–9
16	1 Kings 10–22; 2 Kings 1–8
17	2 Kings 9–25; 1 Chronicles 1–9
18	1 Chronicles 10–29
19	2 Chronicles 1–18
20	2 Chronicles 19–36
21	Ezra 1–10; Nehemiah 1–13
22	Esther 1–10; Mark 1–16
23	Job 1–21
24	Job 22–42
25	Psalms 1–21
26	Psalms 22–44
27	Psalms 45–67
28	Psalms 68–90

Week	Scripture Reading
29	Psalms 91–113
30	Psalms 114–136
31	Psalms 137–150; Proverbs 1–9
32	Proverbs 10–31
33	Ecclesiastes 1–11; Song of Songs 1–8
34	Luke 1–24
35	Isaiah 1–23
36	Isaiah 24–48
37	Isaiah 49–66
38	Romans 1–16
39	Jeremiah 1–20
40	Jeremiah 21–45
41	Jeremiah 46–52; 1 Corinthians 1–16
42	Lamentations 1–5; 2 Corinthians 1–13; Galatians 1–6
43	Ezekiel 1–24
44	Ezekiel 25–48
45	Ephesians 1–6; Philippians 1–4; Colossians 1–4; 1 Thessalonians 1–5; 2 Thessalonians 1–3
46	Daniel 1–12; 1 Timothy 1–6; 2 Timothy 1–4
47	Hosea 1–14; Joel 1–3; Amos 1–9
48	Titus 1–3; Philemon; Hebrews 1–13; James 1–5; 1 Peter 1–5
49	Obadiah; Jonah 1–4; Micah 1–7; Nahum 1–3; Habakkuk 1–3; Zephaniah 1–3; Haggai 1–2
50	Zechariah 1–14; Malachi 1–4; 2 Peter 1–3; 1 John 1–5; 2–3 John; Jude
51	Acts 1–28
52	Revelation 1–22

I Need God to Speak to Me

I need to know that God forgives me.

Psalm 51
Psalm 103:2–5, 11–12
Psalm 130
Isaiah 1:18
Micah 7:18–19
Matthew 9:1–8
Luke 15
John 3:16
John 8:1–11
Acts 2:38–39
Romans 3:21–24
Romans 5:15–19
Romans 8:31–34
2 Corinthians 5:14–21
Galatians 3:10–14
Ephesians 2:4–10
Colossians 1:13–14
1 John 1:7–9

I need hope.

Psalm 27
Psalm 42
Psalm 46
Psalm 71
Isaiah 12:2
Isaiah 40:29–31
Jeremiah 29:11
Romans 8:18–27
Romans 15:4, 13
Philippians 4:13
Hebrews 10:23
1 Peter 1:3–9

I need peace.

Numbers 6:24–26
Luke 2:13–14
John 14:1–4, 27
John 16:33
Romans 5:1–2
Ephesians 2:14–18
Philippians 4:4–7

I need to know God is with me.

Deuteronomy 31:6
Deuteronomy 33:27
Joshua 1:5
Psalm 23
Psalm 28:7–8
Psalm 91
Psalm 121
Isaiah 41:10
Isaiah 58:9

I need direction for my life.

Psalm 1
Psalm 55:22
Proverbs 3:5–6
Proverbs 16:3
Jeremiah 29:11
2 Corinthians 1:8–11
Philippians 2:3–4
1 John 2:15–17

I need help thinking about money.

Psalm 49:16–20
Proverbs 23:5
Ecclesiastes 5:10
Matthew 6:25–34
Matthew 19:23–24
Mark 12:41–44
Luke 12:13–21
Luke 12:32–34
Luke 16:13
1 Corinthians 16:2
1 Timothy 3:3
1 Timothy 6:6–10
Hebrews 13:5

I need to reduce my stress.

Psalm 55:22
Isaiah 40:29–31
Matthew 6:25–34
Luke 12:22–31
Philippians 4:4–7
1 Peter 5:7

I need help facing illness.

Psalm 46
Psalm 50:15
Psalm 73:25–26
Psalm 103:1–5
Psalm 120:1
Matthew 8:14–17
Luke 18:35–43
Romans 5:1–5
2 Corinthians 4:16–18
2 Corinthians 12:7–10
James 1:2–4
James 5:10–11

I need help facing death.

Job 19:25
Psalm 23
Psalm 27:1
Psalm 48:14
Psalm 68:19–20
Matthew 5:4
John 10:27–28
John 11:17–44
John 14:1–4
Romans 8:28–39
1 Corinthians 15:20–22, 35–57
1 Thessalonians 4:13–18
Hebrews 2:14–15
1 Peter 1:3–9
Revelation 7:9–17
Revelation 21:1–7
Revelation 22:12–17

Literary Genres of the Bible

Each genre represents a style of writing selected by the author or poet, and it functions as a contract between the writer and readers. It defines the nature of the communication so as to limit reader misunderstanding.

Types

Historical Narrative

Writers turn an event into a story by carefully selecting and organizing details so that the lesson(s) to be learned from the event becomes more apparent. To that end, the author makes use of plot design, narration, time manipulation, and characterization.

Tip: The plot (conflict evolving to solution) provides an important clue to the lesson(s) being taught.

Hebrew Poetry

Poets speak in more abstract fashion, expressing their ideas in compact bursts of artfully designed, emotion-filled language that trades in sound, metaphor, imagery, and repetition.

Tip: Poetry targets both head and heart. Poetry is designed to be read slowly and repeatedly so as to achieve appreciation of the linguistic artistry and invite thoughtful reflection. Watch for a controlling idea to be emphasized by repetition, contrast, and development.

Law

Law consists of divine directives that contain little if any literary embellishment. In straightforward fashion, they are meant to shape the way God's people think and live.

Tip: The biggest challenge in reading the legal directives in the Bible is to determine which ones are limited in application to a specific time and which are universally applicable throughout all time.

Wisdom

Wisdom combines Hebrew poetry and law, offering generalizations on how to live and think successfully. This poetry can take the form of a proverb or an extended dialogue (Job).

Tip: Wisdom highlights the choices offered in life. Look for options to be offered and direction in making a choice that will result in the highest possible satisfaction in living.

Prophecy

The prophets bring a message from God to people whose immediate circumstances reveal a need for correction, hope, or an insight into the future. The bulk of prophetic literature in the Old Testament is written in the form of Hebrew poetry.

Tip: Learn all that is possible about the circumstances that precipitated the message by examining the historical books, then look for the controlling idea(s) delivered in the poetry.

Parable

The parable takes a well-known image from the writer's everyday surroundings and, by analogy, turns it into a divine truth.

Tip: Learn all you can about the reality of the image being used before attempting to trace the theological truth it teaches.

Letter (Epistle)

As news of Jesus spread into new contexts and cultures, questions arose with regard to lifestyle and theology. These theological and moral issues were clarified in letters addressed to both individuals and groups from respected Christian teachers.

Tip: Because letters jump quickly into the topics they discuss, learn all that is possible about the background of the letters by reading the appropriate section of Acts.

Apocalyptic

Apocalyptic literature makes use of fantastic images and extended visual metaphors in a bid to create hope among those facing difficult days. The message will generally revolve around the theme "Things will get better."

Tip: The coded language of apocalyptic is meant to prevent outsiders from understanding the message. Successful reading of this genre requires that the reader learn the meaning of the symbols being used.

Fifty Key People of the Bible

Aaron	Brother of Moses and Israel's first high priest (Exod. 4:14; 29:4–9; Heb. 7:11)
Abel	Son of Adam and Eve murdered by his brother Cain (Gen. 4:2; Heb. 11:4)
Abraham	Forefather of the Jewish nation and heir of God's promises to use that nation to save the world from sin (Gen. 12:1–3; Heb. 11:8–19)
Adam	First mortal God created (Gen. 2:7; Rom. 5:18–19)
Barnabas	Saw to Saul's (Paul's) welcome in Jerusalem, brought him to Antioch, and participated in the first missionary journey (Acts 9:27; 11:22–26; 13:1–2)
Caiaphas	Jewish high priest who oversaw the religious trial of Jesus (Matt. 26:57; John 11:49–53)
Cain	Son of Adam and Eve who killed his brother Abel (Gen. 4:8; 1 John 3:12)
Daniel	Jewish exile to Babylon who escaped the lions' den and rose to become a key court official in the land of his exile (Dan. 1:6–11; 2:48–49)
David	The second king of Israel, acclaimed poet, and forefather of the Messiah (1 Sam. 16:12–13; 2 Sam. 7:11–16; Ps. 23; Luke 1:26–32; Rev. 22:16)
Deborah	Prophetess and judge in Israel who urged Barak to act (Judg. 4–5)
Elijah	Prophet who battled the prophets of Baal and rode a fiery chariot into glory (1 Kings 18:16–46; 2 Kings 2:1–12; Matt. 17:3–4)
Elisha	Prophet who succeeded Elijah, restored a life in Shunem, and healed the leprosy of Naaman (2 Kings 2:15; 4:8–37; 5:1–19; Luke 4:27; 7:11–17)
Elizabeth	Wife of Zechariah and mother of John the Baptist (Luke 1:5–7, 57)
Esau	Son of Isaac and brother of Jacob who was the forefather of the Edomites (Gen. 25:24–30; 36:43; Heb. 11:20)
Esther	Jewish queen of Persia who saved her people from an extermination plot (Esther 2:7–9; 8:1–13)
Ezra	Learned teacher who taught the returning exiles how to think and live as the people of God in the promised land (Ezra 7:1–10; Neh. 8:1–6)

Hagar	Sarah's servant who became Abraham's second wife, used in Paul's discussion of the covenants made through Abraham and Moses (Gen. 16:1–3; Gal. 4:21–31)
Hannah	Mother of Samuel who dedicated her son to God's service (1 Sam. 1:12–28)
Herod Antipas	Son of Herod the Great who ruled Galilee, executed John the Baptist, and participated in Jesus's trial in Jerusalem (Matt. 14:1–12; Luke 9:7–9; 23:10–12)
Herod the Great	Master politician and architect who ruled the promised land for Rome and whose paranoia led to the execution of children in Bethlehem (Matt. 2:1–18)
Hezekiah	Judean king who pursued a course of aggressive religious reform (2 Kings 18:1–8)
Isaac	Son of Abraham and heir of the covenant promises who was "sacrificed" in a test of his father's faith (Gen. 17:19; 22:1–19; Heb. 11:17–19)
Isaiah	Prophet who spoke often about the coming messiah while warning God's people of the consequences of their covenant disloyalty (Isa. 7:14; 9:1–7; 11:1–5; 53:1–12)
Jacob	Son of Isaac and heir of the covenant promises whose sons become the twelve tribes of Israel (Gen. 28:10–22; 49:1–28; Heb. 11:21)
Jeremiah	Prophet who prepared God's people for exile in Babylon and introduced the idea of a new covenant to come following their return (Jer. 1:9–10; 31:1–34)
Jesus	The son of Mary and Son of God whom the Father sent into the world to save sinners from eternal punishment (Luke 1:26–37).
Job	Man whose suffering creates a dialogue on the reason for the suffering of God's people in this world (Job 1–2; 38–42; James 5:11)
John the Baptist	Promised messenger who prepared the hearts of those among whom Jesus would walk to meet him and who baptized Jesus (Isa. 40:3–5; Matt. 3:13–17; Luke 3:1–18)
Jonah	Reluctant prophet to Nineveh whose life story demonstrated that God's kingdom extended into the gentile world (Jon. 1–4; Matt. 12:39–41)

Joseph	Son of Jacob sold as a slave and elevated to power in Egypt who secured his family's future during a famine by caring for them in Egypt (Gen. 45–46)
Joseph of Nazareth	Husband of Mary who cared for the young boy Jesus and whose family connection made Jesus a son of David (Matt. 1:18–25; Luke 2:1–7)
Joshua	Moses's successor who led Israel into the promised land and defeated the major city-states there before dividing the land among the tribes (Josh. 1:1–5; 18:1–10; Heb. 4:8)
Josiah	Reforming king in Judah who called for covenant renewal after the neglected Book of the Law was found (2 Kings 22:1–23:27)
Judas Iscariot	Dishonest disciple of Jesus who betrayed his Lord for thirty pieces of silver (Matt. 26:14–16; John 12:4–5)
Lazarus	Close friend of Jesus, and brother of Mary and Martha, whom Jesus raised from the dead (John 11:1–44)
Mary, the mother of Jesus	Young girl from Nazareth who gave birth to Jesus, raised him, and remained at his side in death (Luke 1:26–2:52; John 19:25–27)
Mary Magdalene	Woman from whom Jesus drove seven demons; she dedicated her life to supporting Jesus in life and death (Matt. 27:55–56; 28:1; Mark 15:40–47; Luke 8:2; John 19:25; 20:10–18)
Matthew	Tax collector whom Jesus called to be a disciple (Matt. 9:9–10)
Moses	The unique prophet who led Israel out of Egypt, through the wilderness, and to the edge of the promised land (Exod. 3:1–20; Deut. 34:1–12)
Noah	Righteous man who built the great ark that allowed the human race and promises of God to survive the great flood (Gen. 6–9)
Paul	The Way's greatest missionary and the New Testament's most prolific author who was once known as Saul and was a zealous persecutor of Christians (Acts 9:1–16)
Peter	Jesus's fiery student who rose to lead on the day of Pentecost and later convinced the Jewish-Christian church that gentiles were welcome (Matt. 4:18–20; Acts 2:14–41; 10:1–11:18)
Pilate	Roman prefect who presided over the civil trial of Jesus and ordered his execution (Matt. 27:11–26)
Ruth	Moabite who was the daughter-in-law of Naomi, the wife of Boaz, and foremother of David (Ruth 1–4; Matt. 1:5)
Samuel	Prophet of Israel who led a spiritual reformation and anointed the nation's first two kings (1 Sam. 7:2–17; 10:1; 16:13)
Sarah	The former Sarai, wife of Abraham used in Paul's discussion of the covenants made through Abraham and Moses (Gen. 12:5; Gal. 4:21–31)
Saul	Israel's first king, whose rebellion and arrogance led to his rejection by the Lord (1 Sam. 10:1; 15:20–23; Acts 13:21–22)
Solomon	David's son and Israel's third king who was given great wisdom, organized the kingdom, and oversaw a prosperous though less faithful season in Israel's history (1 Kings 3:4–15; 4:1–34; Matt. 6:29; 12:42)
Stephen	Leader in the early church who gave his life in witness to his faith as the first known Christian martyr (Acts 6:8–7:60)
Zechariah	Father of John the Baptist who first sang the song known as the Benedictus (Luke 1:5–25, 57–80)

Fifty Key Places of the Bible

Antioch	This political and commercial center in Syria had a population of more than half a million people. Followers of Jesus were first called "Christians" here (Acts 11:26), and it became the launching point for Paul's three missionary journeys.
Ashdod	*(New Testament: Azotus)* This city had an unhappy experience with the ark of God during the time of the Philistines (1 Sam. 5:1–8) and opposed the rebuilding of the temple in Jerusalem (Neh. 4:7–8) before hearing the gospel from Philip (Acts 8:40).
Babylon	The capital city of the Neo-Babylonian Empire, which defeated Judah, destroyed Jerusalem, and exiled the Jews for seventy years (2 Kings 25:1–21). It became symbolic of the fate of world powers that oppose the advance of God's kingdom (Rev. 18:10, 21).
Beersheba	A city in the Negev frequently used for worship by Abraham's family (Gen. 21:33; 26:23–25; 46:1). When joined with Dan, it was used to mark the northern and southern reaches of the promised land (Judg. 20:1; 2 Sam. 24:2).
Benjamin	The high plateau between the tribal territories of Judah and Ephraim eased travel through the center of the mountainous interior of the promised land. It became the strategic internal crossroads allowing Jerusalem access to the world, and the world access to Jerusalem. Bible events linked with this region will naturally rise in importance (like Josh. 9–10).
Bethany	A village near Jerusalem on the east side of the Mount of Olives often visited by Jesus because it was the home of Mary, Martha, and Lazarus. Jesus raised Lazarus here and ascended into heaven nearby (Luke 24:50; John 11:1, 18; 12:1).
Bethel	A village on the border between Benjamin and Ephraim that became an important worship site for Abraham's family (Gen. 12:8; 28:10–22; 35:1–7). Jeroboam tarnished its reputation by establishing a golden calf sanctuary here (1 Kings 12:28–33).
Bethlehem	A village in Judah near Jerusalem that was the home of Ruth and Naomi, the hometown of David, and the birthplace of Jesus (Ruth 1:1, 22; 1 Sam. 16:1; Mic. 5:2; Luke 2:4–7).
Bethphage	A village on the Mount of Olives, which was the presumed city limits of Jerusalem. Jesus rode a donkey into this village and into Jerusalem, fulfilling Old Testament promises about him (Matt. 21:1–5; Luke 19:28–35).
Bethsaida	This town lay on the north side of the Sea of Galilee and was the home of Philip, Andrew, and Peter (John 1:44). This community had the chance to hear Jesus and see his miracles more frequently than others. Their failure to respond in faith resulted in sharp censure (Matt. 11:21).
Beth Shemesh	A town set aside for the Levites on the east side of the Valley of Sorek (Josh. 21:16) whose residents mishandled the ark of the covenant, illustrating just how badly the faith of Israel had deteriorated before the reforms of Samuel began (1 Sam. 6:19–20).
Caesarea Maritima	This thoroughly Roman port city built on the Mediterranean coast of Israel was the home of Cornelius and the place Peter learned that the gospel was destined for the gentiles (Acts 10:1–35). During his extended detention here, Paul learned how the Roman world worked prior to embarking for Rome (Acts 23:23–26:32).
Caesarea Philippi	A city established at the base of Mount Hermon and at the headwaters of the Jordan River; it was enhanced by Herod Philip to serve as his regional capital. The pagan sanctuaries of this city became the setting for a discussion about Jesus's identity, which led to Peter's great confession (Matt. 16:13–20).
Capernaum	A town built on the northwest shore of the Sea of Galilee near the International Highway that became known as Jesus's "home" (Mark 2:1). Jesus moved here to fulfill Old Testament prophecy, establish a base of operations in Galilee, and provide international access to his message (Matt. 4:13–17; 11:23).
Colossae	This was a leading city in the Roman province of Asia Minor along the east–west trade route that linked Ephesus with cities far to the east along the Euphrates River. Although the city is unmentioned in the book of Acts, believers there received a letter from Paul because of numerous heresies they had adopted (Col. 1:2).

Corinth	Due to its advantageous geography between the Aegean and Adriatic Seas, Corinth became a leading commercial center in ancient Greece. The flow of traffic made it an attractive spot for Paul, who both visited (Acts 18:1–18) and sent letters to the Christians living in this morally challenged city (1–2 Cor.).
Damascus	The capital city of Aram strategically located along ancient transportation routes (Isa. 7:8). Although a frequent opponent of God's kingdom during the Old Testament, the Jews here were quick to recognize Jesus as Messiah (Acts 9:2). When Saul went to address this "problem," Jesus met and converted him just before he arrived (Acts 9:3–22).
Dan	This city was located along the International Highway, the critical lookout station that would first feel an attack from the north (Jer. 8:16). Its name became synonymous with the northern border of the promised land (Judg. 20:1; 2 Sam. 24:2). Jeroboam assured its ongoing censure by establishing a golden calf sanctuary here (1 Kings 12:28–30).
Dead Sea	This unique inland lake formed the eastern border of the promised land (Num. 34:3, 12). It is the lowest place on the earth's surface (1,300 feet below sea level) and void of the kind of life we expect in a lake due to its high salt content (30 percent by weight). Ezekiel speaks of this dead body of water coming to life in the age to come (Ezek. 47:1–7).
Decapolis	A group of sprawling Greco-Roman cities established along important transportation routes. They were marked with unique architecture and cultural experiences meant to sell Hellenism to the locals. For observant Jews this gentile country (east of the Sea of Galilee and associated with Hippos) was the fearsome "other side" (Mark 4:35) in which Jesus reached out to gentiles (Mark 5:20; 8:1–13).
Ephesus	An important Roman city was destined to grow in this location where east–west overland routes meet east–west shipping lanes. Paul spent years at this hub of human movement, which provided a gateway into Asia (Acts 19:1–10; 20:17). Both Paul and John wrote letters to the Christians here (Ephesians; Rev. 2:1–7).
Gath	One of the five major Philistine city-states, Gath was the home of Goliath (1 Sam. 17:4). After this giant's defeat and during the days Saul was seeking David's life, David sought refuge in this city. Here David learned Philistine battle strategies. Ironically he later used this information to defeat the Philistines and seize Gath (1 Sam. 27:2–4; 1 Chron. 18:1).
Gibeah	A town in Benjamin along the central road system in the promised land that became the home of Saul. Its dark past (Judg. 19:12–26) casts a dark shadow across the rise of Israel's first king as Saul makes this town the first capital of Israel (1 Sam. 10:26). It becomes known as "Gibeah of Saul."
Gibeon	Centrally located on a small rise in the middle of the Benjamin plateau, this village superintended the east–west route that connected Jerusalem to the world and the armies of the world to Jerusalem. Deception allowed its residents to maintain some autonomy at the time of Joshua's conquest (Josh. 9). Later this Levitical city became the home of the tabernacle and bronze altar (1 Chron. 16:39; 2 Chron. 1:3, 5), a worship center at which Solomon asked for and received the gift of wisdom (1 Kings 3:4–15).
Hazor	An important intersection of the International Highway just south of Hazor fostered the development of a major city in this location. Although Canaanite Hazor was defeated by Joshua (Josh. 11:10), it rose again to fight against Israel at the time of Deborah and Barak (Judg. 4:2). Solomon later fortified this location for Israel's use (1 Kings 9:15).
Hebron	A town in Judah located along the central Ridge Route. Abram built a memorial altar here to recall the land promises his family had been given (Gen. 13:14–18) and later purchased the cave of Machpelah, which served as the family tomb (Gen. 23:17–20). Its religious role continued as a Levitical city (Josh. 21:11), and it became the capital of David during the time of the civil war that followed Saul's death (2 Sam. 2:11).

Jericho	The area of Old and New Testament Jericho was an oasis on the edge of the Judean wilderness from which roads traveled to the interior of the promised land. The Lord gave this city into Joshua's hands (Josh. 6). Near here Elijah left the stage of history (2 Kings 2:5) and the "new" Elijah, John the Baptist, entered (Matt. 3:1; John 1:28). Jesus healed Bartimaeus (Mark 10:46) and welcomed Zacchaeus into the kingdom of God (Luke 19:1–2).
Jerusalem	This city plays a more powerful role in Bible communication than any other place. It became the political capital of Israel (2 Sam. 5:1–12), the religious center of Judaism, and home of the ark (2 Sam. 6) and the Lord's temple (1 Kings 5–8). "Jerusalem" frequently personifies God's people and their fate (Ps. 87; Lam. 1). It is where Jesus was crucified and raised to life and is the city that anticipates his return in glory (Rev. 21:1–2).
Jezreel Valley	This triangular valley interrupts the central mountain range allowing the easiest east–west passage for international travelers. Its agricultural and transportation advantages were shared by four Israelite tribes. Key cities like Megiddo developed along its perimeter to control military movement and collect tax revenue. The flat terrain and economic value made it a battleground. Saul and Josiah died in battles here (1 Sam. 29:11; 2 Kings 23:29).
Joppa	The Old Testament seaport of Israel via which timber was brought into the promised land for the building of the temple at Jerusalem (2 Chron. 2:16; Ezra 3:7) and from which Jonah fled when directed to go to Nineveh (Jon. 1:3). Here Peter raised Dorcas and received a vision that led him to witness to gentiles in Caesarea Maritima (Acts 9:36–10:23).
Jordan River	This meandering river connects the Sea of Galilee and the Dead Sea. It was the eastern boundary of Canaan (Num. 34:12) mentioned frequently in connection with Israel's entry into the promised land (Deut. 4:14; 11:11; Josh. 1:2) and miraculously dried up ahead of them (Josh. 3–4). Jesus's public ministry began when he was baptized in this river (Mark 1:9).
Judean wilderness	Steep terrain, poor soil, and lack of rainfall make this region hostile to sustained human settlement. David hid here from the murderous hand of Saul (1 Sam. 24:1; 26:1–3). It provided the austere setting for John the Baptist's somber message (Isa. 40:3; Matt. 3:1) and the setting for Jesus's temptation (Matt. 4:1–4).
Kiriath Jearim	A town in the mountains of Judah that became the home for the ark of the covenant for twenty years during the time of Samuel (1 Sam. 6:21; 7:1–2). David brought it from there to Jerusalem (1 Chron. 13:5–6).
Megiddo	The most strategically located city in the ancient world guarding a narrow pass on the edge of the Jezreel Valley and along the International Highway. Although taken by Joshua (Josh. 12:21), Manasseh failed to hold it (Judg. 1:27). Megiddo finally comes to Israelite hands and is fortified by Solomon (1 Kings 9:15). King Josiah died in battle with Egypt here (2 Kings 23:29–30).
Mount Carmel	A thirty-mile mountain ridge that blocks north-south travel on the coastal plain, then channels the flow of traffic through chalk valleys that bisect this ridge and empty into the Jezreel Valley. It became the site of Elijah's contest with the prophets of Baal (1 Kings 18).
Mount Ebal	This mountain rises just north of the Shechem pass and was the geographical focus of the rededication ceremony held by Joshua at the start of the conquest. Here Joshua erected stone pillars inscribed with the law together with an altar (Deut. 27:1–8; Josh. 8:30–32). The tribes announcing the curses for covenant disobedience stood on this mountain (Deut. 27:13; Josh. 8:33–35).
Mount Moreh	This mountain in the Jezreel Valley was used by Gideon as he prepared to attack the Midianite invaders (Judg. 7:1). It also hosted two parallel miracles in villages on its flanks. Elisha raised a boy to life in Shunem (2 Kings 4:8, 32–37). Jesus raised a young man at Nain (Luke 7:11–17).
Mount of Olives	This extended mountain ridge rose east of and higher than the city of Jerusalem. It hosted a number of important events in the last week of Jesus's life, including his riding a donkey into Bethphage (Matt. 21:1), his triumphal entry on Palm Sunday (Luke 19:37), his reflection on the end times (Matt. 24:3), and his struggle in prayer in the garden of Gethsemane (Matt. 26:30).

Mount Sinai	Following the Israelites' extended stay in Egypt, the Lord led them here before he led them to the promised land in order to visually present himself to them and to organize them as his covenant people (Exod. 19:2–16). The mountain became emblematic of the Mosaic covenant (Neh. 9:13; Gal. 4:24–25).
Mount Tabor	This dome-shaped mountain in the Jezreel Valley made it a striking landmark celebrated with Mount Hermon as an iconic symbol of God's creative work (Ps. 89:12). It was the staging area for Barak and Deborah's attack on the Canaanite forces gathered in the valley below (Judg. 4:6, 12, 14).
Nazareth	A small, geographically isolated village on a ridge north of the Jezreel Valley. It was the setting for the announcement of Jesus's unique birth (Luke 1:26) and became the childhood home of Jesus (Luke 2:39). By living there, Jesus fulfilled Old Testament prophecies made about him (Matt. 2:23). Public disdain for those living in Nazareth affected the way people thought about Jesus (John 1:46; 19:19).
Nineveh	This metropolis at the top of the Fertile Crescent's arch was the pagan city to which the Lord sent Jonah to teach him about the breadth of God's kingdom (Jon. 1–4). Jesus used it to drive home this point (Matt. 12:41). It eventually became capital of the empire of Assyria and the focus of the book of Nahum because it wickedly overplayed its role as divine corrector of God's people.
Philippi	This city was a Roman colony and leading city in the district of Macedonia, which was visited by Paul (Acts 16:12; 20:6). He followed up his visits with a letter of thanks and encouragement preserved in Philippians.
Rome	The capital city of the Roman Empire and natural transportation hub that connected its far-flung holdings via sea-lanes and roadways. Pentecost converts carried news of Jesus here (Acts 2:10). Paul wrote the believers a letter (Romans) that anticipates a later visit (Acts 19:21; 23:11). That important visit happened when Paul made an appeal to have his case heard by the emperor in Rome (Acts 25:25; 28:14).
Samaria	Omri made this city the capital of the northern kingdom of Israel (1 Kings 16:24). Ahab and Jezebel built a sanctuary to Baal here (1 Kings 16:32) that brought condemnation of the place from the prophets and started kingdom and capital on a slide that would result in their destruction by Assyria (2 Kings 17:5–6).
Sea of Galilee	This low-elevation, inland lake has a high profile in the Gospels because many days of Jesus's ministry were spent on its waters and shorelines. Jesus called disciples from fishermen plying its waters (Matt. 4:18), miraculously fed thousands on its shoreline (Matt. 15:29), and stilled its storms (Matt. 8:24).
Shechem	This town was the highest profile worship site in the promised land prior to the time Joshua set up the tabernacle at Shiloh. Shechem became intimately linked to the Abrahamic covenant as the site of the first theophany in the promised land (Gen. 12:6–7). It was linked to the Mosaic covenant, as Joshua renewed the covenant here at the close of the conquest (Josh. 24:1–27).
Shiloh	The sanctuary city became the home of the tabernacle at the time of Joshua (Josh. 18:1) and was where the final distribution of the land took place (Josh. 18:8–10). Although Samuel was called to service here (1 Sam. 3), the failure of the priests and people to maintain the sanctity of the site led to its destruction by the Philistines (1 Sam. 2:27–36; Ps. 78:60; Jer. 7:12–14).
Sychar	This New Testament Samaritan village lay adjacent to the site of Old Testament Shechem. Jesus declared himself to be Messiah in this place so intimately linked to the covenants that anticipated his arrival and identified the non-Jewish Samaritans as the field ripe for harvesting (John 4:1–42).
Thessalonica	As the chief port of Macedonia, this city offered the bridge between the Thermaic Gulf and the Egnatian Way. It was an open cultural center in which new ideas would find an interested audience. Paul visited this city and wrote back-to-back letters to the Christians there (Acts 17:1–9; 1–2 Thess.).

Archaeology and the Bible

What is archaeology?

Archaeology is the carefully designed investigation of the past that studies the architecture and artifacts that have survived in the ground. It identifies, recovers, interprets, preserves, and publishes information about those objects.

What value does archaeology have for Bible students?

It enhances and broadens our understanding of historical events.

It expands and amplifies our understanding of ancient culture, that is, human activity and thought.

It sharpens our identification of named places and advances our mapping of the land.

It improves our understanding of the status of and changes in the ancient ecosystems.

How are artifacts and architecture assigned dates in the Middle East?

By noting the metals from which household implements and weapons are made.

By recovering items that have a date on them (i.e., a coin) or items that contain the name of a well-known person whose dates have been confirmed.

By the carbon dating of organic materials.

By examining the pottery recovered at an archaeological site.

Clay was easily shaped and hardened into a variety of household items. The method of manufacture, form, decoration, and ware changed regularly even if a new culture had not arrived at a site. Thus ceramic dating is the most common method used to date artifacts and architecture in the biblical world.

Archaeological Periods

3300–1200 BC The Canaanite Period

3300–2300 Early Bronze Age I–III

Bronze becomes the primary metal for making tools and weapons as writing develops in the Fertile Crescent. Fortified cities complete with temples and palaces develop in Canaan by about 3000 BC. Abraham's family lives in Mesopotamia.

2300–2000 Early Bronze Age IV (Middle Bronze)

The larger urban centers collapse and are replaced by unfortified settlements and camps used by those migrating according to the rhythms of their animals' needs. Abraham's family arrives in Canaan.

2000–1550 Middle Bronze Age

Larger walled cities and greater signs of wealth return to Canaan together with a nomadic people known as the Amorites. Abraham's family lives in Canaan until famine drives them to Egypt.

1550–1200 Late Bronze Age

Egypt's power extends over the Canaanite city-states. Moses leads the Israelites out of Egypt, to Mount Sinai, and then to the edge of the promised land. Joshua leads Israel in the conquest of Canaan. The time of the judges begins.

1200–586 BC The Israelite Age

1200–925 Iron Age I

The Philistines arrive in Canaan. Iron becomes the metal of choice for making tools and weapons. The time of the judges continues and concludes. Samuel anoints Saul and David, Israel's first two kings. Its third king, Solomon, is the last to rule Israel as a united kingdom. By 930 BC the united kingdom has become the divided kingdom.

925–586 Iron Age II

Israel is ruled as two kingdoms, each with its own capital and king yet with a shared spiritual responsibility. As both kingdoms struggle spiritually, the corrective words of prophets like Elijah and Elisha fail to elicit the urgent changes needed in the northern kingdom. The Lord uses the Assyrian Empire to punish Israel. Samaria, its capital, is destroyed in 722 BC; its people are removed from their land and scattered around the Assyrian Empire. The southern kingdom (Judah) also fails to make needed changes when chastised by the prophets but survives the Assyrian assault. It succumbs to the Babylonian Empire, which begins a series of deportations that take Judeans from the promised land to Babylon (605 BC). The siege and destruction of Jerusalem and its temple follow in 586 BC.

586–539 BC The Neo-Babylonian Period

Daniel and Ezekiel speak to God's people exiled to Babylon while a small remnant of Jews remains in the land, all awaiting a return to the promised land, which was to occur seventy years after their exile began.

539–332 BC The Persian Period

The Persians displace Babylon as the empire that controlled the known world. A Jewish girl by the name of Esther becomes queen of Persia for a time as Judah becomes the province of Yehud. Zerubbabel, Ezra, and Nehemiah work to rebuild the temple in Jerusalem, the walls of Jerusalem, and the faithfulness of the returning exiles sent back to their homeland by Cyrus.

332–167 BC Early Hellenistic Period

Alexander the Great conquers Persia and then the world, establishing Greek language and culture as the norm throughout his empire. Upon his death in 323 BC, Alexander the Great's generals and their families take the reins of power; the Ptolemies (Greek kings in Egypt) and Seleucids (Greek kings in Syria) battle one another for the upper hand while the Jews and their land are repeatedly caught in the middle of this fight. The darkest days are associated with the reign of Antiochus IV Epiphanes, whose radical plan of Hellenization seeks to eradicate the worship practices that make the Jews unique.

167–37 BC Late Hellenistic Period (Hasmonean)

Jewish revolutionaries led by the Maccabee family fight back against the radical Hellenization of Antiochus IV, reestablish Jewish political autonomy, cleanse the temple, and liberate the Jews so that they can practice their religion without penalty. Jewish kings (Hasmoneans) again rule Israel and expand the state's land holdings. The destruction of the Samaritan temple on Mount Gerizim creates enmity between Jews and Samaritans that lingers into the time of Jesus. But Hasmonean succession problems bring Rome's unwelcomed presence and the loss of Jewish autonomy by 63 BC.

37 BC–AD 132 Early Roman Period

The Roman senate appoints Herod the Great as King of Judea in 40 BC. This begins his storied political and building career that overlaps with the birth of Jesus. Herod's paranoia over this rival leader leads him to seek the execution of Jesus by ordering the death of the infants in Bethlehem. Upon Herod's death, his kingdom is divided between his three sons: Herod Antipas (Galilee and Perea), Herod Philip (Iturea, Traconitis, and Gaulanitis), and Archelaus (Judah). Archelaus fails so badly that he is removed from office, and Judah is ruled directly by the Romans starting in AD 6. This is the time of Jesus's ministry on earth, the expansion of the kingdom recorded in the book of Acts, and the letters of the New Testament.

Glossary of Archaeological Terms

absolute dating The process of assigning an approximate, chronometric date to an object or structure. This is achieved by its association with a datable object such as a coin or alternative method of age estimation, such as radio carbon dating.

AD/CE Labels that identify something that was made or happened after the date of Jesus's birth. The abbreviation AD stands for *Anno Domini* ("the year of the Lord"). The abbreviation CE stands for "Common Era."

artifact An object made by humans or an object modified for human use that provides insight into the way people lived and thought.

ashlar A building stone that has been harvested from a quarry and then cut into a square or rectangle.

balk/baulk An unexcavated wall allowed to remain between the squares being investigated and that provides a physical record of the strata encountered as the archaeologists dig down into the square.

BC/BCE Labels that identify something that was made or happened before the date of Jesus's birth. BC is the abbreviation for "Before Christ." BCE is an abbreviation for "Before the Common Era."

ceramics Manmade objects formed from clay and baked hard.

chronometric dating Dates that are expressed in years (e.g., 2014).

dendrochronology A system of absolute dating that uses tree ring patterns to more precisely date an object or stratum by comparing known growth patterns of trees in an area with the tree rings evident in a wooden artifact.

flotation A method that places excavated soil in water and then uses the buoyancy of animal and plant remains to discover these materials, which are too small to be easily discovered by sifting.

gufa (**Arabic "basket"**) Rubber basket used for moving excavated materials.

in situ The original position of an artifact when it is first discovered.

locus Location defined in three-dimensional space. Each object discovered or removed from an archaeological site will have its original location identified in this way.

material culture Manmade objects and architectural elements used by people of the past.

ostracon A potsherd that has ancient writing on it.

potsherd A fragment of a broken ceramic vessel also called a "sherd."

radiocarbon dating Dating method that compares the known decay rate of C-14 with the remaining C-14 in an organic object in order to estimate its age (± 50 years).

relative dating A system of dating that uses the location of an artifact and/or its similarity to another artifact to organize material culture from oldest to most recent (chronology) yet without assigning the objects a chronometric date.

sifting The investigation technique that calls for the sifting of all excavated soil through a screen in order to detect any small objects that may have been missed during the excavating of this material.

square Today most archaeological sites are divided into a grid of uniformly spaced, ten-meter-by-ten-meter squares that are separated from adjoining squares by a balk. Each square is assigned to a digging team and square supervisor responsible for its excavation.

stratigraphy The interpretation of the strata or layers in a tel, each of which contains evidence of a single period of human occupation.

tel/tell An artificial hill created when people return to settle on the same location again and again because of the natural advantages the location offers.

toponymy The study that investigates the origin of place names and how those place names are assigned to regions, natural features, and urban centers.

Geographical Zones of the Promised Land

See also the maps "Geographical Zones of the Promised Land" and "Rainfall in the Promised Land."

Coastal Plain

Geography	*Culture*
Low in elevation	Grain agriculture
Generally level terrain close to the Mediterranean Sea	Easily traveled (International Highway)
	Easily invaded

Central Mountains

Geography	*Culture*
High in elevation	Terraced agriculture for olives and fruit
Steep-sided mountains and narrow, V-shaped valleys	Difficult to travel
	Difficult to invade

Jordan Rift Valley

Geography	*Culture*
Elevations below sea level	North: fishing and agriculture
Sea of Galilee, Jordan River, and Dead Sea	South: mining for salt and bitumen
	Lightly traveled due to swamps, large predator attacks, and high temperatures

Transjordan Plateau

Geography	*Culture*
Highest in elevation	North: grain agriculture and cattle
Mountains and high plateaus	Middle: olives and fruit, sheep and goats
	South: camels and trade
	Travel on the King's Highway

Seasons and Culture

Summer Season—May through September

Climate	*Culture*
Stable atmosphere	Overland travel
Sunny skies	Mediterranean shipping
Warmer temperatures (Jerusalem average high 83°F)	Season for war
Pleasant, westerly sea breeze	Maturing of the olives, dates, grapes, and figs
No rain	People look for ways to stay cool
High humidity and dewfall	Cisterns empty and water table drops
	Flowers wither
	Pastures dry out

Winter Season—October through April

Climate	*Culture*
Unstable atmosphere	Overland travel diminishes
Frequent cloudy days	Mediterranean shipping ceases
Cooler temperatures (Jerusalem average high 63°F)	Season of peace
Gusty winds	Maturing and harvesting grain
Rain and occasional snow	People look for ways to warm up
	Cisterns fill and the water table recharges
	Flowers spring to life
	Pastures turn green

Winds of the Promised Land

Pressure-Induced Winds

Source

Created as air moves between high- and low-pressure areas

Cultural Impact

High winds associated with deep lows of the winter season that can destroy structures and threaten shipping on the Mediterranean Sea

Examples

Ezekiel 13:13–14; 27:26; Matthew 7:27; Acts 27:13–14

Mediterranean Sea Breeze

Source

Created during the summer months when air cooled over the Mediterranean Sea moves inland to replace the warm air rising over the land

Cultural Impact

Celebrated winds that provide natural air-conditioning
The predictable breeze that farmers used to winnow their grain

Examples

Job 21:18; Psalm 1:4; Isaiah 17:13

Sharqiya

Source

Created when cool air on the ridges above the Sea of Galilee descends violently into the lake basin

Cultural Impact

The destructive and unpredictable winds that can catch even experienced fishermen off guard and fill them with terror

Examples

Matthew 14:22–24; Mark 4:35–37; Luke 8:22–25

Khamsin

Source

The dry south and southeast winds that bring high temperatures and fill the air with gritty, yellow clouds of dust as the atmosphere changes between seasons

Cultural Impact

Suddenly and totally decimates pastures and wildflowers in early summer
Irritating winds that shorten tempers
Symbol of divine judgment

Examples

Psalm 103:15–16; Isaiah 27:8; Jeremiah 18:17; Hosea 12:1; Luke 12:55

Water in the Promised Land

Rainfall-Dependent World

By contrast to Egypt or Mesopotamia, where major rivers and irrigation provide access to fresh water, the promised land is dependent on rainfall (Deut. 11:10–11).

Because rainfall virtually ceases for seven months of the year (April–October), the rainwater has to be captured, or underground water has to be accessed to assure a yearlong supply.

Sources for Water

Spring

Springs occur naturally when the land's surface coincides with the elevation of the water table.
They offer clean, filtered water with minimum need for development or maintenance.

Well

Wells are shafts dug down to the water table.
Their sides were lined with fieldstones to prevent collapse.
A cap and cover were added to prevent evaporation and contamination.
Yearly maintenance was required.

Cistern

Cisterns were underground chambers dug into bedrock to store runoff water captured during the rainy season.
They have a narrow neck near the surface, which widens into a bell-shaped body.
A cap and cover were added to prevent evaporation and contamination.
Yearly maintenance was required to replace the plaster that waterproofs its sides.

Aqueduct, Tunnel, and Reservoir

These major construction projects undertaken by strong central governments were meant to access, move, and store water at locations more convenient for those living in large cities.
Yearly maintenance was required.

Plants and Trees of the Bible

Acacia Tree

Biology

Various species of this thorny tree grow in the dry desert areas.

Human Connection

It is the only hardwood that grows in the dry wilderness areas and so becomes the wood used by Moses when building the tabernacle and its worship furniture. Its long-burning wood was used for building fires. And because camel saliva can soften its thorns, it provides nourishment for them in settings with little forage.

Bible Examples

Exodus 25:10, 13, 23, 28; 27:1; Isaiah 41:19

Almond Tree

Biology

The almond tree thrives throughout all but the driest areas of the promised land. In January it produces a beautiful pink and white flower ahead of the leaves, an indication that spring has arrived. By March, the flowers fade as the leaves and nuts appear.

Human Connection

Both the green and dried almonds are very rich in nutritional value. Sweet almonds were used as a cough suppressant and a headache remedy. The tree is associated with alert and hopeful expectation.

Bible Examples

Exodus 37:19–20; Numbers 17:8; Ecclesiastes 12:5; Jeremiah 1:11–12

Cedar of Lebanon

Biology

This is a conifer with silvery-blue needles that grow from long branches that reach out like arms from the mature tree's trunk. They are most common in the Lebanon mountains north of the promised land, where they grow more than a hundred feet tall in their one-hundred-plus-year lifespan.

Human Connection

The reddish tones, pleasant aroma, and straight grain made this cedar the standout choice for construction if one could afford the price. It is associated with prestige, power, and beauty.

Bible Examples

2 Samuel 5:11; 1 Kings 5:6–18; 7:1–7; Psalms 29:5; 92:12; Song of Songs 5:15; Ezekiel 31:10–17

Fig Tree

Biology

The fig tree grows throughout the promised land. When its ashen gray trunk is coaxed to life by the winter rains, it produces fruit and small leaves marking the start of spring. The earliest set of fruit is called *page*, but the tree repeatedly bears new sets of fruit into the fall. It is easily distinguished by its massive, lobed leaves.

Human Connection

The leaves provide some of the most effective shade in the region. And the natural sugars in its fruit were used as a sweetener. Dried figs offered an energy boost for travelers. It is a tree associated with the good life (Micah 4:4).

Bible Examples

Genesis 3:7; 1 Kings 4:25; Song of Songs 2:13; Hosea 9:10; Matthew 21:19–21; Mark 13:28

Grapevine

Biology

The grapevine is a deciduous climber that grows throughout the land but thrives particularly in the hill country of Judah, maturing with the aid of dewfall during the dry summer months.

Human Connection

This vine, which grew wild in the promised land, was among the first plants to be domesticated. Its fruit was eaten when fresh and dried into raisins. Its juice was drunk fresh and fermented into wine to supplement the meager supply of fresh water. It was associated with joy and the good life (Micah 4:4). Because it is so intimately linked to the promised land and God's chosen people, it is often used as a symbol for them.

Bible Examples

Numbers 13:24; Psalm 80:8–13; Song of Songs 7:7–8; Isaiah 5:1–7; John 15:1–5

Oak Tree

Biology

Five different species of oak inhabit Israel, all of which produce acorns and all of which grow in widely spaced stands with meadowland between them. They thrive from the mountains of Samaria all the way to Mount Hermon. It is the most widely represented of the wild-growing trees in Israel and also has produced the oldest surviving tree in Israel at a little over five hundred years of age.

Human Connection

The sturdy wood from this tree was used to make tool handles, plows, and yokes. Its chemical properties were used in the tanning of leather and as a traditional folk medicine used to lower blood pressure and cure eye infections. It became a symbol of strength and fertility.

Bible Examples

Joshua 24:26; 2 Samuel 18:9–14; Psalm 29:9; Isaiah 1:29–30; 57:5; Amos 2:9

Olive Tree

Biology

The olive tree thrives in the mountains of Israel, producing the highest quality olives in Samaria. Wild olive trees were domesticated to enhance the olive harvest, which occurs in September.

Human Connection

Both the green and more mature black olives were eaten after processing. Special effort was made to extract the oil from the olives. It was used for cooking, as a medicine, for cosmetics, in the production of soap, to anoint leaders, and as the fuel burned in lamps. The olive tree is associated with beauty, health, stability, nobility, and divine favor.

Bible Examples

Genesis 8:11; Exodus 30:22–25; Job 29:6; Psalm 23:5; Jeremiah 31:12; Matthew 25:3–10; Luke 10:34

Pomegranate Tree

Biology

The pomegranate is one of the signature trees of the promised land (Deut. 8:8). It produces beautiful red flowers in the spring. Its fruit ripens over the dry summer months and is harvested in fall.

Human Connection

The moist, delicious fruit of this tree was enjoyed and celebrated because it ripened just as the cistern water was at its lowest quality. Pomegranate juice was drunk fresh and fermented into wine. According to the rabbis, the pomegranate has 613 seeds. That links it to the Torah, in which the rabbis found 613 laws. This is why Torah scroll handles are adorned with the pomegranate and perhaps why this fruit appears so frequently in the art that adorns the Old Testament sanctuary.

Bible Examples

Exodus 28:33–34; Numbers 13:23; 1 Kings 7:18, 20, 42; 2 Kings 25:17; Song of Songs 6:7; Haggai 2:19

Sycamore Tree

Biology

The biblical sycamore tree is not related to the sycamore trees of the Western world but is rather a type of fig tree. It is a very large tree with a rounded crown that produces a copious amount of shade. While rare today, it was present along the coastal plain and filled the foothills during Bible times.

Human Connection

The small fig produced by this tree along all its external surfaces, including the trunk, is eaten though it is of lower quality than the true fig. Its ripening can be enhanced by puncturing its skin, something shepherds like Amos were often hired to do as they watched their flocks (Amos 7:14). The branches of this tree combine the qualities of lightness and strength; consequently, they were employed as roof rafters.

Bible Examples

1 Kings 10:27; 1 Chronicles 27:28; Psalm 78:47; Isaiah 9:10; Luke 19:4

Tamarisk Tree

Biology

The tamarisk (also called a salt cedar) makes its home in the hottest and driest parts of the promised land where the soil is too salty for many other plants to survive. It extrudes a bit of that salt onto its linear leaves in order to attract moisture from the atmosphere, which it then absorbs through its leaf structures.

Human Connection

As one of the only trees that grows in the arid areas of this land, it was used for cooling. Although its leaves offer precious little shade, a freshening microclimate is created when the excess water that gathers on the salt-laden leaves evaporates in the late morning hours.

Bible Examples

Genesis 21:33; 1 Samuel 22:6; 31:13

Wild Animals of the Bible

Bear

Habitat and Habits

The Syrian brown bear, more tan than brown in color, is an omnivore that lived in the mountain forests of Israel. It was the largest of the large predators that lived in this land with males tipping the scale at more than six hundred pounds. Despite their size, threatened bears could charge at speeds up to thirty-five miles per hour.

Human Connection

While bears generally avoided contact with humans, their size, speed, and unpredictability presented a real threat to shepherds and travelers. The risk increased dramatically if the encounter was with a sow accompanied by her young. The bear was a symbol of power and strength.

Bible Examples

1 Samuel 17:34–37; 2 Samuel 17:8; Proverbs 28:15; Lamentations 3:10–11; Daniel 7:5; Amos 5:19

Deer

Habitat and Habits

Three different types of deer lived in the forests of Israel during Bible times. The red deer was the largest of them, standing five feet tall at the shoulder. Only the males had antlers. The fallow deer was just three feet tall at the shoulder. It was distinguished by the spots that both males and females had on their coats and by the thick, moose-like antlers sported by the males. The roe deer was the smallest of all at less than three feet at the shoulder with short, erect antlers. In all cases, deer used forest cover to remain out of the sight of predators, resorting to their speed and agility when spotted and threatened.

Human Connection

Listed among the clean animals, the deer was eaten by the Israelites. It was a symbol of beauty, agility, and speed.

Bible Examples

Deuteronomy 12:15; 1 Kings 4:23; Psalms 18:33; 42:1; Proverbs 5:19; Song of Songs 2:9, 17; Isaiah 35:6; Habakkuk 3:19

Dog

Habitat and Habits

Dogs are wild pack animals by nature, carnivores, and descendants of the wolf. But some of these canines with a more docile inclination found their way into the company of humans, living in their cities and near their camps. Interbreeding of these more docile animals diminished the wildness in them, opening the door for a closer relationship with humans.

Human Connection

In Egypt and Mesopotamia, dogs were employed as hunting assistants, herd protectors, and watchdogs. References to the last two roles are found in the Bible. But it was the semi-wild, scavenging packs of dogs in Israel that led to their more negative characterization in the Bible. They are pictured not as cuddly companion animals but as menacing creatures that eat untended and unburied bodies. Thus to be associated with a dog was to be regarded as lower class and disgusting.

Bible Examples

Exodus 22:31; 1 Samuel 17:43; 2 Kings 9:36; Job 30:1; Psalm 22:20; Isaiah 56:10–11; Matthew 7:6; 15:26–27

Dove

Habitat and Habits

This medium-sized bird is present in all but the driest locations of Israel. The most common species are the rock dove, collared dove, turtle dove, and laughing dove. The subtle, pastel tones of their plumage make them among the most attractive birds in Israel. These birds are vulnerable when on the ground, and a burst into flight is their only defense against predators.

Human Connection

Doves were quick to abandon natural nesting sites for buildings or dovecotes. Dovecotes are structures built by humans that mimic nesting habitat so that the doves are drawn to build their nests where it is more convenient to gather eggs or doves themselves for food or sacrifice. Their dung was also collected and used to fertilize gardens. Doves symbolized gentle innocence, beauty, and vulnerability.

Bible Examples

Leviticus 1:14; Psalms 55:6; 74:19; Song of Songs 1:15; 2:14; 5:2; Jeremiah 48:28; Hosea 7:11; Matthew 3:16; 10:16

Eagle

Habitat and Habits

Many species of eagles are either resident in Israel or migrate through, including the imperial eagle, short-toed eagle, golden eagle, and Bonelli's eagle. All effortlessly rise on thermals, soaring in search of snakes, birds, small mammals, or carrion for food. They build their nests in remote locations, particularly high rocky outcroppings where they are fiercely protective of their young.

Human Connection

Although the eagle was listed among the unclean animals (Lev. 11:13), the Israelites were captivated by this bird, particularly by the majesty of its flight. The eagle symbolized loving care, youthful vitality, and wondrous speed.

Bible Examples

Exodus 19:4; Deuteronomy 32:11; 2 Samuel 1:23; Proverbs 30:19; Isaiah 40:31; Jeremiah 49:22; Revelation 8:13

Fox

Habitat and Habits

Several species of fox inhabited ancient Israel, but the one mentioned in the Bible is the red fox, which lives in the mountain forests. It is about twenty-four inches in length, with shorter legs and a tail that can be longer than the rest of its body. This dusky red fox is a solitary hunter that will consume everything from small mammals to lizards to insects to fruit. It tends to hunt in a home range, where it establishes multiple holes in which to cache its food.

Human Connection

Among the predators of Israel, the fox barely deserves a rank, viewed more as a nuisance than a mortal threat. In Greek and Roman fables, the fox became a symbol of cunning.

Bible Examples

Judges 15:4–5; Nehemiah 4:3; Song of Songs 2:15; Matthew 8:20; Luke 13:32

Gazelle

Habitat and Habits

The gazelle is a member of the antelope family and has a tan back and lighter underbelly separated by a dark brown side stripe. The larger mountain gazelle is three feet tall at the shoulder and prefers the habitat of northern Israel, where grasses abound. The Dorcas gazelle is just two feet tall at the shoulder with slightly more red in its coat. It prefers the drier southern reaches of Israel, where it acquires the majority of its water from the plants it eats. The male Dorcas gazelle has sweeping horns that form a heart shape when viewed from the front.

Human Connection

The gazelle was consumed as food by the Israelites but appears most frequently in the Bible as a symbol of speed and beauty. When threatened, the gazelle's initial burst of speed can top fifty miles per hour. Its long neck, athletic build, and dark eyes set off by facial stripes assure its place among the most beautiful of God's creatures.

Bible Examples

Deuteronomy 12:22; 2 Samuel 1:19; 2:18; 1 Chronicles 12:8; Song of Songs 2:9, 17; 7:3; Isaiah 13:14

Ibex

Habitat and Habits

The Nubian ibex, or wild goat, has a sandy brown coat with a white underbelly that matches well with the arid environment it calls home. Males are about three times larger than females and sport a striking set of horns that curve gracefully over their backs, achieving a length of more than fifty inches. Food and water call them from the steep mountain slopes, but they quickly return to this near-vertical habitat, which provides security from predators.

Human Connection

The wild goat was hunted and eaten by Israelites. Its handsome appearance made it a symbol of beauty. And its effortless and graceful movement on sheer mountain faces caused mortals to marvel and list it among the wonders of God's created world.

Bible Examples

Genesis 22:13; Deuteronomy 14:5; 1 Samuel 24:2; Job 39:1; Psalm 104:18; Isaiah 13:21; 34:14

Leopard

Habitat and Habits

This eight-foot-long carnivore is distinguished from all others in ancient Israel by its spotted coat. The leopard is a solitary, nocturnal hunter that uses stealth and slow, purposeful movements to get into proximity of its prey. It then pounces and delivers the death blow by using its powerful jaw muscles to break the neck of its victim, whether wild goat, domesticated livestock, or human traveler.

Human Connection

The leopard was among the large predators that ancient travelers and shepherds feared. As the fastest predator in the biblical world, it became a symbol of agility and speed.

Bible Examples

Song of Songs 4:8; Isaiah 11:6; Jeremiah 5:6; 13:23; Daniel 7:6; Hosea 13:7; Habakkuk 1:8; Revelation 13:2

Lion

Habitat and Habits

Tipping the scale at over five hundred pounds, this predator joined with the bear in being the largest carnivores in the region. Rather than relying upon speed and solo hunting tactics, lions hunt in prides, using the cover of darkness and carefully orchestrated attacks to confuse and bring down prey animals with the strength that is their signature trait.

Human Connection

While lion hunting is depicted as a royal sport in Mesopotamia, the residents of Israel lived in fear of this predator mentioned more than any other in the Bible. It attacked sheep as well as ancient travelers. While the lion was feared, its qualities were deeply respected and used as metaphors when speaking about the courage and strength of celebrated mortals. Those who survived encounters with lions were deserving of special recognition.

Bible Examples

Genesis 49:9; Deuteronomy 33:22; Judges 14:5–6; 1 Samuel 17:36–37; 2 Kings 17:25; Psalm 22:13, 21; Isaiah 11:6; 1 Peter 5:8; Revelation 5:5

Owl

Habitat and Habits

Eight species of owl either inhabit or migrate through the promised land. The eagle owl (great owl) is the most easily recognized given its seventy-nine-inch wingspan, piercing orange eyes, and upright ear tufts. The little owl is the most easily seen. This plump bird is the owl most likely to be active during the daylight hours. Owls of all types are generally nocturnal and live secretive lives, preferring to live in ruins or in remote places that allow them to avoid contact with people.

Human Connection

Because of owls' habitat and nocturnal habits, most people would not have seen them, although they may have heard them from time to time. Consequently the owl became a symbol of social isolation or abandonment.

Bible Examples

Leviticus 11:16–18; Job 30:29; Psalm 102:6; Isaiah 14:23; Jeremiah 50:39; Micah 1:8; Zephaniah 2:14

Raven

Habitat and Habits

This member of the crow family is represented in Israel by the common raven (north) as well as the fan-tailed raven and brown-necked raven (south). The common raven stands twenty-five inches tall with a wingspan of fifty-five inches. Its impressive size and glossy black plumage distinguish it from other birds. Ravens are omnivores that eat everything from locusts to frogs to fruit, and they scavenge on carcasses.

Human Connection

Among the Jews, ravens were listed among the unclean animals because of their tendency to eat carrion. Yet there is great respect for this bird's intelligence given their problem-solving skills. It is the intelligence of the raven that likely influences its mention in the lives of Noah, Elijah, and Jesus.

Bible Examples

Genesis 8:7; Leviticus 11:15; 1 Kings 17:6; Job 38:41; Psalm 147:9; Proverbs 30:17; Song of Songs 5:11; Isaiah 34:11; Luke 12:24

Rock Hyrax

Habitat and Habits

The rock hyrax, which resembles a marmot or guinea pig, lives in noisy colonies that can have dozens of members. Hyraxes have a gray-brown furry coat with a creamy underbelly, short ears, and long black whiskers. They also have very distinctive foot pads that allow them to move efficiently about their rocky homes. Their diet consists of vegetation of all kinds, from which they also derive a good share of the water they need. The greater part of their day is spent basking in the sun, never wandering far from the rocky outcroppings where they can quickly find shelter in the rocky crags from eagles patrolling the area for a meal.

Human Connection

The Bible lists the hyrax among the unclean animals. Although it lacks natural defensive skills, its wisdom is celebrated in choosing rocky crags as its home.

Bible Examples

Leviticus 11:5; Deuteronomy 14:7; Psalm 104:18; Proverbs 30:26

Snake

Habitat and Habits

Thirty-six species of snakes reside in the promised land, six of them equipped with poison. These species inhabit all sectors of the land and range in size from one to six feet in length. Their diet consists of insects, lizards, birds, and small mammals. As cold-blooded animals, they regulate their body temperature by changing their environment. They are most likely to be seen when basking in the sun and most likely to strike foot or hand when disturbed while hiding in a cool recess away from the sun.

Human Connection

The ancients regarded the snake as among the shrewdest and most mysterious of the animals. The encounters with poisonous snakes led to the view that snakes were dangerous creatures. Thus *snake* became a derogatory term for someone deemed undesirable and dangerous.

Bible Examples

Genesis 3:1; 49:17; Exodus 7:9–10; Numbers 21:6; Proverbs 23:32; Amos 5:19; Matthew 10:16; 23:33; Mark 16:18; Luke 10:19; Revelation 20:2

Stork

Habitat and Habits

The white stork is the largest member of the stork family, identified by its long red beak and its long red legs, which lift it to a standing height of three feet. It is easily distinguished in flight by its tendency to find thermals on which it soars with wings set in place. In flight, the striking white leading edge of the wing contrasts with the black trailing edge. The white and black storks (the latter having a glossy black back and white belly) migrate through Israel, stopping to feed where they can find shallow standing water around which they hunt for various small animals.

Human Connection

During the migration seasons, the sky can fill with thousands of storks, leaving ground-bound mortals to marvel at their flight. While listing them among the unclean animals, the biblical authors celebrate their choice of season for migrating and energy-saving method of flight.

Bible Examples

Leviticus 11:19; Job 39:13; Psalm 104:17; Jeremiah 8:7; Zechariah 5:9

Vulture

Habitat and Habits

The griffin vulture is the largest of the birds of prey, with a wingspan of up to eight feet; it was the most common vulture in the promised land during Bible times. It leaves the nests it builds on high cliffs each morning to fly on the thermals generated as the ground warms. The heavier vulture flies chiefly by soaring with its wings set in a shallow V shape. It flies to high altitudes from which it can use its highly refined eyesight to spot dead animals, which it consumes.

Human Connection

As a carrion eater, the vulture is listed among the unclean animals. The great majority of Bible references are associated with its method of flight and its passion for settling on dead animals.

Bible Examples

Genesis 15:11; Leviticus 11:13; Job 15:23; Proverbs 30:17; Micah 1:16; Matthew 24:28

Wild Ox

Habitat and Habits

The auroch, or wild ox, was the ancestor of domestic cattle in the promised land, thriving in those places where natural pastures formed. It is now extinct, making it necessary to rely upon ancient descriptions and surviving skeletal remains to re-create the appearance of this animal. The bulls weighed in at 1,500 pounds and stood six feet at the shoulder, carrying horns that were up to thirty-one inches in length and seven inches in diameter.

Human Connection

The wild ox was the largest and most powerful hoofed animal in Israel during Bible times. It was threatening, fierce, and powerful. It came to symbolize vitality, independence, and menacing strength.

Bible Examples

Numbers 23:22; Deuteronomy 33:17; Job 39:9; Psalms 22:21; 29:6; 92:10; Isaiah 34:7

Wolf

Habitat and Habits

The Iranian wolf, which prefers the northern part of Israel, and the Arabian wolf, which prefers the desert south, are both medium-sized wolves at just twenty-six inches tall at the shoulder and between forty and sixty pounds. These are highly effective predators who stalk their prey before striking with jaws that have twice the clamping force of the average domesticated dog. If the initial strike fails, the wolf has the endurance and tenacity to pursue its fleeing prey until exhaustion forces the animal to the ground.

Human Connection

The wolf was a threat to the livestock of those living in Bible times though less dangerous to humans than the lion and the bear. It came to symbolize those who were aggressive, capable, and threatening.

Bible Examples

Genesis 49:27; Isaiah 11:6; Jeremiah 5:6; Ezekiel 22:27; Zephaniah 3:3; Matthew 10:16; John 10:12; Acts 20:29

The Agricultural Year in Israel

Climate

The summer season of drought comes to a close with the increasing chances for rainfall in late September. The peak months for receiving rain are December and January, when the most rain falls in the land; then the chance for rain diminishes again so that there is virtual drought between mid-May and mid-September. During those drought months, evening dewfall becomes an important source of moisture for maturing plants.

Agricultural Calendar

Nov–Dec	Grain fields are plowed and planted
Dec–Mar	Grain fields mature
April	Barley harvest
May	Wheat harvest
June–Aug	Summer fruit matures
July–Sept	Grape harvest (varies with region)
Aug–Sept	Fig, pomegranate, date harvest
Sept–Oct	Olive harvest

Religious Festivals Related to the Agricultural Year

For more on the festivals, see "Holidays and Celebrations" below.

Passover: associated with the barley harvest

Pentecost (Feast of Weeks): associated with the wheat harvest

Feast of Tabernacles: associated with the close of the agricultural year and with the expectation that it will rain again soon

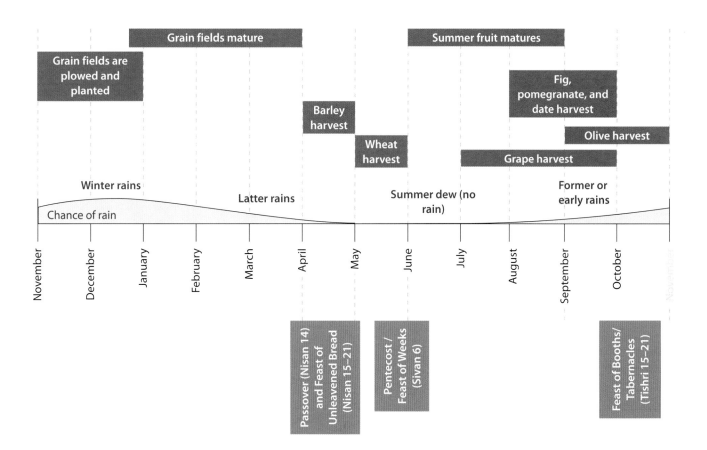

Agriculture

Scratch plow

Threshing floor

Threshing sledge

Winnowing fork

©John A. Beck

Household grain mills

Olive presses

Winepress

Agricultural watchtower

Weights and Measures

Weights

Unit	Relationship to System	Approximate English Equivalent	Approximate Metric Equivalent
Gerah	.05 shekel	.02 ounce	.57 gram
Beka (Bekah)	.5 shekel	.22 ounce	6.2 grams
Pim	.67 shekel	.33 ounce	9.3 grams
Shekel	2 bekahs	.4 ounce	11.3 grams
Litra	30 shekels	12 ounces	.34 kilogram
Mina (pound)	50 shekels	1.25 pounds	.57 kilogram
Talent	3,000 shekels	75 pounds	34 kilograms

Lengths

Unit	Relationship to System	Approximate English Equivalent	Approximate Metric Equivalent
Finger	.25 of a handbreadth	.75 inch	1.9 centimeters
Handbreadth	4 fingers	3 inches	7.6 centimeters
Span (spread fingers)	3 handbreadths	9 inches	23 centimeters
Cubit (elbow to fingertip)	2 spans	18 inches	46 centimeters
Pace (stride length)	.5 of a fathom	3 feet	.91 meter
Fathom	2 paces	6 feet	1.8 meters
Kalamos (reed)	3 paces	9 feet	2.7 meters
Stadion (furlong)	200 paces	600 feet	183 meters
Sabbath Day's walk	6 stadia	.68 mile	1.1 kilometers
Milion (mile)	8 stadia	.92 mile	1.5 kilometers

Liquid Volume

Unit	Relationship to System	Approximate English Equivalent	Approximate Metric Equivalent
Log	.014 bath	.67 pint	.3 liter
Xestēs (pot)	.13 hin	1.2 pints	.57 liter
Kab (cab)	4 logs	2.67 pints	1.3 liters
Hin	3 cabs	1 gallon	3.8 liters
Bath (ephah)	6 hins	5.8 gallons	22 liters
Metretes (measure)	10 hins	10 gallons	38 liters
Cor (homer)	10 baths	60 gallons	227 liters

Dry Volume

Unit	Relationship to System	Approximate English Equivalent	Approximate Metric Equivalent
Xestēs (pot)	.5 cab	1.1 pints	.5 liter
Kab (cab)	.06 ephah	1.3 quarts	1.2 liters
Omer	.10 ephah	2.3 quarts	2.2 liters
Seah (measure)	.33 ephah	7.7 quarts	7.3 liters
Modios	4 omers	9.5 quarts	9 liters
Ephah (bath)	10 omers	23 quarts	22 liters
Lethek	5 ephahs	116 quarts	110 liters
Cor (homer)	10 ephahs	233 quarts	220 liters

Prophets of the Bible (Nonwriting)

Prophet	Role	Scripture References
Abraham	Father of the Jewish nation and of the Messiah who taught his family in word and action what it meant to trust the Lord.	Genesis 20:7
Moses	Led Israel out of Egypt and to the border of the promised land. Received and authored the Torah.	Deuteronomy 34:10
Miriam	The sister of Moses who joined with him and Aaron to lead Israel. She led the Israelite women in song after the crossing of the Red Sea.	Exodus 15:20; Micah 6:4
Deborah	A leader in Israel who directed the actions of Barak in his battle with Hazor.	Judges 4:4
Samuel	As the final judge of Israel, he led a spiritual reformation in advance of anointing Israel's first two kings.	1 Samuel 3:20
Nathan	Appears as David and Solomon's personal, spiritual counselor.	2 Samuel 7:2; 12:25; 1 Kings 1:34
Gad	David's "seer" who advised him on how to elude Saul and later confronted the king over his unauthorized military census.	1 Samuel 22:5; 2 Samuel 24:11
Ahijah	Told Jeroboam that he would rule the ten northern tribes of Israel and also announced his downfall.	1 Kings 11:29; 14:18
Jehu	Announced God's judgment on Baasha, king of Israel.	1 Kings 16:7, 12
Huldah	After the Book of the Law is rediscovered at the time of King Josiah, she defines the consequences of Judah's paganism.	2 Kings 22:14–20
Shemaiah	Tells King Rehoboam of Judah that the Egyptian attack under Shishak was sponsored by the Lord.	2 Chronicles 12:5
Azariah	Tells King Asa of Judah that the Lord was with him and would support his efforts at spiritual reform in Judah.	2 Chronicles 15:8
Micaiah	Told King Ahab that his campaign to control Ramoth Gilead would end in disaster.	2 Chronicles 18:7
Oded	Tells the Israelite army to return the prisoners and plunder they seized in a battle with Judah.	2 Chronicles 28:9
John the Baptist	Forerunner to the Messiah who prepared Israel to meet their savior.	Matthew 14:5; Luke 1:76
Anna	On the day of Jesus's dedication at the temple, she recognized Jesus as the expected redeemer.	Luke 2:36
Agabus	Spoke of Paul's coming arrest in Jerusalem.	Acts 21:10
Jesus	The best of all the prophets who not only spoke for God but was God.	Deuteronomy 18:15–18; Matthew 21:11, 46; Luke 7:16; John 6:14; 7:40; Acts 3:22; 7:37

PART TWO

OLD TESTAMENT

Old Testament Time Line

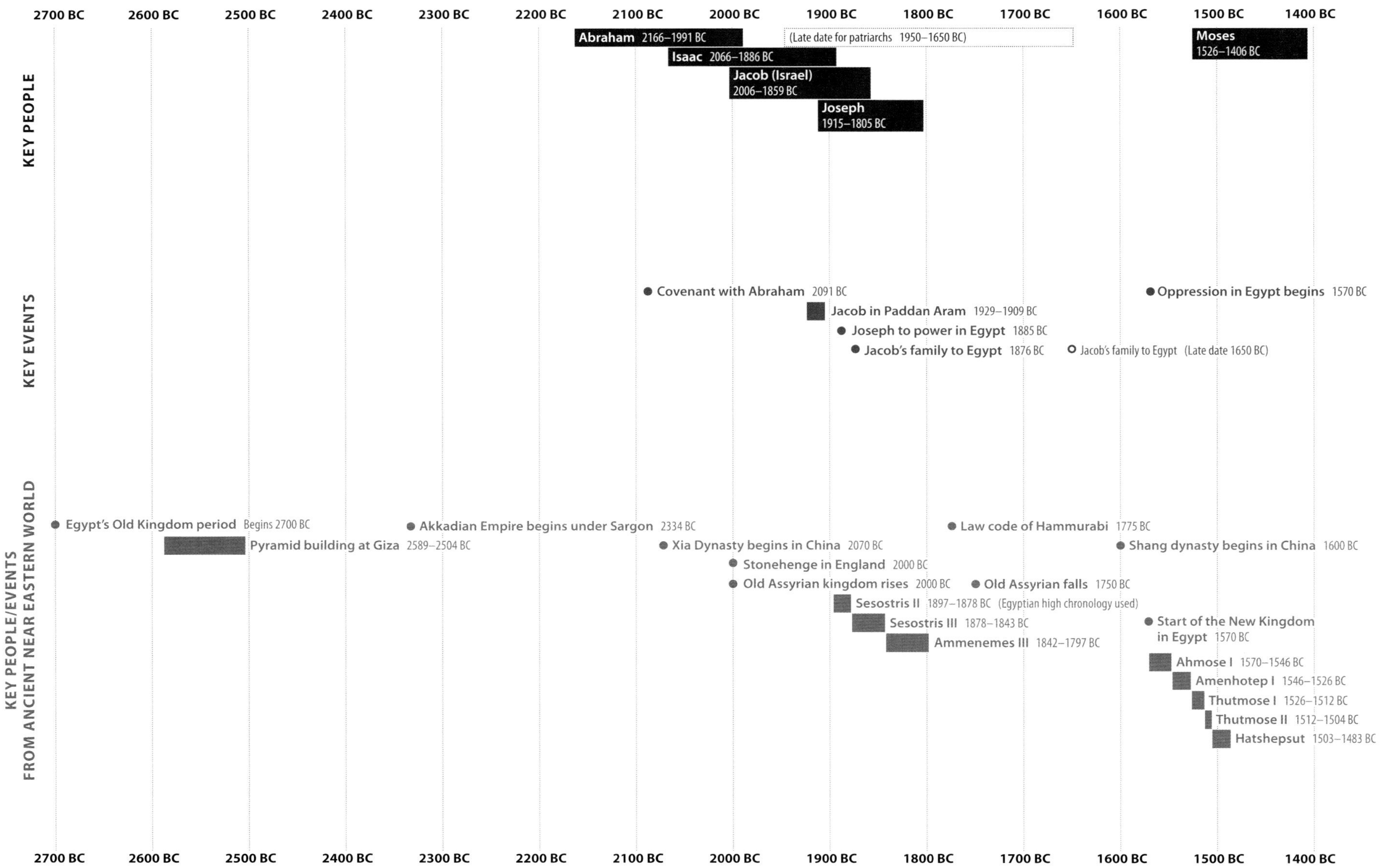

	2700 BC	2600 BC	2500 BC	2400 BC	2300 BC	2200 BC	2100 BC	2000 BC	1900 BC	1800 BC	1700 BC	1600 BC	1500 BC	1400 BC

KEY PEOPLE

Abraham 2166–1991 BC

Isaac 2006–1886 BC

Jacob (Israel) 2006–1859 BC

Joseph 1915–1805 BC

(Late date for patriarchs 1950–1650 BC)

Moses 1526–1406 BC

KEY EVENTS

● Covenant with Abraham 2091 BC

● Jacob in Paddan Aram 1929–1909 BC

● Joseph to power in Egypt 1885 BC

● Jacob's family to Egypt 1876 BC

● Oppression in Egypt begins 1570 BC

○ Jacob's family to Egypt (Late date 1650 BC)

KEY PEOPLE/EVENTS FROM ANCIENT NEAR EASTERN WORLD

● Egypt's Old Kingdom period Begins 2700 BC

● Pyramid building at Giza 2589–2504 BC

● Akkadian Empire begins under Sargon 2334 BC

● Xia Dynasty begins in China 2070 BC

● Stonehenge in England 2000 BC

● Old Assyrian kingdom rises 2000 BC

Sesostris II 1897–1878 BC

Sesostris III 1878–1843 BC

Ammenemes III 1842–1797 BC

● Law code of Hammurabi 1775 BC

● Old Assyrian falls 1750 BC

(Egyptian high chronology used)

● Shang dynasty begins in China 1600 BC

● Start of the New Kingdom in Egypt 1570 BC

Ahmose I 1570–1546 BC

Amenhotep I 1546–1526 BC

Thutmose I 1526–1512 BC

Thutmose II 1512–1504 BC

Hatshepsut 1503–1483 BC

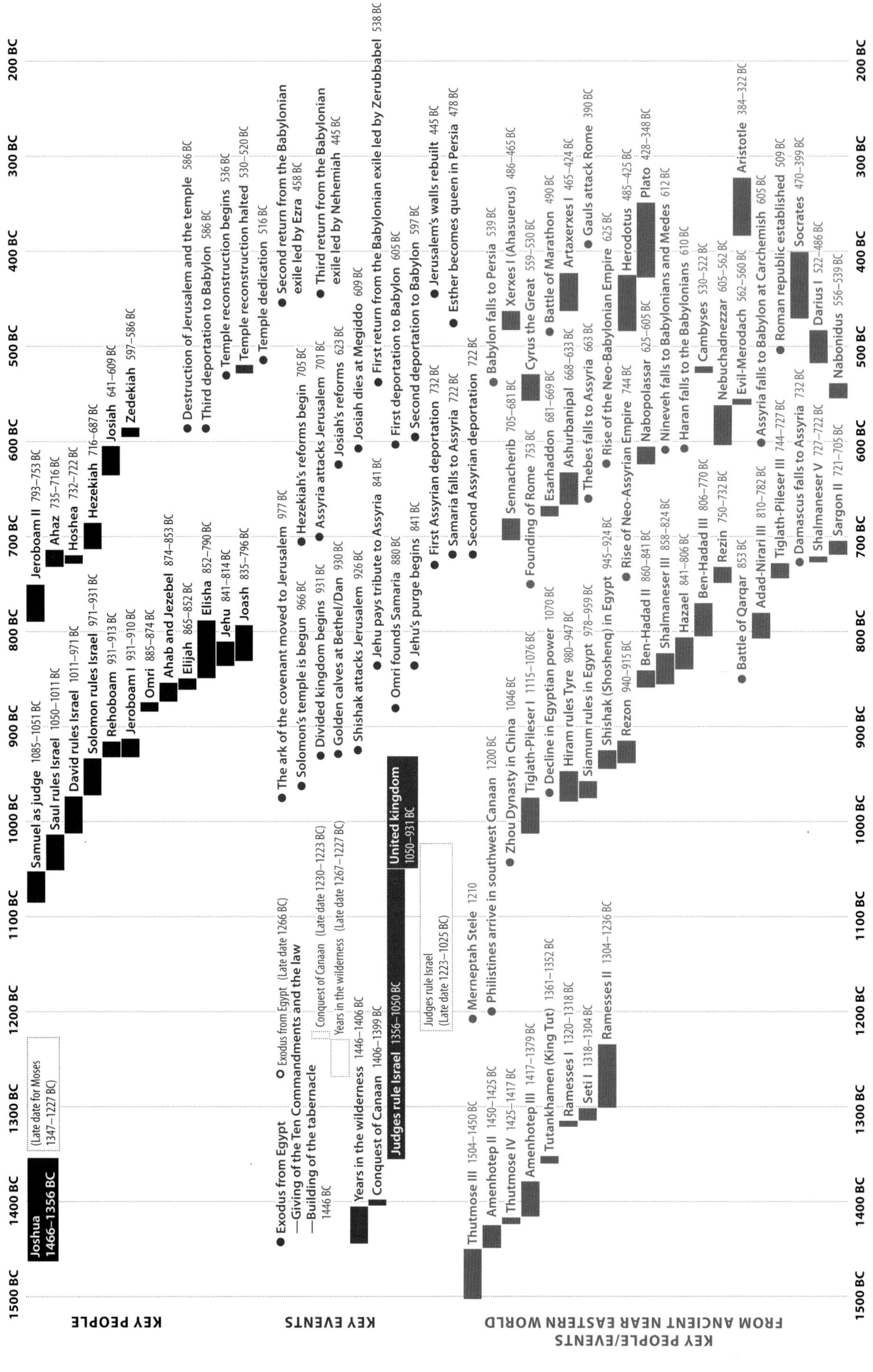
KEY PEOPLE
KEY EVENTS
KEY PEOPLE/EVENTS FROM ANCIENT NEAR EASTERN WORLD
1500 BC
1400 BC
1300 BC
1200 BC
1100 BC
1000 BC
900 BC
800 BC
700 BC
600 BC
500 BC
400 BC
300 BC
200 BC
Joshua 1466–1356 BC
(Late date for Moses 1347–1227 BC)
Samuel as judge 1085–1051 BC
Saul rules Israel 1050–1011 BC
David rules Israel 1011–971 BC
Solomon rules Israel 971–931 BC
Rehoboam 931–913 BC
Jeroboam I 931–910 BC
Omri 885–874 BC
Ahab and Jezebel 874–853 BC
Elijah 865–852 BC
Elisha 852–790 BC
Jehu 841–814 BC
Joash 835–796 BC
Jeroboam II 793–753 BC
Ahaz 735–716 BC
Hoshea 732–722 BC
Hezekiah 716–687 BC
Josiah 641–609 BC
Zedekiah 597–586 BC
Exodus from Egypt
—Giving of the Ten Commandments and the law
—Building of the tabernacle
1446 BC
Exodus from Egypt (Late date 1266 BC)
Conquest of Canaan (Late date 1230–1223 BC)
Years in the wilderness (Late date 1267–1227 BC)
Years in the wilderness 1446–1406 BC
Conquest of Canaan 1406–1399 BC
Judges rule Israel 1356–1050 BC
Judges rule Israel (Late date 1223–1025 BC)
United kingdom 1050–931 BC
The ark of the covenant moved to Jerusalem 977 BC
Solomon's temple is begun 966 BC
Divided kingdom begins 931 BC
Golden calves at Bethel/Dan 930 BC
Shishak attacks Jerusalem 926 BC
Jehu pays tribute to Assyria 841 BC
Omri founds Samaria 880 BC
Jehu's purge begins 841 BC
Hezekiah's reforms begin 705 BC
Assyria attacks Jerusalem 701 BC
Josiah's reforms 623 BC
Josiah dies at Megiddo 609 BC
First return from the Babylonian exile led by Zerubbabel 538 BC
First deportation to Babylon 605 BC
Second deportation to Babylon 597 BC
First Assyrian deportation 732 BC
Samaria falls to Assyria 722 BC
Second Assyrian deportation 722 BC
Destruction of Jerusalem and the temple 586 BC
Third deportation to Babylon 586 BC
Temple reconstruction begins 536 BC
Temple reconstruction halted 530–520 BC
Temple dedication 516 BC
Second return from the Babylonian exile led by Ezra 458 BC
Third return from the Babylonian exile led by Nehemiah 445 BC
Jerusalem's walls rebuilt 445 BC
Esther becomes queen in Persia 478 BC
Thutmose III 1504–1450 BC
Amenhotep II 1450–1425 BC
Thutmose IV 1425–1417 BC
Amenhotep III 1417–1379 BC
Tutankhamen (King Tut) 1361–1352 BC
Ramesses I 1320–1318 BC
Seti I 1318–1304 BC
Ramesses II 1304–1236 BC
Merneptah Stele 1210
Philistines arrive in southwest Canaan 1200 BC
Zhou Dynasty in China 1046 BC
Tiglath-Pileser I 1115–1076 BC
Decline in Egyptian power 1070 BC
Hiram rules Tyre 980–947 BC
Siamun rules in Egypt 978–959 BC
Shishak (Shoshenq) in Egypt 945–924 BC
Rezon 940–915 BC
Rise of Neo-Assyrian Empire 744 BC
Ben-Hadad II 860–841 BC
Shalmaneser III 858–824 BC
Hazael 841–806 BC
Ben-Hadad III 806–770 BC
Rezin 750–732 BC
Battle of Qarqar 853 BC
Adad-Nirari III 810–782 BC
Tiglath-Pileser III 744–727 BC
Damascus falls to Assyria 732 BC
Shalmaneser V 727–722 BC
Sargon II 721–705 BC
Sennacherib 705–681 BC
Founding of Rome 753 BC
Esarhaddon 681–669 BC
Ashurbanipal 668–633 BC
Thebes falls to Assyria 663 BC
Rise of the Neo-Babylonian Empire 625 BC
Nabopolassar 625–605 BC
Nineveh falls to Babylonians and Medes 612 BC
Haran falls to the Babylonians 610 BC
Nebuchadnezzar 605–562 BC
Evil-Merodach 562–560 BC
Assyria falls to Babylon at Carchemish 605 BC
Roman republic established 509 BC
Darius I 522–486 BC
Nabonidus 556–539 BC
Babylon falls to Persia 539 BC
Xerxes I (Ahasuerus) 486–465 BC
Cyrus the Great 559–530 BC
Battle of Marathon 490 BC
Artaxerxes I 465–424 BC
Gauls attack Rome 390 BC
Herodotus 485–425 BC
Plato 428–348 BC
Cambyses 530–522 BC
Aristotle 384–322 BC
Socrates 470–399 BC

Abraham and His Family in the Promised Land

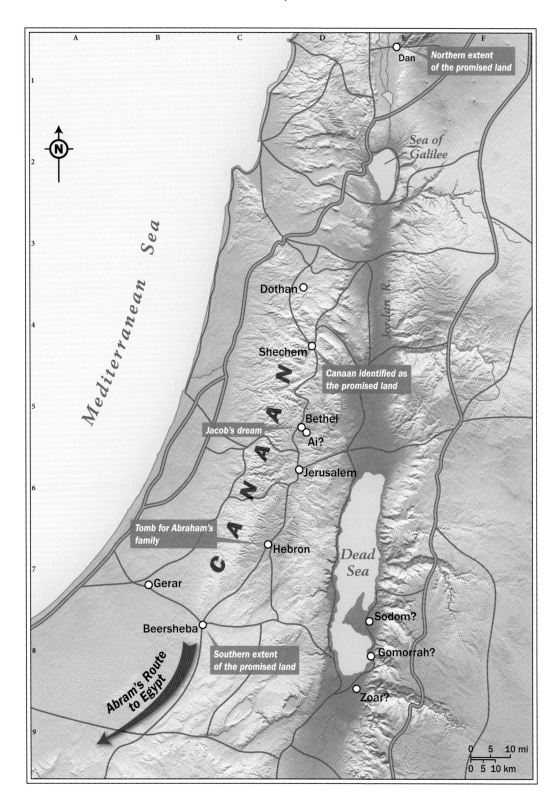

Dan
Northern extent of the promised land

Sea of Galilee

Mediterranean Sea

Jordan R.

Dothan

Shechem

Canaan identified as the promised land

Bethel
Jacob's dream
Ai?

Jerusalem

Tomb for Abraham's family

Hebron

Dead Sea

Gerar

C A N A A N

Sodom?

Beersheba

Gomorrah?

Southern extent of the promised land

Abram's Route to Egypt

Zoar?

0 5 10 mi
0 5 10 km

Journeys of Abraham

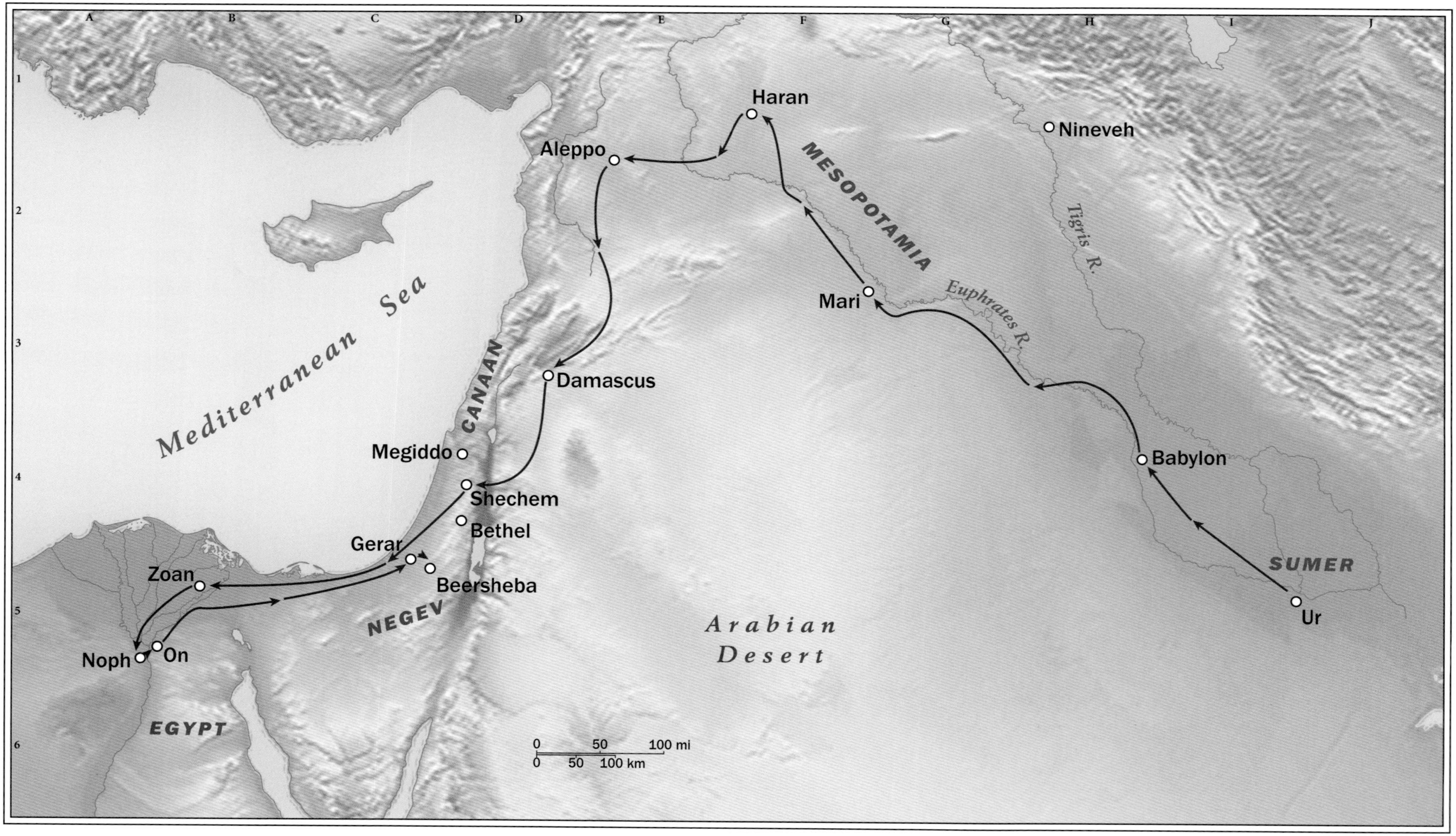

Nineveh

Tigris R.

Euphrates R.

SUMER

Ur

Babylon

MESOPOTAMIA

Mari

Haran

Aleppo

Damascus

Shechem

Bethel

Beersheba

Megiddo

Gerar

CANAAN

NEGEV

Arabian Desert

Mediterranean Sea

Zoan

On

Noph

EGYPT

100 mi
50   100 km
0   50   100 km

Exodus and Desert Wanderings

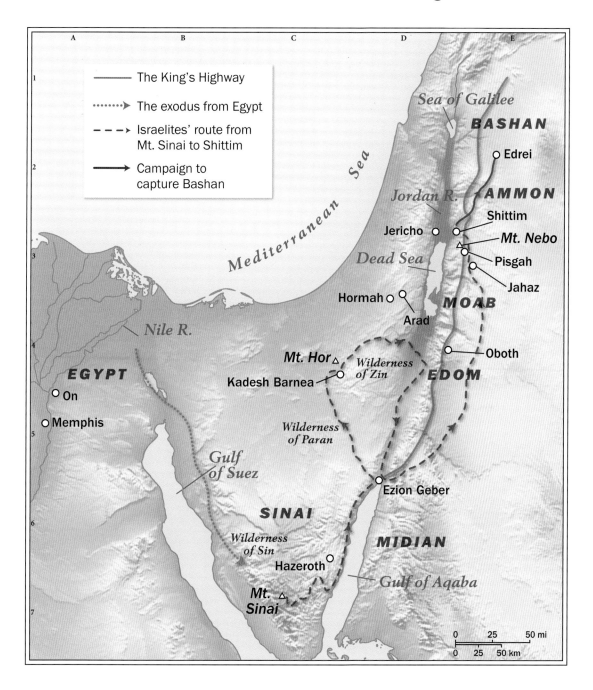

Legend:
- —— The King's Highway
- ·····▶ The exodus from Egypt
- – – ▶ Israelites' route from Mt. Sinai to Shittim
- —▶ Campaign to capture Bashan

Sea of Galilee
BASHAN
Edrei
Jordan R.
AMMON
Shittim
Jericho
Mt. Nebo
Dead Sea
Pisgah
Jahaz
Hormah
Arad
MOAB
Mediterranean Sea
Wilderness of Zin
Oboth
Mt. Hor
EDOM
Kadesh Barnea
Nile R.
EGYPT
On
Memphis
Wilderness of Paran
Gulf of Suez
Ezion Geber
SINAI
MIDIAN
Wilderness of Sin
Hazeroth
Gulf of Aqaba
Mt. Sinai

0   25   50 mi
0   25   50 km

Conquest

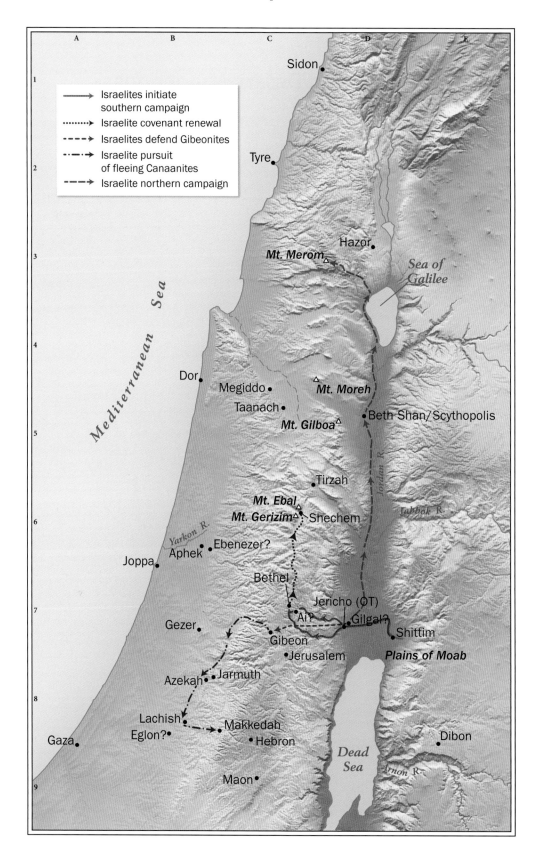

Legend:
- → Israelites initiate southern campaign
- ····→ Israelite covenant renewal
- ----→ Israelites defend Gibeonites
- -·-·→ Israelite pursuit of fleeing Canaanites
- -- --→ Israelite northern campaign

Sidon
Tyre
Hazor
Mt. Merom
Sea of Galilee
Mediterranean Sea
Dor
Megiddo
Taanach
Mt. Moreh
Mt. Gilboa
Beth Shan / Scythopolis
Tirzah
Mt. Ebal
Mt. Gerizim Shechem
Jordan R.
Jabbok R.
Yarkon R.
Aphek Ebenezer?
Joppa
Bethel
Jericho (OT)
Ai? Gilgal?
Gezer
Gibeon Shittim
•Jerusalem *Plains of Moab*
Azekah• Jarmuth
Lachish
Eglon?• Makkedah
Gaza •Hebron Dibon
Maon• *Dead Sea*
Arnon R.

Tribal Divisions

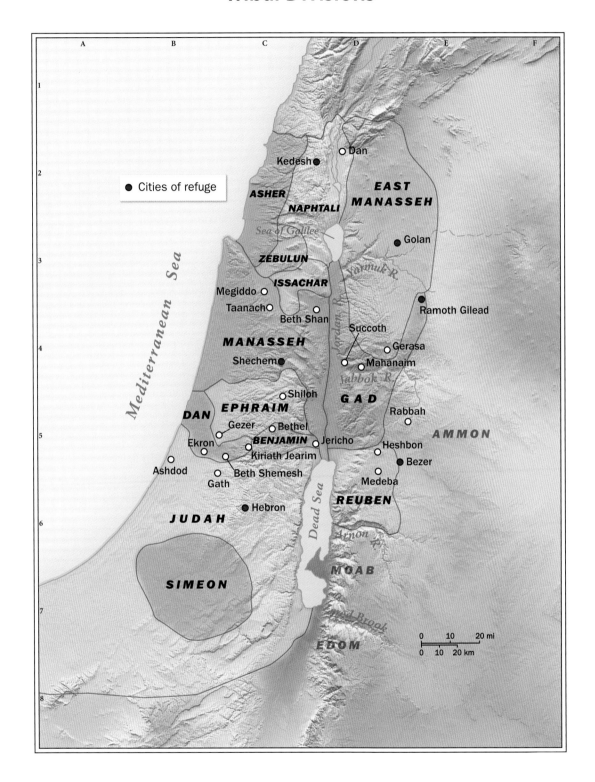

A B C D E F

1

Dan

Kedesh

2

● Cities of refuge

ASHER

NAPHTALI

EAST MANASSEH

Sea of Galilee

Golan

3

ZEBULUN

ISSACHAR

Megiddo

Taanach

Beth Shan

Yarmuk R.

Ramoth Gilead

Succoth

4

MANASSEH

Shechem

Gerasa

Mahanaim

Jabbok R.

Jordan R.

Mediterranean Sea

Shiloh

EPHRAIM

GAD

DAN

Gezer

Bethel

Rabbah

5

Ekron

BENJAMIN

Jericho

Heshbon

AMMON

Kiriath Jearim

Bezer

Ashdod

Beth Shemesh

Medeba

Gath

REUBEN

Hebron

6

JUDAH

Dead Sea

Arnon R.

MOAB

7

SIMEON

Zered Brook

EDOM

0   10   20 mi
0   10   20 km

Judges

United Kingdom

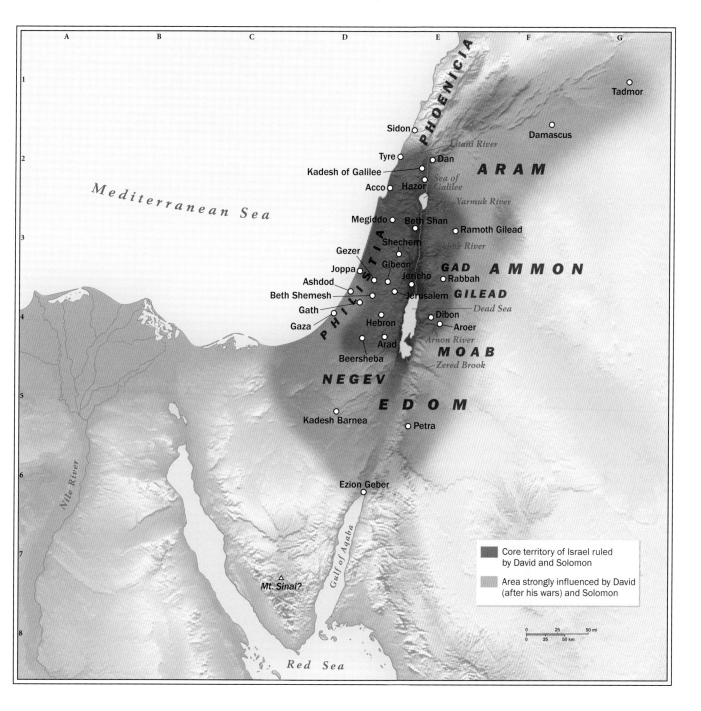

Core territory of Israel ruled by David and Solomon

Area strongly influenced by David (after his wars) and Solomon

Map labels:

Mediterranean Sea

PHOENICIA
Sidon
Tyre
Kadesh of Galilee
Acco
Litani River
Dan
Hazor
Sea of Galilee
ARAM
Damascus
Tadmor
Yarmuk River
Megiddo
Beth Shan
Ramoth Gilead
Shechem
Gezer
Jabbok River
Gibeon
Joppa
Jericho
GAD
AMMON
Ashdod
Rabbah
Beth Shemesh
Jerusalem
GILEAD
Gath
Dibon
Dead Sea
Gaza
Hebron
Aroer
Arad
Arnon River
Beersheba
MOAB
Zered Brook
NEGEV
EDOM
Kadesh Barnea
Petra
Ezion Geber
Nile River
Gulf of Aqaba
Mt. Sinai?
Red Sea
PHILISTIA

0   25   50 mi
0   25   50 km

Divided Kingdom

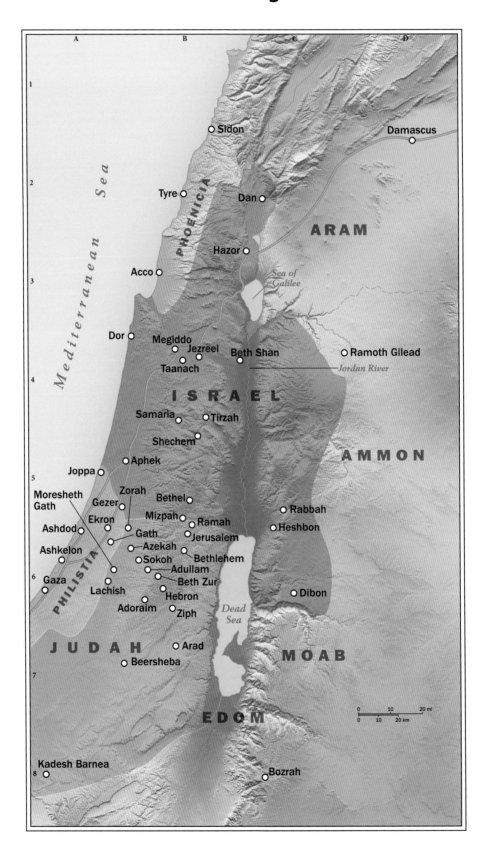

Exile and Return

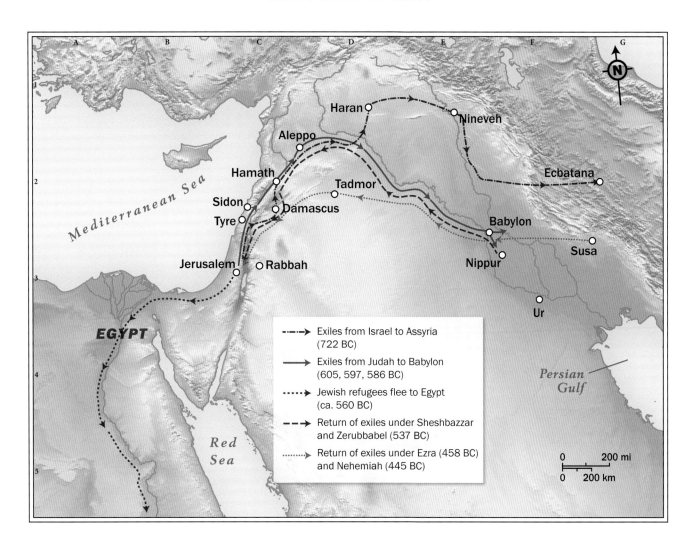

Mediterranean Sea

Haran · Nineveh · Ecbatana

Aleppo

Hamath · Tadmor

Sidon · Damascus · Babylon

Tyre · Susa

Jerusalem · Rabbah · Nippur

EGYPT

Ur

Red Sea

Persian Gulf

Legend:

- – · – → Exiles from Israel to Assyria (722 BC)
- —→ Exiles from Judah to Babylon (605, 597, 586 BC)
- ····→ Jewish refugees flee to Egypt (ca. 560 BC)
- – – → Return of exiles under Sheshbazzar and Zerubbabel (537 BC)
- ·······→ Return of exiles under Ezra (458 BC) and Nehemiah (445 BC)

0 ———— 200 mi
0 ———— 200 km

Assyrian Empire

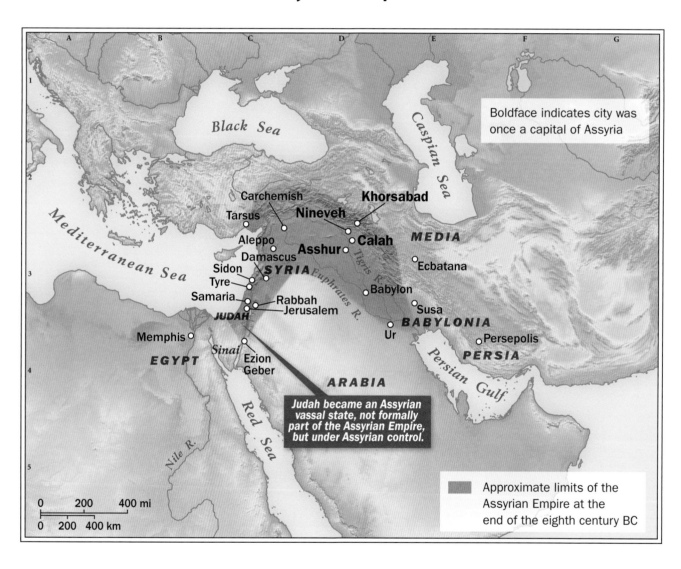

Boldface indicates city was once a capital of Assyria

Black Sea

Caspian Sea

Mediterranean Sea

Carchemish

Tarsus

Khorsabad

Nineveh

Aleppo

Asshur

Calah

MEDIA

Damascus

SYRIA

Tigris R.

Sidon

Euphrates R.

Ecbatana

Tyre

Babylon

Samaria

Rabbah

JUDAH

Jerusalem

Susa

BABYLONIA

Memphis

Ur

Persepolis

Sinai

PERSIA

EGYPT

Ezion Geber

ARABIA

Persian Gulf

Judah became an Assyrian vassal state, not formally part of the Assyrian Empire, but under Assyrian control.

Red Sea

Nile R.

0   200   400 mi

0   200   400 km

Approximate limits of the Assyrian Empire at the end of the eighth century BC

Babylonian Empire

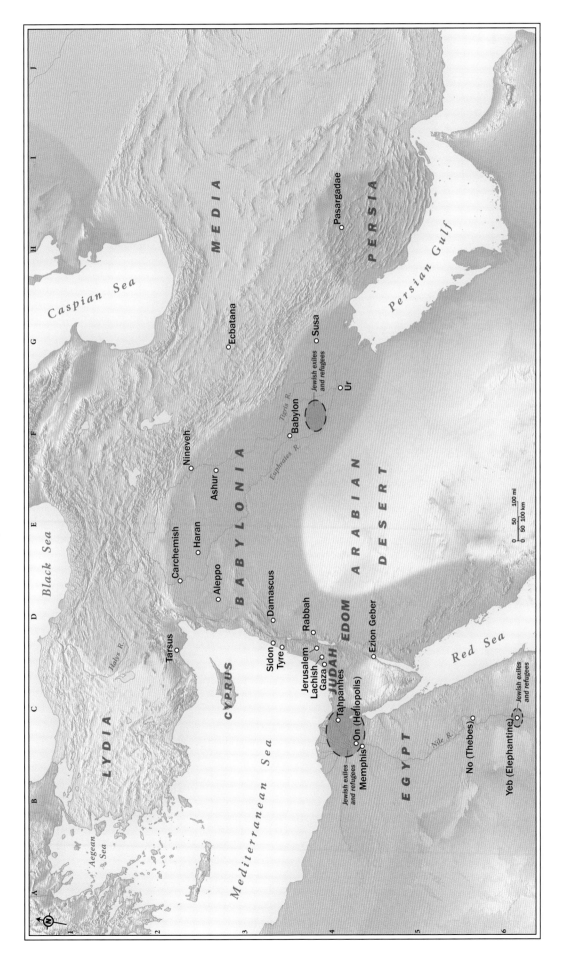

Persian Empire

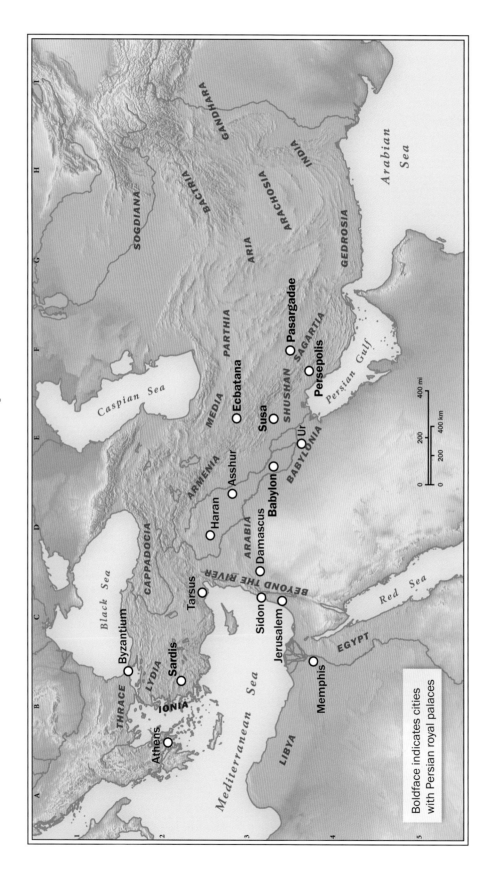

Boldface indicates cities
with Persian royal palaces

THRACE
IONIA
LYDIA
CAPPADOCIA
ARMENIA
MEDIA
PARTHIA
SOGDIANA
BACTRIA
GANDHARA
INDIA
ARACHOSIA
ARIA
GEDROSIA
SAGARTIA
SHUSHAN
BABYLONIA
ARABIA
BEYOND THE RIVER
EGYPT
LIBYA

Athens
Sardis
Byzantium
Tarsus
Sidon
Jerusalem
Memphis
Damascus
Haran
Asshur
Babylon
Ur
Susa
Ecbatana
Persepolis
Pasargadae

Black Sea
Caspian Sea
Mediterranean Sea
Red Sea
Arabian Sea
Persian Gulf

400 mi
400 km
200
200
0
0

Jerusalem during the Time of the Old Testament

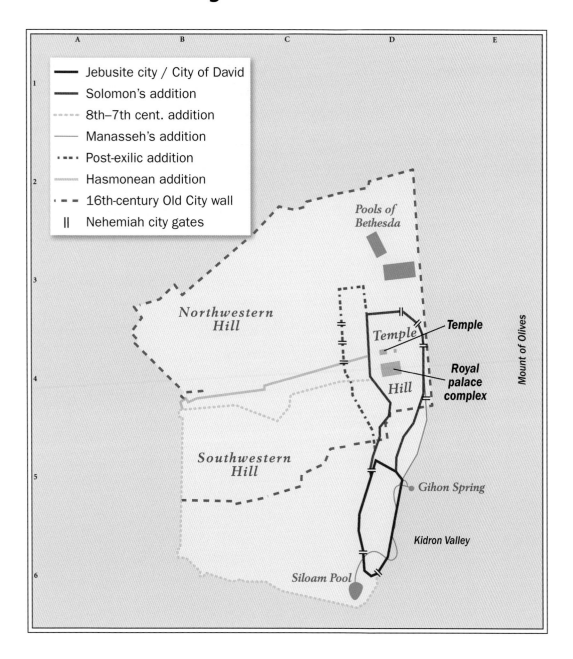

Legend:
- Jebusite city / City of David
- Solomon's addition
- 8th–7th cent. addition
- Manasseh's addition
- Post-exilic addition
- Hasmonean addition
- 16th-century Old City wall
- Nehemiah city gates

Pools of Bethesda

Northwestern Hill

Temple

Temple

Royal palace complex

Hill

Mount of Olives

Southwestern Hill

Gihon Spring

Kidron Valley

Siloam Pool

Canon Division and Organization of the Old Testament

A Sacred Collection Takes Shape

The idea of a sacred collection surfaced as soon as Moses began to write (Deut. 31:24–26).

In Jesus's day, the sacred collection was organized into three categories: the Law, the Prophets, and the Psalms [or Writings] (Luke 24:44).

No specific ordering of individual books was required so long as the sacred texts existed as separate scrolls.

Ordering the books became a practical necessity when the Bible was published in a codex (book with a binding), which began in the second and third century AD.

English Protestant Canon

Pentateuch

Genesis	Leviticus	Deuteronomy
Exodus	Numbers	

Historical Books

Joshua	1–2 Samuel	Ezra
Judges	1–2 Kings	Nehemiah
Ruth	1–2 Chronicles	Esther

Poetry

Job	Proverbs	Song of Songs
Psalms	Ecclesiastes	

Major Prophets

Isaiah	Lamentations	Daniel
Jeremiah	Ezekiel	

Minor Prophets

Hosea	Jonah	Zephaniah
Joel	Micah	Haggai
Amos	Nahum	Zechariah
Obadiah	Habakkuk	Malachi

Hebrew Canon

Torah

Genesis	Leviticus	Deuteronomy
Exodus	Numbers	

Prophets

Joshua	Hosea	Habakkuk
Judges	Joel	Zephaniah
1–2 Samuel	Amos	Haggai
1–2 Kings	Obadiah	Zechariah
Isaiah	Jonah	Malachi
Jeremiah	Micah	
Ezekiel	Nahum	

Writings

Psalms	Song	Daniel
Job	Ecclesiastes	Ezra
Proverbs	Lamentations	Nehemiah
Ruth	Esther	1–2 Chronicles

The Baker Book of Bible Charts, Maps, and Time Lines

Ancient Additional Sources

Royal Records

Title	Presumed Content	Number of References	Example
Annals of the Kings of Israel	Court records from the northern kingdom that may have included royal correspondence, military records, genealogies, and other archival material.	19	1 Kings 14:19
Annals of King David	Court records from the administration of King David that may have included royal correspondence, military records, genealogies, and other archival material.	1	1 Chronicles 27:24
Book of the Kings of Israel and Judah	A composite court record including key data from the rulers of the northern and southern kingdoms that may have included genealogies, select royal correspondence, military records, and other archival material.	4	1 Chronicles 9:1
Book of the Kings of Judah and Israel	A composite court record including key data from the rulers of the northern and southern kingdoms that may have included genealogies, select royal correspondence, military records, and other archival material.	4	2 Chronicles 16:11
Annotations on the Book of Kings	A commentary that interpreted information found in the official court records.	1	2 Chronicles 24:27

Prophetic Literature

Title	Presumed Content	Number of References	Example
Records of Samuel the Seer	A record of key events with theological importance from the time of David created by the prophet Samuel.	1	1 Chronicles 29:29
Records of Nathan the Prophet	A record of key events with theological importance from the time of David and Solomon.	2	1 Chronicles 29:29
Records of Gad the Seer	A record of key events with theological importance from the time of David.	1	1 Chronicles 29:29
Prophecy of Ahijah the Shilonite	A record of events and observations associated with the transition from united to divided kingdom by the prophet who announced that this was the Lord's doing.	1	2 Chronicles 9:29
Writings of Iddo the Seer	A record of events with theological importance that concerns the transition from united kingdom to divided kingdom.	3	2 Chronicles 9:29
Records of Shemaiah the Prophet	A record of the transition from united to divided kingdom that paid particular attention to genealogies associated with the ruling house of Judah.	1	2 Chronicles 12:15
Records of the Seers	A theologically informed record that included the prayer offered by Manasseh and the locations of pagan high places he had established.	1	2 Chronicles 33:19

Religious Poetry

Title	Presumed Content	Number of References	Example
Book of Wars of the Lord	A compilation of military victory songs that in this case defines the northern geographical border of Moab.	1	Numbers 21:14
Book of Jashar	A compilation of songs, each of which commemorated important Old Testament events.	2	Joshua 10:13; 2 Samuel 1:18

Holidays and Celebrations

Passover (*Pesach*)

Scripture: Exodus 12:1–13; Leviticus 23:5
Date: Nisan 14 (spring)

Origin

The first Passover is linked to the final plague in Egypt, when every firstborn son was to die. The Lord spared ("passed over") those households where lamb's blood was put on the door frames at his direction.

Summary

Passover commemorates the exodus from Egypt. As the family gathers in their home, an oral review of this event is coupled with a meal whose components (bitter herbs, unleavened bread, and lamb) assist in recalling the details of the exodus.

New Testament Connection

As a Jew, Jesus traveled to Jerusalem for the celebration of Passover many times during his life. Prior to his death on Good Friday, Jesus ate a Passover meal with his disciples and used its components to initiate the meal known as the Lord's Supper (Matt. 26:17–30). Christians linked the death of Jesus with the death of the Passover lamb (1 Cor. 5:7–8).

Feast of Unleavened Bread (*Hag Hamatzot*)

Scripture: Exodus 12:14–20; Leviticus 23:6–8
Date: Nisan 15–21 (spring)

Origin

This feast also began with the exodus from Egypt when the Lord directed his people to remove yeast from their homes. All baked goods were to be made without the use of yeast.

Summary

Together with Passover, the activities of the Feast of Unleavened Bread are meant to commemorate the exodus from Egypt. For one week, yeast is meticulously removed from the home and all the bread eaten is unleavened bread (Hebrew *mazot*). This is to be a week when regular work is suspended and special worship services are enjoyed.

New Testament Connection

Jesus would have joined the Jewish families who streamed to Jerusalem for this weeklong celebration in the holy city. The negative connotations associated with yeast in this festival led "yeast" to be used as a metaphor for something bad (Matt. 16:12; Luke 12:1; 1 Cor. 5:7).

Feast of Weeks / Pentecost (*Shavuot*)

Scripture: Exodus 23:16; Leviticus 23:15–21
Date: Sivan 6 (spring)

Origin

This became part of the Israelite annual calendar at Mount Sinai.

Summary

Fifty days after Passover (the prefix *pente-* means "fifty"), God directed his people to give thanks for the wheat harvest during this agricultural festival. In order to remind them of the source of this blessing and encourage them to give thanks for God's role in providing this essential component of the ancient diet, God's people were to bring an offering of grain products to the temple. After the Old Testament era, this festival also commemorated the giving of the law on Mount Sinai.

New Testament Connection

The Jews who heard and responded to Peter's Pentecost sermon had traveled to Jerusalem and were at the temple to participate in this festival (Acts 2).

Feast of Trumpets (*Rosh Hashanah*)

Scripture: Leviticus 23:23–25; Numbers 29:1–6
Date: Tishri 1 (fall)

Origin

This became part of the Israelite annual calendar at Mount Sinai.

Summary

The sounding of the ram's horn (*shofar*) marks the beginning of the Jewish year. On this day regular work was to cease, and special worship was to commence to begin the year with the appropriate state of mind. It came to mark the start of a ten-day period of sober reflection and repentance leading to the Day of Atonement.

New Testament Connection

No specific reference to the Feast of Trumpets is made in the New Testament.

Day of Atonement (*Yom Kippur*)

Scripture: Leviticus 16:1–34
Date: Tishri 10 (fall)

Origin

This became part of the Israelite annual calendar at Mount Sinai.

Summary

This was the holiest day in the Hebrew calendar when the people were "cleansed of their sins" (Lev. 16:30). It was a day for fasting and prayer among the people. The high priest entered the holy of holies to sprinkle blood on the atonement seat of the ark of the covenant, putting blood between the place where God made his presence known above the ark and the law code kept within the ark. The high priest also confessed the sins of the people over a scapegoat that was then driven into the wilderness.

New Testament Connection

The imagery of this day is used in Hebrews to speak of the way in which the blood of Jesus and his sacrifice bring final atonement to the world in the way that the offering on the Day of Atonement did not (9:11–28).

Feast of Booths/Tabernacles (*Sukkot*)

Scripture: Leviticus 23:33–44; Numbers 29:12–40
Date: Tishri 15–21 (fall)

Origin

This became part of the Israelite annual calendar at Mount Sinai.

Summary

During the fall fruit harvest, God's people were to suspend regular work and spend extra time in worship for seven days. This was a time to reflect on the years the Israelites spent in the wilderness prior to their arrival in the promised land. The portable shelters (*sukkah*) made from branches reminded them of the "booths" in which their ancestors lived during this part of their history (Neh. 8:14–17). Prayers were offered for the anticipated coming of the winter rains, and a priest carried water from the Siloam pool and poured it out at the base of the great altar.

New Testament Connection

Jesus attended this festival and used its symbolism to teach about his identity as the Messiah (John 7:1–39).

Feast of Dedication (*Hanukkah*)

Scripture: John 10:22
Date: Kislev 25 (winter)

Origin

During the intertestamental period, the temple in Jerusalem was liberated from pagan hands and rededicated to the Lord's service by the Maccabees in 164 BC (1 Macc. 4:52–59). Tradition holds that during the eight-day celebration that followed, there was insufficient untainted olive oil to keep the temple menorah burning. Yet a one-day supply of oil miraculously lasted eight days.

Summary

This is a time of celebration and reflection on the rededication of the temple. In time various rituals were added to the celebration, including the use of the Hanukkah candleholder.

New Testament Connection

Jesus faced a hostile crowd in the temple complex during this festival, a crowd ready not to celebrate but to stone him for his claims to be God (John 10:22).

Purim (*Purim*)

Scripture: Esther 9
Date: Adar 13–14 (winter)

Origin

When the ungodly Haman plotted the destruction of the Jews throughout the Persian-ruled empire (selecting the day by casting of the *purim*, or "lots"), the Lord used the godly influence of Esther to prevent the atrocity. The day of the intended destruction and realized deliverance became the Jewish festival of Purim.

Summary

This day of celebration and gift giving recalls the divine mercy that turned a day associated with mourning into a day of joy, a day when the Lord saved the Jews from their enemies.

New Testament Connection

No specific reference to Purim is made in the New Testament.

Covenants

Definition

A covenant is an agreement between two or more parties that defines obligations, benefits, and penalties.

Covenant Initiated at Creation (Covenant of Works)

Bible Reference

Genesis 2:15–17

Summary

The Creator promised temporal well-being and eternal salvation to mortals who remained sinless as demonstrated in the moral correctness of their thoughts, desires, and actions.

Covenant Initiated with Noah and All Living Things

Bible Reference

Genesis 9:8–17

Summary

The Lord unilaterally promised Noah and all living things that he would never again subject the earth to a universal flood. This promise indicates that God has another way of dealing with a sin-ruined world that stands in sharp contrast to a destructive flood. And because all living things in the natural world are corecipients of this promise, it motivates a respectful nurturing of the environment in God's people.

Covenant Initiated with Abraham

Bible Reference

Genesis 12:1–3; 13:14–16; 15:9–21; 17:1–14

Summary

The Lord unilaterally and unconditionally promised salvation for sin-ruined mortals through a descendant of Abraham who would bless all nations with work accomplished in the land promised to Abraham's descendants. Circumcision of the males in Abraham's family became a sign of this covenant.

Covenant Initiated with Moses

Bible Reference

Exodus 19–24; Deuteronomy 27–30

Summary

To aid Abraham's family in the role they would play in bringing the covenant with Abraham to its culmination, God made a conditional agreement with Israel. God promised them his special attention, peace, health, and prosperity in exchange for obedience to the unique law code given to shape their thinking and actions. Disobedience would be met with violence, illness, famine, and divine retribution.

Covenant Initiated with David

Bible Reference

2 Samuel 7:5–16

Summary

This covenant narrows the scope of the promises given to Abraham. The messiah would not just be a descendant of Abraham but also a descendant of David, and not just a descendant of David but one regarded as the son of God (7:14). The Lord had promised Abraham that one of his descendants would be a blessing for all nations, and now David finds the execution of this "blessing" linked to his family (7:29). One of his descendants would be the eternal King who would rule an eternal kingdom.

Covenant Initiated with Jeremiah (New Covenant)

Bible Reference

Jeremiah 31:31–34

Summary

The failure of the Israelites to uphold their side of the agreement initiated at Mount Sinai was about to result in their deportation from the promised land. This old covenant was so much on their mind that hope had all but been extinguished; they had lost sight of the even older covenant made with Abraham. The new covenant initiated with Jeremiah is not a brand-new covenant but a renewal of the covenant initiated with Abraham and David. Its refreshing tone pointed ahead to the days of the Messiah who would offer the very last sacrifice needed for sin, making the unconditional blessing of forgiveness available to all nations (Heb. 10:13–18).

Ancient Near Eastern Deities and the Bible

Asherah

Canaanite female deity identified as the consort of the chief Canaanite god, El, and as the mother of the gods.

Mentioned frequently in the Old Testament in parallel with worship of Baal.

The Asherah pole was a wooden device associated with worship of Asherah. The Israelites were to remove them from the land but instead added to their number by building their own (Exod. 34:13; 2 Kings 17:10).

Ashtoreth (Astarte, Ishtar)

The chief female deity of Tyre and Sidon, the beautiful daughter of the chief Canaanite deity, El, and the sensual, female consort of Baal.

Thought to influence a variety of dimensions of life, including sexuality, fertility, weather, and war.

Israelite affection for this deity came with Solomon's alliance with Phoenicia—one of the abuses that precipitated the division of his kingdom (1 Kings 11:33).

Baal

Male deity worshiped throughout the biblical region under a variety of subregional names including Baal-Berith, Baal Peor, Baal Zaphon, and Hadad.

Expressed himself in the thunder, lightning, rain, and dewfall that made agriculture and pastoralism possible in Canaan.

Baal is mentioned more often than any other deity in the Old Testament, and the Israelites learned to worship him as they learned how to farm the land from their Canaanite neighbors.

Because both the Lord and Baal claimed to control the rain and dew, conflict between the two naturally followed (e.g., Deut. 11:10–17; Judg. 6:36–40; 1 Kings 18:16–46).

Chemosh (Kemosh)

The national god of Moab thought to control its well-being and destiny, particularly in war (Judg. 11:24; Jer. 48:46).

Solomon built a high place for Chemosh on the Mount of Olives just east of the Lord's temple, an act that precipitated the division of his kingdom (1 Kings 11:1, 33).

Molek (Molech)

National deity of Ammon.

Child sacrifice influenced this deity's disposition and action, a detestable practice mentioned repeatedly with the deity's name (Lev. 18:21; 20:2–4).

Solomon built a sanctuary of Molek on the Mount of Olives just east of the Lord's temple, an act that precipitated the division of his kingdom (1 Kings 11:5, 7, 33).

Dagon (Dagan)

National deity of the Philistines adopted upon their arrival in Canaan.

Thought to influence the health of the grain harvest in the prime grain-growing land of the Philistine plain.

Perceived to have bested the Lord when Samson was enslaved (Judg. 16:23) and when the Philistines put the captured ark of the covenant in the temple of Dagon (1 Sam. 5:2), notions quickly dispelled.

Marduk (Bel)

As the creator god, Marduk was identified as the chief god of the Babylonian pantheon.

While the Israelite exile to Babylon made Marduk appear superior to the Lord, Jeremiah announced that Babylon's destruction would reveal Bel's true worth (Jer. 50:2).

Nebo

Son of the chief Babylonian god, Marduk.

Thought to influence wisdom and writing.

Mentioned once by name (Isa. 46:1) as Isaiah describes the fall of Babylon; this deity would be as humbled as his adherents.

Tammuz

Sumerian deity associated with fertility.

The death of this deity is associated with the infertility of the land that mourns his passing. His restoration is associated with the return of fertility.

Adherents practice ritual weeping to encourage his return (Ezek. 8:14).

Old Testament Expectations Fulfilled by Jesus

Expectation	References	Fulfilled by Jesus	References
A descendant of Eve would give birth to the Messiah.	Genesis 3:15	Mary gave birth to Jesus.	Luke 2:7; 3:38; Galatians 4:4
The Messiah would defeat the devil.	Genesis 3:15	Jesus defeated the devil.	Hebrews 2:14; 1 John 3:8
The Messiah would be a descendant of Abraham.	Genesis 12:3	Jesus was a descendant of Abraham.	Matthew 1:1; Luke 3:34; Galatians 3:16, 29
The Messiah's saving mission would benefit all nations.	Genesis 12:3; Isaiah 42:6; 49:6; 55:4–5	Jesus's saving work extends to all people of all time.	Luke 2:32; John 3:16; Acts 2:39; 26:23; 2 Corinthians 5:19
The Messiah would be a descendant of Isaac.	Genesis 26:3–4	Jesus was a descendant of Isaac.	Matthew 1:2; Luke 3:34; Hebrews 11:18
The Messiah would be a descendant of Jacob.	Genesis 28:14	Jesus was a descendant of Jacob.	Matthew 1:2; Luke 3:34
The Messiah would be a descendant of Judah.	Genesis 49:10; Micah 5:2	Jesus was a descendant of Judah.	Matthew 1:3; Luke 3:33; Hebrews 7:14; Revelation 5:5
The Messiah would rule as a king.	Genesis 49:10; Numbers 24:17; 2 Samuel 7:16; Psalm 2:6; Isaiah 9:7; Micah 5:2	Jesus rules as king.	Matthew 28:18; John 18:36–37; 1 Corinthians 15:24–25; Revelation 19:16
The Messiah would be like the Passover lamb.	Exodus 12:1–11, 46; Isaiah 53:3	Jesus is like the Passover lamb.	John 1:29; 19:36; 1 Corinthians 5:7; Revelation 5:12
The Messiah would be a prophet.	Deuteronomy 18:15–19	Jesus was a prophet.	Matthew 21:11; Luke 7:16; John 6:14; 7:40
The Messiah would be a descendant of David.	2 Samuel 7:12–13; Isaiah 9:7; Jeremiah 23:5	Jesus was a descendant of David.	Matthew 1:1; Luke 2:4
The Messiah would face strong opposition from those in power.	Psalms 2:1–2; 22:12–13	Jesus faced strong opposition from those in power.	John 11:47–53; Acts 4:25–27
The Messiah was the Son of God.	Psalm 2:7	Jesus is the Son of God.	Matthew 3:17; Acts 13:32–33; Hebrews 5:5; 2 Peter 1:17
The Messiah would overcome all who oppose him.	Psalms 2:9; 110:1–2; Isaiah 63:1–6; Daniel 2:44–45	Jesus overcomes all who oppose him.	Revelation 19:15–16

Expectation	References	Fulfilled by Jesus	References
The body of the Messiah would not decay after death.	Psalm 16:8–10	Jesus's body did not decay after his death.	Acts 2:25–32; 13:32–37
The Messiah would be undistinguished and shown considerable disrespect.	Psalm 22:6–7; Isaiah 53:1–3	Jesus was undistinguished and shown considerable disrespect.	Matthew 27:37–44; John 1:46
The Messiah would be pierced.	Psalm 22:16; Isaiah 53:5	Jesus was pierced.	Matthew 27:31; John 19:34, 37; Revelation 1:7
The Messiah's clothing would be divided by casting lots.	Psalm 22:18	Jesus's clothing was divided by the casting of lots.	Matthew 27:35; John 19:23–24
The Messiah would be a priest like the non-Levite Melchizedek.	Psalm 110:4	Jesus was a priest like the non-Levite Melchizedek.	Hebrews 5:6–10; 6:20; 7:1–22; 10:11–14
The Messiah would join himself physically to the human race.	Psalm 40:6–8; Isaiah 7:14; 9:6	Jesus was physically joined to the human race.	Matthew 1:22–23; Luke 2:7; Galatians 4:4; Hebrews 10:5–9
The Messiah would bring light to dark places.	Isaiah 9:1–2; 60:1–3	Jesus brings light to dark places.	Matthew 4:14–16; Luke 2:30–32; John 8:12
The Holy Spirit would rest on the Messiah.	Isaiah 11:2	The Holy Spirit rested on Jesus.	Matthew 3:16
The Messiah would bring in a season of peace.	Isaiah 11:6–11; 65:17–25	Jesus brings a season of peace.	Matthew 11:28–30; John 14:27; Revelation 7:14–17; 21:1–5
The Messiah would heal the disabled.	Isaiah 35:5–6	Jesus healed the disabled.	Matthew 11:5; Luke 7:21–22
The Messiah would appear east of Jerusalem.	Isaiah 40:1–5	Jesus was baptized east of Jerusalem and often entered Jerusalem from the east.	Matthew 3:1–3, 13; 21:1–11, 17–18
The Messiah would be like a good shepherd.	Isaiah 40:10–11	Jesus is like a good shepherd.	John 10:14; Hebrews 13:20
The Messiah would conduct his life in great humility.	Isaiah 42:1–4	Jesus conducted his life in great humility.	Matthew 12:17–21; John 13:4–5
The Messiah would be the saving substitute for sin-ruined mortals.	Isaiah 53:4–6, 12	Jesus was the saving substitute for sin-ruined mortals.	Matthew 8:16–17; Romans 4:25; 5:6–8; 1 Corinthians 15:3; 2 Corinthians 5:21

Expectation	References	Fulfilled by Jesus	References
The Messiah would be assigned a criminal's grave only to be buried in a wealthy man's grave.	Isaiah 53:9	Jesus was assigned a criminal's grave and then buried in a wealthy man's grave.	Matthew 27:57–60
The Messiah would bring good news to the poor and brokenhearted to comfort all who mourn.	Isaiah 61:1–3	Jesus brought good news to the poor and brokenhearted and comforted those who grieved.	Matthew 5:3–4; Luke 4:16–21
The Messiah would initiate a new covenant.	Jeremiah 31:31–34	Jesus initiated a new covenant.	Luke 22:20; Hebrews 10:13–18
The Messiah would appear as the Son of Man coming on the clouds of heaven.	Daniel 7:13–14	Jesus is the Son of Man who will come on the clouds of heaven.	Matthew 24:30; 25:31; 26:64; Acts 1:9–11; Revelation 1:7
The days of the Messiah's coming would be coupled with an outpouring of the Holy Spirit.	Joel 2:28–32	The ascension of Jesus was followed by an outpouring of the Holy Spirit.	John 14:15–17; Acts 2:17–21
The Messiah would be born in Bethlehem.	Micah 5:2	Jesus was born in Bethlehem.	Matthew 2:1–6; Luke 2:4–11
The Messiah would enter Jerusalem riding on a donkey.	Zechariah 9:9	Jesus entered Jerusalem riding on a donkey.	Matthew 21:1–7; John 12:13–15
The Messiah's arrival would be announced by a forerunner.	Isaiah 40:3; Malachi 3:1; 4:5–6	Jesus's arrival was announced by John the Baptist.	Matthew 3:1–3; 11:10–14; Luke 1:17; 7:27

Old Testament Weapons

Battle Ax

The battle ax was an adaptation of the household axe whose metal head assumed a variety of shapes, from duckbill to crescent to rectangle. The handle of this short-range weapon acted like a lever, increasing the force with which the sharpened edge of the head could be driven into an enemy soldier.

Mace

The mace was an adaptation of the battle ax. The handle terminated in a round stone or metal ball that had no sharpened edge. It also took advantage of the principle of the lever but instead of cutting was meant to break bones and crush the skulls of enemy soldiers.

Sword

Prior to the time of the judges in Israel, the sword of the Bible was most likely the sickle sword. The handle of the sickle sword terminated in a curved blade whose outer edge was sharpened. This made it very effective for slashing. As the Iron Age dawned, this weapon changed in both shape and composition. Bronze gave way to iron, and the sickle sword gave way to the straight sword. The straight sword had a shorter handle and a longer blade sharpened on both sides so that it could be used for both slashing and stabbing. In time, a raised rib was added down the middle of the blade to strengthen it.

Dagger

The dagger was similar in design to the straight sword but shorter in length, making it easier to conceal and more agile than the longer sword so that it might be more effective in a close-quarter fight.

Spear

The spear was composed of a wood shaft whose length corresponded to the height of the soldier who used it. The wood shaft terminated in a metal point that was sharpened on both sides. It was primarily designed as a thrusting weapon rather than a weapon that was thrown, designed to engage the enemy soldier before their sword, ax, mace, or dagger could threaten.

Javelin

The javelin looked like the spear but was made to be lighter and carried a more streamlined head. It was the medium-range weapon that was meant to be thrown at the approaching enemy soldiers. Experiments from the time of Napoleon indicated an effective range of about 65 feet; however, with an added looped cord, the range increased to 260 feet.

Bow and Arrow

The bow and arrow was a long-range weapon meant to engage approaching enemies long before their handheld weapons were in range to do harm. At first the bow was made from a single piece of bent wood. But in time this simple bow was replaced by the composite bow. In both cases, it is the physics that allows the soldier to extend the distance the arrow could travel by harnessing the energy of the rebounding wood bow when the string was released. With the composite bow, the effective range of this weapon extends to 200 yards. While one arrow might be easily avoided, archers were grouped so that they could release a hail of arrows that caused carnage and panic when they arrived.

Sling

The sling and the slingshot are not the same thing. The biblical sling consisted of two cords of leather or wool attached to a pouch into which the projectile was placed. Once the clay, wood, or stone projectile was loaded, the slinger would grasp the free ends of the two cords and rotate the weapon either overhead or at the side. After two or three rotations, one of the cords would be released, allowing the projectile to exit the pocket at speeds well over 100 miles per hour. This high-speed projectile was more difficult to see coming and was effective at more than 200 yards, capable of engaging the enemy even before the archers.

Creation Week Cycle in Genesis 1:1–2:4

DAY ONE (1:3–5)

Light is created to distinguish daylight from dark.

DAY TWO (1:6–8)

The atmosphere of earth and the sea become distinct from one another.

DAY THREE (1:9–13)

Dry land is extracted from the sea and filled with life-giving vegetation.

DAY FOUR (1:14–19)

Light carriers (sun, moon, and stars) are created to distinguish daylight from dark.

DAY FIVE (1:20–23)

Birds that fly in the atmosphere and creatures that live in the sea are created.

DAY SIX (1:24–31)

Animals that live on dry land and people are created.

DAY SEVEN (2:2–3)

God rests and blesses the seventh day.

Abraham's Descendants

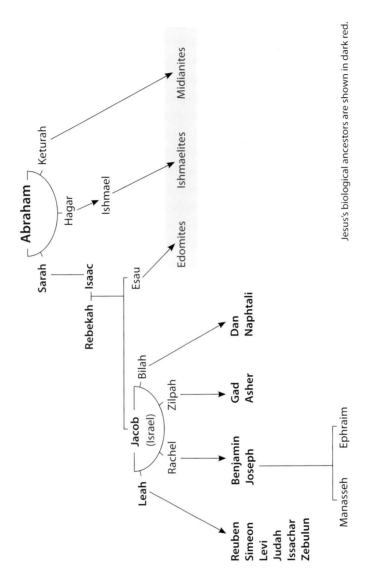

Abraham

- Sarah — Isaac
- Hagar — Ishmael → Ishmaelites
- Keturah → Midianites

Rebekah — Isaac

Jacob (Israel) / Esau → Edomites

- **Leah** → Reuben, Simeon, Levi, Judah, Issachar, Zebulun
- **Rachel** → Benjamin, Joseph → Manasseh, Ephraim
- **Zilpah** → Gad, Asher
- **Bilah** → Dan, Naphtali

Lot (nephew of Abraham)
- → Moabites
- → Ammonites

Jesus's biological ancestors are shown in dark red.

Key Theophanies in Genesis

Theophany			Content of the Theophany						
Text	Receiver	Location	Promised Land	Family to Nation	Divine Blessing	Enhanced Reputation	Blessing to All Nations	Security	Circumcision
12:1–3	Abram	Haran	•	•	•	•	•	•	
12:6–7	Abram	Shechem	•						
13:14–18	Abram	?	•	•					
15:1–21	Abram	?	•	•	•			•	
17:1–22	Abraham	?	•	•	•				•
18:1–33	Abraham	Hebron		•			•	•	
21:11–13	Abraham	Beersheba		•					
22:15–18	Abraham	Moriah	•	•	•		•	•	
26:1–6	Isaac	Gerar	•	•	•		•		
26:23–25	Isaac	Beersheba		•	•				
28:10–15	Jacob	Bethel	•	•			•	•	
31:3	Jacob	Paddan Aram	•		•			•	
32:22–29	Jacob	Jabbok River			•			•	
35:9–13	Jacob	Bethel	•	•	•				
46:1–4	Jacob	Beersheba	•	•				•	

Plagues, Deities, and the Egyptian Economy

Plague	Exodus	Egyptian Worship	Egyptian Economy
Nile to blood	7:14–24	Khnum (Chnum): water provision Hapi: associated with the agricultural rehabilitation of the land during the annual flooding of the Nile	Productivity drops as workers abandon usual tasks in order to dig wells that provide drinking water
Frogs	8:1–15	Heqet (Keket): represented as a frog and linked with fertility	Distraction of workers, lowering productivity
Gnats	8:16–19		Distraction of workers, lowering productivity
Flies	8:20–32		Distraction of workers, lowering productivity
Diseased livestock	9:1–7	Hathor: cow-headed goddess associated with health, fertility, and beauty Ptah (Pteh): linked to the Apis bull and provider of fertility and protection	Death of animals used for transportation, draft work, and food
Boils on livestock and animals	9:8–12		Disabling of animals used for transportation and draft work as well as disabling of workers
Severe thunderstorms and hail	9:13–35	Set (Seth): the storm god associated with thunderstorm phenomena	Injury of livestock and workers, destruction of field crops and fruit trees
Locusts	10:1–20	Osiris: deity associated with the underworld and agriculture	Distraction of workers and destruction of the remaining field crops and fruit trees
Darkness that was felt	10:21–29	Re (Ra or Amun-Re): sun god and patron of the pharaoh	Outdoor work stops, and indoor workers are distracted
Death of firstborn sons	11:1–12:30	As head of Egypt's religious leaders, Pharaoh was to use his divine influence to maintain the Egyptian principle of *ma'at*, which assured personal well-being and social justice.	Personal tragedy compounded with the stress of the previous plagues totally disables the nation, its leadership, and the notion of royal succession.

Date of the Exodus

Source	Evidence	Thirteenth-Century Date	Fifteenth-Century Date
1 Kings 6:1	Solomon began building the temple in Jerusalem in 966 BC, "480 years" after the exodus from Egypt.	The figure 480 is a figurative expression for twelve generations (12 x 40 = 480). Assuming a generation is closer to twenty-five than forty years, this 480 should be understood as three hundred years. Three hundred years earlier than 966 BC yields a 1266 BC exodus date.	The figure 480 is a literal date used to identify the founding of the most important building in Jerusalem. Calculating 480 years earlier than 966 BC yields a 1446 BC exodus date.
Exodus 1:11	The Israelites were forced to build the Egyptian city of Ramesses.	This city was named after its famed builder Ramesses II, who ruled Egypt 1304–1236 BC.	The name "Ramesses" predates this famous pharaoh and is called a "store city" rather than a royal residence.
Judges 11:26	Jephthah observes that the Israelites have occupied key cities near the Arnon River gorge for three hundred years.	Jephthah is exaggerating the number, using hyperbole as he argues with the king of Ammon over who has the right to the land between the Arnon and Jabbok Rivers.	Jephthah (about 1100 BC) is using a rounded but literal number when saying that it has been about three hundred years since the Israelites had arrived in the land. Note that 1100 + 300 + 40 (years in the wilderness) = 1440 BC.
Tel el-Amarna Tablets	A portion of this archive dating to about 1400 BC includes correspondence from Syro-Palestine leaders complaining to Egypt about the invasion of "Habiru."	The term *Habiru* is very broad and is not necessarily connected to the arrival of the Israelites in this region.	While the term *Habiru* does not narrowly point to the Israelites, the activity of the Habiru described in the tablets closely parallels the biblical description of the invading Israelites.
Merneptah Stele	This Egyptian monument dating to the reign of Pharaoh Merneptah (1213–1203 BC) formally mentions "Israel" as an opponent he engaged in Canaan.	The language of the monument suggests that "Israel" is a people group less well established in the land than other groups mentioned on the stele. This would be true if the Israelites had arrived more recently in the land.	In order for Israel to be worthy of mention as an opponent on this monument, it must have been established in Canaan for a longer period of time.
Thirteenth-century archaeology of Canaan	Many archaeological sites in Canaan dating to the thirteenth century BC show signs of significant destruction.	This destruction is consistent with the military invasion of Joshua and the Israelites.	This destruction is not consistent with the way Joshua describes the Israelite advance into Canaan since only a handful of cities faced significant destruction. The thirteenth-century destruction is consistent with the description in Judges, which speaks of multiple attacks on Israelite holdings by invaders like the Philistines and of warfare between the Israelite tribes.

Animals, Insects, and the Israelite Diet

Type	Clean	Unclean	Texts
Mammals	Mammals that have both a split hoof and chew the cud	Mammals that have a split hoof but do not chew the cud, such as the pig Mammals that chew the cud but do not have a split hoof, such as the camel Mammals that walk on four legs with paws, like the dog, bear, or cat A kid cooked in its mother's milk All rodents Mammals found dead Blood of mammals	Leviticus 11:1–8, 27, 29, 42; 19:26; 22:8; Deuteronomy 14:1–8, 21
Birds	All birds unless otherwise prohibited	Birds of prey Fish-eating birds Carrion scavengers Hoopoe Bat Bird found dead Blood of a bird	Leviticus 11:13–19; 19:26; 22:8; Deuteronomy 14:11–18, 21
Water creatures living in lakes, seas, or streams	All water creatures that have both fins and scales	All water creatures that do not have both fins and scales, such as eel, clam, or crab All water creatures found dead Blood of a water creature	Leviticus 11:9–12; 19:26; 22:8; Deuteronomy 14:9–10, 21
Insects	Only insects that hop using jointed legs like the locust, cricket, and grasshopper	All other flying or walking insects Insect found dead	Leviticus 11:20–23; 22:8; Deuteronomy 14:21
Reptiles	None	Particularly all lizards and snakes	Leviticus 11:29–30, 42

Biblical and Ancient Near Eastern Worldviews

Biblical Worldview	Ancient Near Eastern Worldview
There is only one God.	There are many gods.
God's existence is eternal and presumed at the time of this world's creation.	The gods are not eternal and evolved into being over time.
God is never in error.	The gods are prone to making mistakes.
God is always moral and just in his thoughts and actions.	The gods are frequently immoral and unjust in their thoughts and actions.
God's actions and mood are predictable.	The actions and moods of the gods are erratic.
God's story is revealed in history.	The story of the gods is revealed in mythology.
God created the natural world.	The gods represent components of the natural world.
Mortals are the honored crown of God's creation.	Mortals are an afterthought, created to be the lowly slaves of the gods.
The primary role of mortals is to give glory to God.	The primary role of mortals is to provide for the needs of the gods.
God forbids the manufacture and use of idols.	The gods sponsored and required the use of idols to mediate interaction with mortals.
God is sovereign and cannot be manipulated by the use of sympathetic magic.	The gods are dependent on mortals and subject to the use of sympathetic magic.
God's expectations are clearly communicated in writing.	The expectation of the gods is hidden and must be intuited from personal experience and through the use of omens.
Sacrifices are worship tools that recall the dependence of mortals upon God and model the solution for sin.	Sacrifices provide the gods with food, which they need to survive.

Old Testament Sacrifices

Name	References	Personal Item Brought	Reason
Burnt offering	Leviticus 1; 6:8–13	Male from the flock/herd that has no visible defect For those of lower economic status, a dove or pigeon	To provide atonement and assurance of forgiveness for general sins To signal complete surrender and dedication of one's life to God
Grain offering (meal offering, tribute offering)	Leviticus 2; 6:14–23	Fine flour mixed with oil, salt, and incense Baked cakes made with fine flour, salt, and oil but without yeast or honey Roasted heads of grain sprinkled with oil, incense, and salt	To give thanks for the blessing of the Lord on the grain and fruit harvest
Fellowship offering (peace offering)	Leviticus 3; 7:11–36	Male or female from the herd or flock with no visible defect Thank offerings are accompanied by baked cakes.	To express thankfulness for one's relationship with the Lord and the peace he provides To solemnize a vow To express thankfulness for particular blessings received
Sin offering	Leviticus 4:1–5:13; 6:24–30	Male or female animal from the herd or flock with no visible defect, doves and pigeons, or fine flour without oil or incense added; type is socioeconomic and situation specific.	To restore purity, to secure atonement, and to provide assurance of forgiveness for those who have committed unintentional sins
Guilt offering	Leviticus 5:14–6:7; 7:1–10	Ram without visible defect	To restore purity, to secure atonement, and to provide assurance of forgiveness for those who have committed unintentional sins where restitution to the harmed individual is possible. Restitution is paid to the one harmed at 120 percent of loss.

Israelite March and Camp

Order of the Tribes When Traveling (Num. 10)

| Rear | 6
Northern tribes
(Dan, Asher, Naphtali)
(vv. 25–27) | 5
Western tribes
(Ephraim, Manasseh, Benjamin)
(vv. 22–24) | 4
"Holy things" Levites
(Kohathites)
(v. 21) | 3
Southern tribes
(Reuben, Simeon, Gad)
(vv. 18–20) | 2
"Tabernacle" Levites
(Gershonites, Merarites)
(v. 17) | 1
Eastern tribes
(Judah, Issachar, Zebulun)
(vv. 14–16) | Front |

Positions of the Encamped Tribes

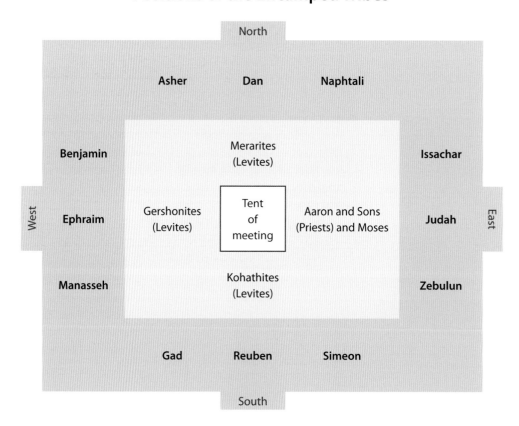

North

Asher   Dan   Naphtali

Benjamin

Merarites
(Levites)

Issachar

West

Ephraim

Gershonites
(Levites)

Tent
of
meeting

Aaron and Sons
(Priests) and Moses

Judah

East

Manasseh

Kohathites
(Levites)

Zebulun

Gad   Reuben   Simeon

South

The Numbers in Numbers

Issue

The Hebrew word אלף is used in reporting the census data at both the beginning and end of the book of Numbers (1:46; 26:51).

The word אלף can reference either the number "one thousand" (Gen. 20:16) or a "military unit" of approximately ten to fifteen soldiers, those constituted by a social unit larger than a household but smaller than a tribe (Judg. 6:15).

Differences

"One Thousand"	"Military Unit"
Results in over 600,000 Israelite soldiers	Results in about 7,000–10,000 Israelite soldiers
Results in a total Israelite population of over 2,000,000 Israelites	Results in a total Israelite population of 28,000–40,000 Israelites
Follows the lead of Jewish religious scholars working between the fifth and tenth centuries AD (Masoretes) who understood the word in this way	Uses contemporary linguistics and a more advanced understanding of the Hebrew language to consider the ways in which individual words are given meaning
Makes the Israelite army over six and a half times larger than the assumed size of the Egyptian army at the time, explaining the fear that seized Egypt	Makes the Israelite army about one-third the assumed size of the Egyptian army at the time, explaining both the nervousness of the Egyptians and the fear of the Israelites
Makes the miracle of survival in the wilderness more dramatic	Makes movement through the wilderness from Egypt to the promised land more manageable
Makes the number fit with the data on the half-shekel tax collected from every Israelite male twenty years of age and older (Exod. 38:25–26)	Makes the Israelites smaller than the nations they would displace from the promised land, keeping their comparative size in line with Moses's assessment (Deut. 7:1, 7)
Explains why the Canaanite city-states banded together to resist the Israelite invasion of their land	Keeps the freshwater resources of the promised land in tune with the number of people entering the land

Similarities

Both solutions respect the authority and integrity of the biblical text.

Both solutions illustrate that God fulfilled his promise to Abraham, allowing his small family to become a great nation.

Both solutions require a divine miracle to sustain the number of people traveling in the wilderness.

Both solutions treat the information as census data derived from the time of Moses rather than an exaggeration whose numbers are drawn from a later era.

Conquest in Joshua

Location	Text	Strategic Importance	Theological Importance
Jericho	Joshua 6:1–27; 12:9	Primary eastern gateway from the Jordan River valley to Canaan's interior	Strategic gateway that Israel was to leave unfortified as mark of their faith in the Lord's protection (Josh. 6:26)
Ai (near Bethel)	Joshua 8:1–29; 12:9	Control of Benjamin plateau and Jericho-Gezer Road	Jacob's dream and memorial pillar (Gen. 28:10–22)
Shechem	Joshua 8:30–35; 24	Controls mountain pass between Mt. Ebal and Mt. Gerizim along the Ridge Route	Promised land identified for Abram (Gen. 12:6–7); location of Joseph's tomb; covenant renewal site during and after Joshua's conquest
Gibeon	Joshua 9:1–10:28	Control of Benjamin plateau and Jericho-Gezer Road	Future home of the tabernacle and altar of burnt offering (1 Chron. 21:29)
Jerusalem	Joshua 12:10	Controls of Benjamin plateau and Jericho-Gezer Road	Abram and Melchizedek (Gen. 14:18); Israel's future religious and political center
Hebron	Joshua 12:10	Controls movement into Judah's hill country from the Negev along the Ridge Route	Tomb of Abraham/Sarah, Isaac/Rebekah, Jacob/Leah (Gen. 23:1–20)
Jarmuth	Joshua 12:11	Near Elah Valley route from Shephelah to interior of Judah	
Lachish	Joshua 12:11	Controls key intersection between Shephelah and Hebron	
Eglon	Joshua 12:12	Along secondary road linking Shephelah with Hebron	
Gezer	Joshua 12:12	Controls entrance to Aijalon Valley, the primary route from the coast to the Benjamin plateau and Jerusalem	
Debir	Joshua 12:13	Along secondary route from Negev to Hebron	
Geder	Joshua 12:13	Location uncertain	
Hormah	Joshua 12:14	Along the Transjordan-Gaza trade route in the Negev	Lesson in failed faith at the time of Moses (Num. 14:45)
Arad	Joshua 12:14	Along the Transjordan-Gaza trade route in the Negev	Israelite victories at the time of Moses (Num. 21:1–3)
Libnah	Joshua 12:15	Along the secondary route from the coast to Hebron via the Shephelah	

Location	Text	Strategic Importance	Theological Importance
Adullam	Joshua 12:15	Along the route from the Elah Valley to Ridge Route, linking coast and interior	
Makkedah	Joshua 12:16	Along a secondary route between coast and Hebron	
Bethel	Joshua 12:16	Control of Benjamin plateau and Jericho-Gezer Road	Jacob's dream and memorial pillar (Gen. 28:10–22)
Tappuah	Joshua 12:17	City in Ephraim near Ridge Route	
Hepher	Joshua 12:17	City on the north side of the Dothan Valley along route linking the coast and the Jezreel Valley	
Aphek	Joshua 12:18	Key water source on the Sharon plain along International Highway	
Lasharon	Joshua 12:18	Location uncertain	
Madon	Joshua 12:19	Location uncertain	
Hazor	Joshua 12:19	Major city overseeing key junction on the International Highway north of the Sea of Galilee	
Shimron Meron	Joshua 12:20	Location uncertain	
Akshaph	Joshua 12:20	Location uncertain	
Taanach	Joshua 12:21	Gateway city to the Jezreel Valley	
Megiddo	Joshua 12:21	Most strategic city in the ancient world along International Highway, controlling passage to the Jezreel Valley	
Kedesh	Joshua 12:22	Town in Naphtali along International Highway	
Jokneam in Carmel	Joshua 12:22	Gateway city to Jezreel Valley	
Dor (Naphoth Dor)	Joshua 12:23	Port city on the Mediterranean Sea with access to the Jezreel Valley	
Goyim in Gilgal	Joshua 12:23	Location uncertain	
Tirzah	Joshua 12:24	City at intersection of the Wadi Farah (Fariah) and the Ridge Route linking the Jordan Valley with the interior of Samaria	

Holy War

In holy war, the commander of the armies of heaven clearly identifies himself as the commander of the army on earth (Josh. 5:13–15).

In holy war, the Lord expressly reveals his intentions to go to war to his subordinate commander on the ground (Josh. 1:1–6).

In holy war, the Lord provides public miracles associated with the subordinate commander on the ground to confirm that this commander has been authorized to conduct such a war (Josh. 4:14–24; 6:8–20).

In holy war, the Lord gives both general and very specific instructions on how war is to be waged (Deut. 7:1–6; 20:1–20; Josh. 1:7–9; 6:2–5).

In holy war, a victorious outcome is certain if the divine directions are followed (Deut. 20:1–4; Josh. 1:5–6; but see Josh. 7:10–12 and 9:14).

In holy war, it is necessary for the people to consecrate themselves before battle as a reminder that such war serves and glorifies God, not mortals (Josh. 3:5; compare Exod. 19:10, 14–15; Josh. 8:30–35).

In holy war, the Lord determines the fate of the opposing city structures, their residents, and their possessions (Deut. 20:19–20; 21:10–14; Josh. 6:21; 8:1–2; 11:6; but note the exception in Josh. 6:25).

Literary Cycle in Judges

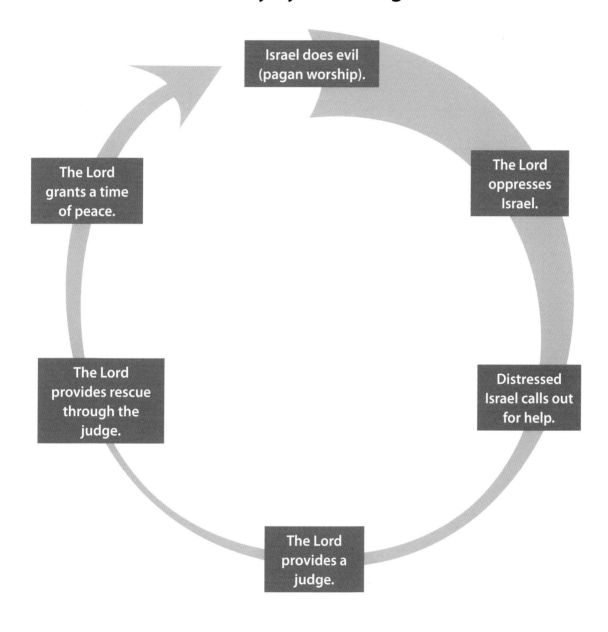

Israel does evil (pagan worship).

The Lord oppresses Israel.

Distressed Israel calls out for help.

The Lord provides a judge.

The Lord provides rescue through the judge.

The Lord grants a time of peace.

Judges

Judge	Text	Years of Service	Accomplishments
Othniel	Judges 3:7–11	40	Ended eight years of Aramean oppression by defeating King Cushan-Rishathaim.
Ehud	Judges 3:12–30	80	Ended eighteen years of oppression by using a ruse to kill King Eglon of Moab by retaking Jericho from Moab and by overseeing the defeat of the Moabite army.
Shamgar	Judges 3:31	Unreported	Ended a time of Philistine oppression by striking down six hundred soldiers with an oxgoad.
Deborah	Judges 4–5	40	Ended twenty years of oppression by joining with Barak to defeat Jabin, the king of Hazor, and his general, Sisera, with his iron-clad chariots in the Jezreel Valley.
Gideon	Judges 6–8	40	Ended seven years of Midianite oppression by demonstrating that Baal was a fraud and by leading three hundred soldiers chosen by the Lord at the Harod Spring into battle against thousands of Midianites camped in the Jezreel Valley.
Tola	Judges 10:1–2	23	Unreported
Jair	Judges 10:3–5	22	Unreported
Jephthah	Judges 10:6–12:7	6	Ended eighteen years of Ammonite oppression in Gilead by attacking Ammonite cities and subduing them.
Ibzan	Judges 12:8–10	7	Unreported
Elon	Judges 12:11–12	10	Unreported
Abdon	Judges 12:13–15	8	Unreported
Samson	Judges 13–16	20	Ended forty years of Philistine oppression by provoking the Philistines with a marriage contract to one of their own, killing thirty men in Ashkelon, burning their grain fields in the Valley of Sorek, killing "a thousand men" in Judah with a donkey's jawbone, and collapsing the temple of Dagon at Gaza, killing many Philistine worshipers there.
Samuel	1 Samuel 1–16, 19	Over 90	The prophet/judge who listened to God's voice when no one else did, oversaw the defeat of the Philistines at Mizpah, and provided the transition to the Israelite monarchy, anointing both Saul and David as the first two kings of Israel.

Ark of the Covenant on the Move

Location	Text	Circumstances
Mount Sinai	Exodus 25:10–22; 40:1–3	Moses is given directions for the construction of the ark and places it in the tabernacle.
On the move in the wilderness	Numbers 4:4–6	The Lord makes the Kohathites responsible for packing and moving the ark as the Israelites travel toward the promised land.
Jordan River	Joshua 3:1–4	The ark leads the Israelites across the Jordan River and into the promised land.
Jericho	Joshua 6:2–7	The ark leads the fighting men in their walks around Jericho.
Valley between Mt. Ebal and Mt. Gerizim	Joshua 8:33	Joshua places the ark in the center of the covenant renewal ceremony at Shechem.
Shiloh	Joshua 18:1	The ark finds a home with the tabernacle in Shiloh as the final division of the promised land takes place.
Bethel	Judges 20:27–28	The ark is temporarily moved to Bethel near their war camp so that the Israelites might ask the Lord how to respond to the crimes committed by Gibeah of Benjamin.
Shiloh	1 Samuel 1:3; 3:3	Samuel's family worships and Samuel serves at the tabernacle in Shiloh.
Ebenezer near Aphek	1 Samuel 4:1–4	The Israelites take the ark into battle against the Philistines, treating it like a talisman that will bring them victory.
Ashdod	1 Samuel 5:1	The Philistines capture the ark and take it to the temple of Dagon.
Gath	1 Samuel 5:8	When the ark brings trouble to Ashdod, the Philistines move it to Gath.
Ekron	1 Samuel 5:10	When the ark brings trouble to Gath, the Philistines move it to Ekron.
Beth Shemesh	1 Samuel 6:13–15	The Philistines of Ekron quickly design a way to return the ark to the Israelites via the Valley of Sorek to Beth Shemesh.
Kiriath Jearim	1 Samuel 7:1	When the Israelites of Beth Shemesh mishandle the ark, it is moved to Kiriath Jearim, where it remains for twenty years.
Household of Obed-Edom	2 Samuel 6:7–11	As David moves the ark toward the city of David, Uzzah's irreverent act and death causes a three-month delay.
City of David	2 Samuel 6:16–17	David successfully moves the ark to the city of David.
Temple Mount in Jerusalem	1 Kings 8:1–5	Solomon places the ark in the temple he has completed.

Kingship

Permitted Similarities between Israelite and Non-Israelite Kings

Both had symbols of leadership that included thrones and crowns.	Both collected tariffs on trade goods.
	Both collected tribute from defeated enemies.
Both had royal palaces.	Both had administrations that participated in governing daily affairs of the state.
Both had capital cities.	
Both integrated a religious worldview with politics.	Both played a role in the judicial system.
Both collected taxes from their citizens.	Both were regarded as the nation's military leader.

Mandated Differences between Israelite and Non-Israelite Kings

Israelite Kings	Non-Israelite Kings
Came to power when God designated them for service	Came to power by using influence, manipulation, and force to leverage the support of the pagan clergy and/or aristocrats
Were to have a personal copy of the divine law code in their possession that they read every day and that became the constitution that informed the way they ruled	Ruled without a written constitution and acquired divine direction via divination
Were to be chosen only from those who were Israelites and eventually only from the descendants of King David	Could be anyone with sufficient personal ambition and power to acquire the office
Were to rule with humility, never considering themselves better than their subjects	Arrogantly distinguished themselves from their subjects in every way possible, including building monuments to their own accomplishments
Were not to acquire horses as a sign of their prestige	Acquired horses as a sign of their prestige
Were not to develop a royal harem as a sign of their prestige	Developed royal harems as a sign of their prestige
Were to limit the amount of wealth they accumulated	Sought to accumulate as much wealth as possible
Were to respect private land rights	Confiscated private land and added it to their royal estates
Could not function as priests	Functioned as priests
Were to trust in the Lord, who would maintain their national security	Trusted foreign alliances and military assets to maintain their national security
Forced only non-Israelites from defeated nations to work on public works projects	Forced both captured slaves and their own citizens to work on public works projects
Were to respect the integrity of the local village and its young people	Took the best and brightest young people from the local villages and compelled them to work for the state
Used prayer to make national decisions	Used divination as the tool in making and validating national decisions

King Saul, Successes and Failures

Successes

Rescued Jabesh Gilead from Ammon and humbly gave the Lord credit for the victory	1 Samuel 11:1–13
Defeated the Philistine army, which had penetrated into the heartland of his kingdom	1 Samuel 14:16–23
Conducted successful military campaigns against Moab, Ammon, Edom, the Philistines, the Amalekites, and the kings of Zobah	1 Samuel 14:47–48

Failures

Acted as a priest by offering a sacrifice	1 Samuel 13:9–12
Allowed the Philistines to establish a military camp in the heart of Israel	1 Samuel 13:16–22
Foolishly instructed his soldiers not to eat during the battle with the Philistines, an order that nearly cost his son, Jonathan, his life	1 Samuel 14:24–45
Set up a monument to honor his own accomplishments	1 Samuel 15:12
Arrogantly failed to follow divine directions in the battle with the Amalekites	1 Samuel 15:10–23
Failed to act or inspire action in the face of the challenge hurled at Israel by Goliath	1 Samuel 17:11
Repeatedly tried to kill David in a jealous attempt to keep David from replacing him as king	1 Samuel 18:11, 20–27; 19:10–15; 23:15; 24:2; 26:2
Killed the priests at Nob and their families when he suspected them of conspiring with David	1 Samuel 22:6–19
Sought the services of a medium at Endor when he wanted to speak to the deceased Samuel	1 Samuel 28:7–19
Lost a decisive battle to the Philistines, which put the survival of the kingdom at great risk	1 Samuel 31:1–7
Ordered the death of Gibeonites, who had protected status	2 Samuel 21:1

David's Family

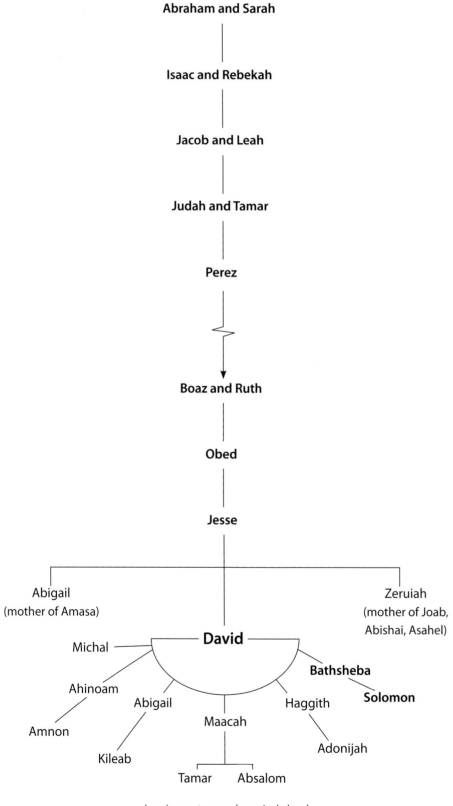

Abraham and Sarah

Isaac and Rebekah

Jacob and Leah

Judah and Tamar

Perez

Boaz and Ruth

Obed

Jesse

Abigail
(mother of Amasa)

Zeruiah
(mother of Joab,
Abishai, Asahel)

David

Michal

Ahinoam

Amnon

Abigail

Kileab

Maacah

Tamar   Absalom

Haggith

Adonijah

Bathsheba

Solomon

Jesus's ancestors are shown in dark red.

The Baker Book of Bible Charts, Maps, and Time Lines

King David, Successes and Failures

Successes

Comforted the tormented King Saul with music	1 Samuel 16:23
Defeated Goliath and the Philistines in the Elah Valley	1 Samuel 17:1–53
Became a celebrated commander in the Israelite army	1 Samuel 18:13–14, 30; 19:8
Rescued Keilah when it was being harassed by the Philistines	1 Samuel 23:1–5
Spared Saul's life in a cave at En Gedi	1 Samuel 24:1–21
Spared Saul's life in the Desert of Ziph	1 Samuel 26:1–24
Learned the military technology and tactics of the Philistines while living among them for sixteen months	1 Samuel 27:1–7
Wrote a stirring lament upon the deaths of Saul and Jonathan	2 Samuel 1:17–27
Became king of Judah at Hebron	2 Samuel 2:1–4
Became king of all Israel	2 Samuel 5:1–4
Captured Jebus and made it his capital city of Jerusalem	2 Samuel 5:6–12
Brought the ark of the covenant to Jerusalem	2 Samuel 6:1–23
Received the promise that a Davidic dynasty had begun and that one of his descendants would be the promised messiah	2 Samuel 7:11–16
Provided national security by defeating the surrounding states that threatened his kingdom	2 Samuel 8:1–14; 21:15–22
Returned to Jerusalem to reclaim the throne following the takeover attempt by his son Absalom	2 Samuel 19:11–39
Composed and sang beautiful songs that expressed his faith	2 Samuel 22:1–51; Psalm 23

Failures

Committed adultery with Bathsheba	2 Samuel 11:1–5
Killed Uriah, the husband of Bathsheba, in an attempt to cover up his sin	2 Samuel 11:6–17
Failed to see and respond well to moral failures in his family	2 Samuel 13:1–38
Failed to see and respond quickly to the conspiracy of Absalom	2 Samuel 15:1–12
Conducted an unnecessary military census	2 Samuel 24:1–17

Parallel Presentation of Saul and David

The biblical authors introduce us to Saul and David using a similar outline, which allows us to more efficiently compare and contrast them as leaders.

Outline	King Saul	King David
Divine designation	Anointed by Samuel (1 Sam. 10:1)	Anointed by Samuel (1 Sam. 16:12–13)
Successful military campaign	Saves the city of Jabesh Gilead threatened by Ammon (1 Sam. 11:1–11)	Saves the Elah Valley, threatened by a Philistine invasion (1 Sam. 17:1–53)
Confirmation as king	Public confirmation at Gilgal (1 Sam. 11:14–15)	Public confirmation at Hebron, first as king of Judah and then as king of all Israel (2 Sam. 2:4; 5:1–5)
Examples of covenant disloyalty, flawed character, and failed leadership	Acts as a priest (1 Sam. 13:9–12) Allows the Philistines to establish a military camp in the heartland of Israel (1 Sam. 13:16–22) Sets up monument in his own honor (1 Sam. 15:12) Arrogantly ignores divine directions in the battle with the Amalekites (1 Sam. 15:13–23) Repeatedly attempts to kill David (1 Sam. 18:11, 20–27; 19:10–15; 23:15; 24:2; 26:2) Kills Israelite priests and their families at Nob (1 Sam. 22:6–19) Employs a medium at Endor (1 Sam. 31:1–7) Loses a decisive battle that allows the Philistines to cut his kingdom in half (1 Sam. 31:1–7) Orders the death of Gibeonites who had protected status (2 Sam. 21:1)	Commits adultery with Bathsheba and arranges the death of her husband (2 Sam. 11:1–17) Fails to respond to the rape of Tamar, his daughter (2 Sam. 13:1–22) Fails to respond to the murder of Amnon, his son (2 Sam. 13:23–38) Fails to respond quickly to Absalom's conspiracy (2 Sam. 15:1–18) Orders an unnecessary military census (2 Sam. 24:1–4)

King Solomon, Successes and Failures

Successes

Dealt effectively with those who threatened his succession to the throne: Adonijah, Abiathar, Joab, and Shimei	1 Kings 2:22–46
Sought and received the gift of extraordinary wisdom from the Lord	1 Kings 3:4–15
Set up an effective administrative structure for governing his growing state	1 Kings 4:1–19
Presided over a strong national economy	1 Kings 4:20–28
Strengthened the spiritual well-being of the state by building the temple	1 Kings 5–6
Distinguished his state with public works projects throughout the kingdom	1 Kings 7:1–12; 9:15
Understood and owned the covenants that guided Israel's relationship with the Lord	1 Kings 8:22–61
Secured international trade routes in order to establish Israel as a world trading partner and tariff collector	1 Kings 9:15–19, 26–28; 10:1–29

Failures

Acquired horses as a sign of prestige	1 Kings 10:26
Developed a royal harem as a sign of prestige	1 Kings 11:3
Sealed international alliances with marriages, which brought pagan ideology into his life	1 Kings 11:1–6
Built pagan sanctuaries on the ridge east of the temple	1 Kings 11:7–8
Allowed inequity in the tax and labor levies to alienate the northern administrative districts	1 Kings 12:4

Israel's Neighbors

Ammonites

Relation to Israel

Related to Israel through Abraham's nephew, Lot (Gen. 19:38)

Geography

Occupied the east-central Transjordan plateau encompassing the headwaters and tributaries of the Jabbok River (Deut. 3:16; Josh. 12:2). *See the map "Tribal Divisions."*

Special Promises/Responsibilities

The Ammonites received a land grant from the Lord. In return, the Lord expected them to support Israel in accomplishing its sacred mission (Deut. 2:19–21).

Significant Interaction

Oppressed Israel for eighteen years until Jephthah defeated them (Judg. 10:6–33)

Threatened Jabesh Gilead until defeated by King Saul (1 Sam. 11:1–11)

Subjugated from the time of Saul through the time of Solomon (1 Sam. 14:47; 2 Sam. 11:1; 12:26–31; 1 Kings 11:1)

Freedom from Israel gained and lost during the divided kingdom (2 Chron. 20:1; 26:8; 27:5)

Menaced Nehemiah during the rebuilding of Jerusalem's walls and gates (Neh. 2:10, 19; 4:7; 6:1, 12, 14)

Subject of prophetic criticism (Jer. 49:1–6; Ezek. 25:1–7; Amos 1:13; Zeph. 2:8–11)

Moabites

Relation to Israel

Related to Israel through Abraham's nephew, Lot (Gen. 19:37)

Geography

Occupied the Transjordan between the Arnon and Zered Rivers, although they often pressed north of the Arnon River into land assigned to Reuben (Num. 21:12–13, 26; Deut. 2:9–13). *See the map "Tribal Divisions."*

Special Promises/Responsibilities

The Moabites received a land grant from the Lord. In return, the Lord expected them to support Israel in accomplishing its sacred mission (Deut. 2:9).

Significant Interaction

Hired Balaam to put a curse on Israel (Num. 22–24)

Moabite women seduced Israelite men into sexually immoral worship (Num. 25:1–5).

Oppressed Israel for eighteen years until defeated by Ehud (Judg. 3:12–30)

The Moabite Ruth joined an Israelite family, traveled to Bethlehem, and became the great-grandmother of David (Ruth 1–4).

Subjugated from the time of Saul to the time of Solomon (1 Sam. 14:47; 2 Sam. 8:2; 1 Kings 11:1)

Freedom from Israel gained and lost during the divided kingdom (2 Kings 1:1; 3:4–27; 2 Chron. 20:1–30)

Subject of prophetic criticism (Isa. 15–16; 25:10–12; Ezek. 25:8–11; Amos 2:1–3; Zeph. 2:8–11)

Edomites

Relation to Israel

Related to Israel through Abraham's grandson Esau (Gen. 25:30)

Geography

Occupied the southern Transjordan from the Zered River to the Gulf of Aqaba (Gen. 36:8; Deut. 2:5). *See the map "Tribal Divisions."*

Special Promises/Responsibilities

The Edomites received a land grant from the Lord. In return, the Lord expected them to support Israel in accomplishing its sacred mission (Deut. 2:4–6).

Significant Interaction

Refused the Israelites passage as they traveled toward the promised land (Num. 20:14–21)

Subjugated from the time of Saul to the time of Solomon (1 Sam. 14:47; 2 Sam. 8:13–14; 1 Kings 11:1, 15–16; 1 Chron. 18:12)

Freedom from Israel gained and lost during the divided kingdom (2 Kings 8:21; 14:7, 22; 2 Chron. 20:1; 21:8–10; 25:11–12; 28:17)

Harassed Israelites and confiscated their property as the Babylonians led the Israelites into exile (Obad. 11–14)

Subject of prophetic criticism (Isa. 34:5–17; Jer. 49:7–22; Ezek. 25:12–14; Obad. 1–21)

Philistines

Relation to Israel

This segment of the Sea Peoples came to the promised land from the Aegean world and had no blood relationship to Israel.

Geography

Occupied the southern coastal plain of the promised land ruling from five city-states: Gaza, Ashkelon, Ashdod, Ekron, and Gath. *See the map "Divided Kingdom."*

Special Promises/Responsibilities

None

Significant Interaction

Oppressed the Israelites for forty years until Samson defeated them (Judg. 14–16)

Defeated Israel at Aphek and seized the ark of the covenant (1 Sam. 4–6)

Defeated and subdued during the days of Samuel (1 Sam. 7:2–14)

Persistent invasion threat at the time of Saul with the Philistines winning the ultimate victory at the close of his life (1 Sam. 13–14, 17, 31)

Defeated and subdued by David (2 Sam. 5:17–25; 8:1, 12)

A less common and less potent threat during the divided kingdom (2 Kings 18:8; 2 Chron. 17:10–11; 21:16–17; 26:6–7; 28:18)

Subject of prophetic criticism (Isa. 14:29–31; Ezek. 25:15–17; Amos 1:6–8; Zeph. 2:4–7; Zech. 9:5–7)

Dynasties of the Northern Kingdom (Israel)

Dynasty of Jeroboam

King	Accession	Dates	Evaluation
Jeroboam I	Popular selection	931–910 BC	Evil, initiated golden calf worship
Nadab	Inherited	910–909 BC	Evil, encouraged pagan worship

Dynasty of Baasha

King	Accession	Dates	Evaluation
Baasha	Via assassination	909–886 BC	Evil, encouraged pagan worship
Elah	Inherited	886–885 BC	Evil, encouraged pagan worship

Dynasty of Zimri

King	Accession	Dates	Evaluation
Zimri	Via Assassination	885 BC (seven days)	Evil, encouraged pagan worship

Dynasty of Omri

King	Accession	Dates	Evaluation
Omri	Appointed by army	885–874 BC	More evil than those before him, encouraged pagan worship, particularly of Baal
Ahab	Inherited	874–853 BC	More evil than those before him, encouraged pagan worship, particularly of Baal
Ahaziah	Inherited	853–852 BC	Evil, encouraged pagan worship, particularly of Baal
Jehoram (Joram)	Inherited	852–841 BC	Evil, encouraged pagan worship, particularly of Baal

Dynasty of Jehu

King	Accession	Dates	Evaluation
Jehu	Via assassination	841–814 BC	Evil, destroyed Baal worship but still encouraged golden calf worship
Jehoahaz	Inherited	814–798 BC	Evil, encouraged pagan worship
Jehoash (Joash)	Inherited	798–782 BC	Evil, encouraged pagan worship
Jeroboam II	Inherited	793–753 BC	Evil, encouraged pagan worship
Zechariah	Inherited	753–752 BC	Evil, encouraged pagan worship

Dynasty of Shallum

King	Accession	Dates	Evaluation
Shallum	Via assassination	752 BC (one month)	Evil (highlighted in actions)

Dynasty of Menachem

King	Accession	Dates	Evaluation
Menahem	Via assassination	752–742 BC	Evil, encouraged pagan worship
Pekahiah	Inherited	742–740 BC	Evil, encouraged pagan worship

Dynasty of Pekah

King	Accession	Dates	Evaluation
Pekah	Via assassination	752–732 BC	Evil, encouraged pagan worship

Dynasty of Hoshea

King	Accession	Dates	Evaluation
Hoshea	Via assassination	732–722 BC	Evil, but not like kings before him

Rulers of the Southern Kingdom (Judah)

Dynasty of David

Ruler	Dates	Evaluation and Highlights	
Rehoboam	931–913 BC	Strengthened Judah's borders but tolerated pagan worship and had an uneven record of personal commitment to the Lord; he lost the national treasury to the Egyptian invader, Shishak.	■
Abijah	913–911 BC	His rule mixed loyalty and disloyalty to the Lord; he found himself frequently at war with Jeroboam and the northern kingdom.	■
Asa	911–870 BC	Reforming king commended for his dedication to the Lord; he fortified Judah's northern border but was criticized for making a treaty with Aram rather than trusting the Lord.	▲
Jehoshaphat	872–848 BC	Reforming king who did what was right in the eyes of the Lord. He initiated a statewide Torah education program and appointed judges to foster justice.	▲
Jehoram	853–841 BC	Evil king who married Athaliah, the daughter of Ahab and Jezebel; executed his own family members perceived as a threat; and enabled pagan worship.	▼
Ahaziah	841 BC	Evil king who patterned his life on the model of Ahab and Omri; ruled only one year.	▼
Athaliah	841–835 BC	Daughter of Ahab and Jezebel who killed all family rivals and seized the throne after her son died; evil ruler who sponsored Baal worship.	▼
Joash (Jehoash)	835–796 BC	In his early years was a reforming king who repaired the temple, but later tolerated pagan worship and ordered the death of Zechariah, a priest of the Lord, who challenged this pagan policy.	■
Amaziah	796–767 BC	Did what was right in the eyes of the Lord but not wholeheartedly; victory over Edom led to worship of their deities. Pride led to battle with northern kingdom, a horrible loss, and subsequent destruction of Jerusalem's defensive wall.	■
Azariah (Uzziah)	792–740 BC	Relatively faithful to the Lord, strong military leader with well-trained/equipped army who subdued Philistines and Ammonites; refortified Jerusalem. He died a leper when he pridefully assumed the role of a priest.	▲

Ruler	Dates	Evaluation and Highlights	
Jotham	750–732 BC	Did what was right in the eyes of the Lord; subjugated Ammon.	▲
Ahaz	735–716 BC	Among the most unfaithful of Judah's kings who worshiped pagan deities and repeatedly violated the law of Moses. He added a pagan altar to the temple complex before closing it down completely.	▼
Hezekiah	716–687 BC	Among best of the reforming kings who destroyed pagan sanctuaries and reopened the temple. Enhanced the size and defensibility of Jerusalem as well as its water systems. Led his people with faithful words and actions.	▲
Manasseh	697–643 BC	Evil king who encouraged pagan worship, desecrated the temple, and shed innocent blood. After he was temporarily taken by Assyria as a captive, he became a reforming king who restored worship at the temple.	▬
Amon	643–641 BC	Evil king who encouraged pagan worship throughout his life.	▼
Josiah	641–609 BC	Among the best of reforming kings who thoroughly removed pagan worship sites and objects from the promised land. Led people in covenant renewal when the Book of the Law was rediscovered during the temple's renovation.	▲
Jehoahaz	609 BC (three months)	Evil king who encouraged pagan worship. He was dethroned by the Egyptian king and exiled to Egypt after a reign of only three months.	▼
Jehoiakim	609–598 BC	Evil king who encouraged pagan worship. He was placed on the throne by the king of Egypt and later became vassal to the king of Babylon. Rebellion resulted in his exile to Babylon.	▼
Jehoiachin	598–597 BC (three months)	Evil king who encouraged pagan worship; exiled to Babylon along with other significant leaders and artisans of Judah.	▼
Zedekiah	597–586 BC	Evil king who encouraged pagan worship; Babylonian appointee whose rebellion led to the final deportation to Babylon and destruction of Jerusalem.	▼

▲ = generally positive record ▼ = generally negative record ▬ = mixed record in regard to covenant faithfulness

Kings of Israel and Judah

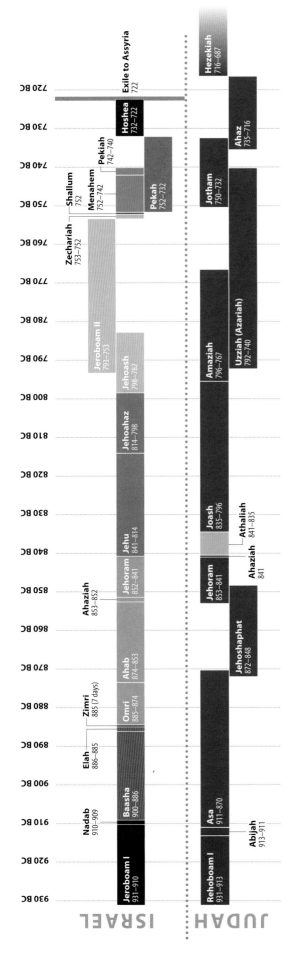

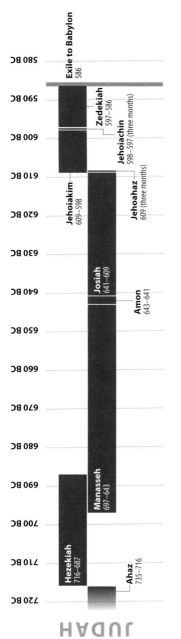

Kings of Syria

King	Dates	Bible Reference	Interaction with Israel and Judah
Rezon (Hezion)	940–915 BC	1 Kings 11:23–25	Adversary of King Solomon
Tabrimmon	915–900 BC	1 Kings 15:18–19	Made a treaty with King Abijah of Judah
Ben-Hadad I	900–860 BC	1 Kings 15:18–20	Bribed by King Asa of Judah to break his alliance with King Baasha of Israel Conquered key locations, impacting the commerce and security of the northern kingdom
Ben-Hadad II	860–841 BC	1 Kings 20:1–34; 2 Kings 6:24; 8:7–10	Attacked Samaria multiple times during the reign of King Ahab Defeated by King Ahab multiple times, resulting in loss of territory won by Ben-Hadad I and an Israelite presence in the markets of Damascus Consulted Elisha near the time of his death
Hazael	841–806 BC	1 Kings 19:15–17; 2 Kings 8:7–15, 28–29; 10:32–33; 12:17–18; 13:3, 22–25	Designated as ruler by Elijah/Elisha Played supporting role in ridding Israel of Baal worship Cruelly threatened both kingdoms through the time of King Joram, King Jehu, and King Jehoahaz of Israel Put Jerusalem under siege at the time of King Joash Took control of the Transjordan away from the northern kingdom and controlled commerce on the King's Highway
Ben-Hadad III	806–770 BC	2 Kings 13:3, 24–25; Jeremiah 49:27; Amos 1:4	Harassed Israel during the time of King Jehoahaz Repeatedly defeated by King Jehoash, who recovered Israelite towns from Aram Subject of prophetic condemnation
Rezin	750–732 BC	2 Kings 15:37; 16:5–9; Isaiah 7:1–8	Joined King Pekah of Israel in an alliance meant to subjugate King Ahaz and Jerusalem

Kings of Assyria

King	Dates	Key History
Tiglath-Pileser I	1115–1076 BC	Campaigned westward to Phoenicia on the Mediterranean Sea
Various inconsequential rulers	1076–934 BC	Royal power eroded in the face of Aramean migrations and Assyrian campaigns ceased
Ashur-Dan II	935–912 BC	Rebuilt Assyria within its traditional homeland
Adad-Nirari II	912–889 BC	Eight campaigns against Aram
Tukulti-Ninurta II	889–884 BC	
Ashurnasirpal II	884–858 BC	Initiated Assyrian practice of one military campaign per year to finance state projects Collected tribute from Tyre and Sidon
Shalmaneser III	858–824 BC	Battle of Qarqar 853 BC
Shamsi-Adad V	824–810 BC	
Adad-Nirari III	810–782 BC	Defeated Damascus and Aram
Shalmaneser IV	782–773 BC	
Ashur-Dan III	772–754 BC	Time of Assyrian weakness
Ashur-Nirari V	754–745 BC	
Tiglath-Pileser III (Pul)	744–727 BC	Campaigns to the west resumed with the goal of controlling all trade routes between the desert and the sea Fall of Damascus 732 BC
Shalmaneser V	727–722 BC	Siege and fall of Samaria 722 BC
Sargon II	721–705 BC	Multiple campaigns into the Levant
Sennacherib	705–681 BC	Siege of Jerusalem 701 BC
Esarhaddon	681–669 BC	Conquered Egyptian delta 671 BC
Ashurbanipal	668–633 BC	Fall of Thebes 663 BC
Ashur-Etil-Ilani	633–622 BC	
Sin-Shur-Ishkun	621–612 BC	Fall of Asshur 614 BC
Ashur-Uballit	612–608 BC	Fall of Nineveh 612 BC Fall of Haran 610 BC

Break in sequence

Assyria, Israel, and Judah

Date	Event	Bible Reference
853 BC	King Ahab of Israel fights with a coalition seeking to halt the westward movement of Shalmaneser III at Qarqar.	Not recorded
841 BC	Shalmaneser III invades and requires tribute from King Jehu of Israel.	Not recorded
805 BC	Adad-Nirari III captures Damascus and invades the coast of the promised land, requiring King Jehoahaz of Israel to pay tribute.	Not recorded
743–738 BC	Tiglath-Pileser III invades the promised land and requires King Menahem of Israel to pay tribute.	2 Kings 15:19–20
734–732 BC	Tiglath-Pileser III invades and seizes large segments of the northern kingdom during the reign of King Pekah, deporting some of its residents.	2 Kings 15:29
734 BC	Responding to an invitation from King Ahaz of Judah, Tiglath-Pileser III attacks Damascus. Ahaz makes religious adjustments in Jerusalem in deference to the Assyrian king.	2 Kings 16:7–18
722 BC	Shalmaneser V annexes the remainder of Israel, taking Samaria at the time of King Hoshea. Northern tribes go into exile.	2 Kings 17:1–6
712 BC	Sargon II takes Ashdod, and King Hezekiah of Judah pays tribute.	Isaiah 10:27–32; 20:1–6
701 BC	Sennacherib invades Judah and puts Jerusalem under siege at the time of King Hezekiah.	2 Kings 18–19; Isaiah 36–37

Kings of Neo-Babylonia

King	Dates	Key Events	Bible Reference
Nabopolassar	625–605 BC	623 BC Gains independence from Assyria 614 BC Defeat of Asshur 612 BC Defeat of Nineveh 610 BC Defeat of Haran	
Nebuchadnezzar	605–562 BC	605 BC Final defeat of Assyria at Carchemish; demands tribute from King Jehoiakim and deports many of Jerusalem's best and brightest, including Daniel 604 BC Daniel interprets the king's dreams and achieves a high rank in government; Shadrach, Meshach, and Abednego survive the fiery furnace. 602 BC Responds to King Jehoiakim's rebellion with a show of force 597 BC Responds to King Jehoiachin's rebellion with another deportation, which includes Ezekiel; removes all the treasures from the palace and temple 588–586 BC Responds to King Zedekiah's rebellion with a siege of Jerusalem, which culminates in the utter destruction of the city, including the temple and a final deportation of Judah's citizens	2 Kings 24–25; 2 Chronicles 36; Daniel 1–4; Ezekiel 1:1–3
Evil-Merodach	562–560 BC	561 BC Releases King Jehoiachin from prison	2 Kings 25:27–30; Jeremiah 52:31–34
Nergal-Sharezer	560–556 BC	Babylonian official at the time of Jerusalem's fall who marries the daughter of Nebuchadnezzar, opening his path to the throne	Jeremiah 39:3, 13
Labashi-Marduk	556 BC		
Nabonidus	555–539 BC (co-regent)		
Belshazzar	555–539 BC (co-regent)	Writing on the wall predicts the loss of his kingdom to the Medes and Persians.	Daniel 5

Kings of Persia

King	Dates	Key Events	Bible Reference
Cyrus	559–530 BC	539 BC Persia defeats and captures Babylon 538 BC First Israelite return from Babylonian exile under Zerubbabel 537 BC Altar rebuilt in Jerusalem 536 BC Foundation of temple in Jerusalem laid; Daniel's vision of the days to come 536 BC Opposition to rebuilding the temple grows	2 Chronicles 36:22–23; Ezra 1; Isaiah 44:28; 45:1; Daniel 1:21; 10–11
Cambyses	530–522 BC	530–520 BC Rebuilding the temple at Jerusalem stops because of opposition	Ezra 4:24
Darius I	522–486 BC	521 BC Builds palaces at Susa 520 BC Temple construction restarts; word of the Lord to Haggai; word of the Lord to Zechariah 516 BC Temple construction completed 490 BC Greeks defeat Persians at Marathon	Ezra 5–6; Haggai 1:1; Zechariah 1:1, 7
Xerxes I (Ahasuerus)	486–465 BC	486 BC Begins to build palaces at Persepolis 478 BC Esther becomes queen of Persia 480–479 BC Greeks defeat Persians with battles at Thermopylae and Salamis	Esther; Daniel 11:2
Artaxerxes I	465–424 BC	458 BC Israelite return from Babylon under Ezra 445 BC Israelite return from Babylon under Nehemiah Defensive wall of Jerusalem restored 433–407 BC Nehemiah travels back to Persia then returns to Judah for a second term as governor	Ezra 7–8; Nehemiah 2:1–9; 2:11–6:16; 13:6–7
Darius II	423–404 BC	Time of intrigue and corruption	
Artaxerxes II	404–359 BC	Restores the palaces at Susa Athens and Sparta weakened as a result of the Peloponnesian War (431–404 BC)	
Artaxerxes III	359–338 BC	Ends sixty-five years of Egyptian independence before his assassination by Bagoas	
Arses	338–335 BC	Puppet king placed on throne by Bagoas, who subsequently assassinates him	
Darius III	335–331 BC	Puppet king placed on throne by Bagoas 334–331 BC Alexander the Great invades and ends the Persian Empire	Daniel 11:3

Old Testament Prophets

Who Was a True Prophet?

An Israelite

Called by God

Authorized to speak on God's behalf to individuals (such as a king) or to a group (such as citizens of a city or nation)

What Did They Say?

They could offer detailed instructions on how to handle a specific situation. For example, they might give instructions on the building of the Lord's temple or how to respond militarily to a national threat.

They interpreted what was happening in their age in light of Israel's loyalty to the Mosaic covenant. For example, they linked crop failure, economic instability, and military occupation to covenant disobedience.

They called Israel to repent of covenant disloyalty.

They assured people of the Lord's eternal love for them by directing their attention to the enduring promises made to Abraham and David.

How Did They Say It?

The prophet's message could be delivered in a life's story, like that of Jonah. But more often their message was shared in symbolic actions or oracles (speeches).

Types of Prophetic Oracles

Indictment Oracles

These speeches criticize attitudes and actions like the worship of pagan deities, insincere religious ritual, and social injustice.

Judgment Oracles

These speeches announce the divine response to covenant disloyalty and include things such as crop failure, foreign invasion, and even exile from the promised land.

Instruction Oracles

These speeches are meant to inform and encourage God's people on how to build greater harmony between their lives and the Mosaic covenant.

Salvation Oracles

These forward-looking speeches speak of better days to come, pointing to things like rescue from military occupation, a return to prosperity, return from exile, and the coming of the messiah.

Types of Psalms

An individual psalm contains a variety of thoughts but often emphasizes one subject more than any of the others. It is that emphatic focus on one subject that leads to the following classification of the psalms.

Type of Psalm	Description	Examples
Confession	Vividly describes feelings of guilt, expresses deep sorrow over personal sins or national failures, which are joined with a plea for God's forgiveness	Psalms 6; 32; 38; 51; 130
Lament	A moving expression of grief that flows from the experiences of an individual or community. It typically describes the poet's plight, expresses a plea for help, and makes a declaration of trust.	Psalms 3; 12; 39; 123; 142
Hymn of praise	Poetic expression of praise and thanksgiving for divine blessings received by an individual or a community	Psalms 8; 30; 113; 150
Wisdom	Reflection on successful living that offers general advice on how to live with a greater sense of purpose and well-being	Psalms 1; 14; 37; 112
Royal	A celebration of David's dynasty, recognizing that the Lord was in the process of fulfilling the promises made in 2 Samuel 7	Psalms 45; 72; 132
Messianic	Offers a vivid description of the messiah's nature, mission, or coming experiences	Psalms 2; 16; 22; 110
Imprecatory	A call for divine judgment on an individual or community that has actively opposed the advance of God's kingdom, often bringing personal harm to the psalmist in the process	Psalms 35; 109

Reading Old Testament Poetry

How Is Old Testament Poetry Different from Prose?

The poet uses fewer words and less space but seeks to say more with less by carefully selecting and artfully organizing a handful of words.

The basic unit of communication in Old Testament poetry is the colon rather than the sentence, with two or three bound together in a set.

The declarative sentences of prose, which are efficient at *informing*, give way to a stylized tapestry of words designed to solicit *feeling and reflection*.

The specific event or situation that lies behind the poet's words is often hidden from view, allowing us to move more quickly into the thought world of the poet.

The physical setting of the poem can jump quickly and without warning between heaven and earth.

Time can move forward, backward, and reverse again within poetry.

The poet uses many more literary devices and metaphors than we find in prose.

Guidelines for Reading and Interpreting Old Testament Poetry

Read the poetry of the Old Testament more *slowly* than prose, paying careful attention to every word and turn of phrase.

Read the poetic piece *repeatedly*, carefully weighing the nature and intent of each word and phrase.

Pause between readings to allow time for reflection and for feelings to arise.

Actively *search for the larger idea* that is introduced, developed, and applied within the poetry.

Watch for the emphasis or development of an idea to occur via its strategic manipulation. The idea can be emphasized or matured by

repeating the idea—"I wait for the Lord more than watchmen wait for the morning, more than watchmen wait for the morning" (Ps. 130:6);

contrasting the idea—"For the LORD watches over the way of the righteous, but the way of the wicked leads to destruction" (Ps. 1:6);

expanding the idea—"Blessed is the one who does not *walk in step* with the wicked or *stand* in the way that sinners take or *sit* in the company of mockers" (Ps. 1:1); or

presenting the idea in a metaphor—"That person is like a tree planted by streams of water, which yields its fruit in season and whose leaf does not wither—whatever they do prospers. Not so the wicked! They are like chaff that the wind blows away" (Ps. 1:3–4).

Wisdom Literature

Definition

Wisdom is the collection of ideas that directs the thoughts, actions, and attitudes of God's people so that they might achieve greater happiness and success while living on earth.

Location

Individual psalms present these ideas (Pss. 1, 37, 49, 112).

Entire books present these ideas (Job, Proverbs, Ecclesiastes, Song of Songs).

Characteristics

Wisdom is anchored in a reverential respect for the Lord.

"The fear of the Lord is the beginning of wisdom, and knowledge of the Holy One is understanding" (Prov. 9:10).

Wisdom grows from the conviction that there is a divine order in this created world that can be discovered. This divine order can be discovered by thoughtful observation of and reflection on life.

Wisdom directs both actions and attitudes.

Wisdom is practical, addressing the most basic dimensions of life, including agricultural practices, marriage relationships, friendship, and personal finances.

Wisdom celebrates moral virtues like humility, honesty, and charity.

Wisdom can take the form of a treatise or a proverb, which is a short, memorable declaration about life and living.

"The glory of young men is their strength, gray hair the splendor of the old" (Prov. 20:29).

"Better to be a nobody and yet have a servant than pretend to be somebody and have no food" (Prov. 12:9).

Treatises are longer investigations of one or more challenging dimensions of life such as human suffering, the prospering of the wicked, or the meaning of life.

Exiles and Returns

Exiles from the Promised Land

Date	Empire	King	Exiles	Bible References
734–732 BC	Assyria	Tiglath-Pileser III	Israelites from Galilee, Gilead, and Naphtali	2 Kings 15:29; 1 Chronicles 5:26
722 BC	Assyria	Shalmaneser V and Sargon II	Israelites from the ten northern tribes	2 Kings 17:1–6
605 BC	Babylon	Nebuchadnezzar	Judeans including Daniel	Daniel 1:1–5
597 BC	Babylon	Nebuchadnezzar	Some ten thousand Judean officers, fighting men, craftsmen, and artisans, including Ezekiel	Ezekiel 1:1–3; 2 Kings 24:13–17
586 BC	Babylon	Nebuchadnezzar	All but the most impoverished Judeans	2 Kings 25:11–12

Returns to the Promised Land

Date	Empire	King	Returnees	Bible References
538 BC	Persia	Cyrus	Judeans led by Sheshbazzar and Jeshua	2 Chronicles 36:22–23; Ezra 1–2
458 BC	Persia	Artaxerxes I	Judeans led by Ezra	Ezra 7–8
445 BC	Persia	Artaxerxes I	Judeans led by Nehemiah	Nehemiah 2:1–9

Nebuchadnezzar's Dream and Daniel's Visions

Nebuchadnezzar's Dream	Bible Reference	Daniel Vision 1	Bible Reference	Daniel Vision 2	Bible Reference	Kingdom	Dates
Statue with head of pure gold	Daniel 2:31–32, 36–38	Lion with eagle's wings	Daniel 7:3–4			Babylonia	605–539 BC
Statue with chest and arms of silver	Daniel 2:32, 39	Bear raised up on one side with three ribs in its mouth	Daniel 7:5	Ram with two horns	Daniel 8:3–4, 20	Medo-Persia	539–332 BC
Statue with belly and thighs of bronze	Daniel 2:32, 39	Leopard with four wings and four heads	Daniel 7:6	Goat with prominent horn that becomes four horns	Daniel 8:5–12, 21–25	Greeks with Alexander the Great and his four successors	332–63 BC
Statue with legs of iron and feet of iron and baked clay	Daniel 2:33, 40–43	Wild beast with iron teeth and ten horns	Daniel 7:7–8, 23–25			Rome	63 BC–AD 476
Rock uncut by human hands smashes the statue and becomes a huge mountain filling the earth	Daniel 2:34–35, 44–45	Ancient of Days gives a son of man coming on the clouds of heaven the authority to rule an everlasting kingdom	Daniel 7:9–14, 26–27			Birth of Jesus and the coming of the kingdom of God	Everlasting

Archaeology of the Old Testament

	Artifact/Structure	Date	Description	Value
1	Gilgamesh Epic (Tablet 11)	1300–1000 BC	An ancient epic tale about the semimythical King Gilgamesh of Uruk, which has been preserved on clay tablets	Includes the story of an ancient flood sent by the gods, a seagoing vessel designed to save humans and animals, a Noah-like figure, Utnapishtim, and other details similar to those in Genesis 6–8
2	Standard of Ur	ca. 2600 BC	Artistically depicts life in Mesopotamia, with one panel dedicated to the culture of war and the other to the culture of peace	A look into the way people lived and thought about life in Mesopotamia over four hundred years before the time of Abraham
3	Mari tablets	1700s BC	Royal archive discovered near Haran that includes economic and administrative texts as well as personal letters	Mention of cultural practices similar to those in Genesis regarding adoption, inheritance, and the ritual use of animals during covenant making
4	Beni Hasan tomb painting	ca. 1892 BC	Egyptian tomb painting that depicts Asiatic merchants carrying personal items and merchandise to Egypt	Confirms the economic ties between the promised land and Egypt; also illustrates the dress, hairstyle, household goods, and weapons known by the family of Abraham
5	Gatehouse at Tel Dan	1800–1750 BC	Remains of the Middle Bronze Age gatehouse that provided access to the city of Laish (Dan)	The earliest known gate associated with an Israelite city, dating to the time of Abraham's family

	Artifact/Structure	Date	Description	Value
6	Yahweh inscription from Soleb	ca. 1400 BC	The artwork of a New Kingdom temple at Soleb includes a cartouche that has been translated, "the land of the *Shasu* of Yahweh."	*Shasu* is the Egyptian term for nomads of the Sinai and southern Palestine who were permitted to graze their animals in the eastern part of the Egyptian delta (Goshen). This represents the earliest mention of the Lord's name, Yahweh, in a setting other than the Bible.
7	Rekhmire tomb paintings	ca. 1500–1425 BC	Tomb paintings from the tomb of the governor of Thebes depicting scenes of daily life during the New Kingdom era	Illustrates the Egyptian culture that surrounded the Israelites during the last decades of their stay in Egypt. Of special interest is the depiction of brick making.
8	Hittite suzerainty covenants	1400–1200 BC	Written agreements that define expectations and responsibilities of lords and their vassals	The format and outline of these covenants uniquely corresponds to the outline and format of the covenant the Lord established with Israel at the time of Moses.
9	Four-horned altar	700s BC	An altar with stone projections at each of its four corners recovered from Beersheba	Illustrates what is meant by the repeated mention of the "horns of the altar" (e.g., Exod. 29:12)
10	Deir ʿAlla inscription	ca. 750–700 BC	Inscription painted in red and black ink on a plastered wall from Jordan that contains a prophecy of Balaam	Possible connection to Balaam, son of Beor (Num. 22:5)

© Bridgeman Images

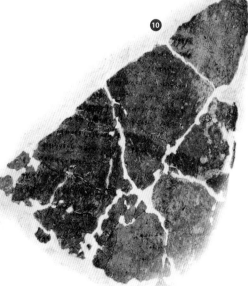

	Artifact/Structure	Date	Description	Value
11	Tel el-Amarna tablets	ca. 1400–1370 BC	Diplomatic correspondence between Syro-Palestine leaders and their overlords in Egypt, a portion of which complains about marauding *Habiru*	Insights into the geopolitical world of Canaan at the time of Israel's entry into Canaan following their extended stay in Egypt
12	Merneptah Stela	1210 BC	Egyptian monument that celebrates Merneptah's victories over Libyans and others of the Levant, including a people group called "Israel"	The earliest mention of "Israel" in an ancient source other than the Bible
13	Egyptian scarab from Khirbet el-Maqatir	1455–1418 BC	A scarab most similar in design to other fifteenth-century Egyptian scarabs, which was discovered in the context of four Late Bronze I pottery sherds just east of the gate guarding the fifteenth-century BC fortress	This recent discovery by the Associates for Biblical Research confirms the fifteenth-century BC date of the fortification identified as the site of Ai attacked during the conquest (Josh. 7:2–5; 8:1–29). The dating of this fortress lends further support to an early date for the exodus.
14	Egyptian maritime battle with the Sea Peoples	1175–1150 BC	The artistic rendering of an Egyptian sea battle with the Sea Peoples from the Medinet Habu tomb of Rameses III at Thebes (Luxor)	Illustrates the manner of dress and weapons used by the Philistines (a subgroup of the Sea Peoples)
15	Ugarit (Ras Shamra) tablets	1400–1200 BC	More than 1,500 clay tablets, which include religious texts that present the mythological stories of deities like El, Asherah, and Baal	This literature advances our understanding of Hebrew, biblical literary forms, and culture within Canaan. This includes insights into the nature of pagan worship and religious thought within Canaan about the time of Israel's entry into the land.

Photo by Michael C. Luddeni, Kh. el-Maqatir Excavation
© Associates for Biblical Research

© De Agostini Picture Library / Bridgeman Images

© Zev Radovan / Bridgeman Images

The Baker Book of Bible Charts, Maps, and Time Lines

	Artifact/Structure	Date	Description	Value
16	Shiloh tabernacle site	1400–1104 BC	The level area on the north side of Shiloh is where the tabernacle was most likely pitched.	This unassuming plateau was the focus of Israel's public religious life from the time of Joshua until the time of Samuel.
17	Palace at Gibeah	1050–971 BC	Near the uncompleted palace of Jordan's King Hussein on Tel el-Ful, we find the remains of a large, palace-like structure.	This is likely the administrative palace of Saul at Gibeah, which served as Israel's first capital city.
18	Pool at Gibeon	1018 BC	A broad cylindrical shaft that includes an embedded staircase cut through bedrock to the water table in order to provide the residents of ancient Gibeon with water	The seven-year civil war that prevented David from assuming the throne as king of all Israel following the death of Saul began at the location of this pool (2 Sam. 2:12–13).
19	Pool Tower and Spring Tower	1011 BC	These towers guarded the Gihon spring and its associated collection pool, which provided water for residents of the city. These towers assured access to the water supply without exiting the city's fortifications.	The water system most likely employed in the capture of Jebus (2 Sam. 5:6–8), a non-Israelite city that became the City of David and Israel's enduring capital
20	David's palace at Jerusalem	ca. 1000 BC	Foundation of a large palace-like structure on the northeast side of the City of David	Presumed to be the palace of King David built in his newly founded capital of Jerusalem (2 Sam. 5:11–12). Here the Lord connected messianic expectation with David's family (2 Sam. 7:1–16).

	Artifact/Structure	Date	Description	Value
21	Tel Dan Stela / House of David inscription	ca. 841 BC	Plaque that celebrates an Aramean victory over the king of "Israel" and the king of the "house of David"	The earliest mention of David and his dynasty in a piece of ancient literature that is not part of the Bible
22*	Tel Qeiyafa	1020–980 BC	A single-period site which has the distinction of being built with two gatehouses and boasting a 10,000-square-foot, multistory palace-like structure at its core	This is likely the Shaaraim ("two gates") referred to in 1 Samuel 17:52. Its monumental architecture demonstrates that a strong and financially capable central government was at work at the time of King David.
23	Six-chambered gate at Gezer	950–925 BC	Massive gatehouse foundation with six opposing guard rooms and a system for draining the city of its water without compromising the security of the city	Illustrates the distinctive gatehouse architecture employed by Solomon (1 Kings 9:15)
24	Gezer Calendar	ca. 950 BC	Small limestone tablet that contains a poetic overview of the agricultural season in Israel written in ancient Hebrew script	One of the earliest examples of Hebrew writing. The calendar provides insights into the agricultural tasks that occupied farmers during various months of the year in the promised land.
25	House of Yahweh Ostracon	500s BC	Pottery sherd from Tel Arad that includes the phrase "He is staying in the house of YHWH" written in early Hebrew script	This unassuming tablet provides the earliest extrabiblical mention of Solomon's temple in Jerusalem.

*Not pictured

© Baker Publishing Group and Dr. James C. Martin. The British Museum.

	Artifact/Structure	Date	Description	Value
26	Sanctuary at Arad	ca. 900 BC	This sanctuary at a small Israelite outpost in southern Israel included an altar of uncut stones, holy place, and holy of holies.	The only surviving Judean sanctuary from the Old Testament era that illustrates the general floor plan of the temple in Jerusalem
27*	Stela of Shishak from Megiddo	925 BC	Corner fragment of a stela discovered at Megiddo that includes the name Shoshenq (Shishak)	This evidence of Egyptian military presence at one of Solomon's fortified cities corroborates the Bible's description of Shishak's invasion during the reign of King Rehoboam (2 Chron. 12:2–9).
28	High place at Dan	930–732 BC	Foundation of the temple and associated worship plaza built by Jeroboam I to facilitate veneration of the golden calf images	Illustrates and corroborates the religious syncretism of the northern kingdom sponsored by their leaders and so often criticized by the biblical authors as they evaluate these kings (1 Kings 12:28–29; 16:2, 31)
29	Samaria ivories	885–722 BC	Approximately five hundred ivory pieces, which likely functioned as furniture inlays, recovered from the palace at Samaria	This rare, imported commodity illustrates the lavish lifestyle of the elite in the northern kingdom; the prophets used ivory as a symbol of misplaced priorities (1 Kings 22:39; Amos 3:15; 6:4–7).
30	Kurkh Stela of Shalmaneser III	853 BC	Stela discovered in southeastern Anatolia that describes Assyrian military campaigns up to 853 BC	This stela affirms the power and influence of King Ahab by describing an event unrecorded in the Bible. It notes that in the battle at Qarqar, Ahab, the Israelite, contributed a substantial two thousand chariots and ten thousand troops to the coalition of forces fighting against Shalmaneser III.

*Not pictured

© Baker Publishing Group and Dr. James C. Martin. The British Museum.

© Baker Publishing Group and Dr. James C. Martin. The British Museum.

	Artifact/Structure	Date	Description	Value
31	Palace at Samaria	875–722 BC	Ruins of the royal palace in the capital city of Samaria from which the northern kingdom was ruled until 722 BC	Home of the most notorious ruling duo of the northern kingdom, Ahab and Jezebel, who sanctioned the worship of Baal in the capital city (1 Kings 16:29–33)
32	Moabite Stone (Mesha Stela)	ca. 835 BC	Monument discovered in the capital city of Moab that celebrates King Mesha's building program and military accomplishments	This monument mentions Omri, alludes to Ahab, and highlights Mesha's view that the Moabite god Kemosh had bested Yahweh in liberating Moab from Israelite control.
33	Black Obelisk	827 BC	Four-sided, black limestone monument that show-cases the conquered bringing tribute to the Assyrian king Shalmaneser III.	In one of the registers, King Jehu of Israel is pictured bowing before Shalmaneser III, with an inscription that reads "Tribute of Jehu, son of Omri."
34*	Tel al-Rimah Stela	797 BC	Stela that portrays the Assyrian king, Adad-Nirari III standing in profile with inscriptions carved into his clothing commemorating his victories	This stela mentions Joash (Jehoash) of Samaria, an Israelite king, as one of those who paid tribute to Assyria. Ironically Adad-Nirari III is likely the "deliverer for Israel" the Lord provided when Aram was oppressing the northern kingdom in the years just before Joash ruled (2 Kings 13:5).
35	Shema Seal	793–753 BC	Stamp seal from Megiddo with an image of a lion and inscribed "(Belonging) to Shema, a servant of Jeroboam"	An item belonging to a member of the royal court of Jeroboam II, one of the most militarily and economically successful kings of Israel (2 Kings 14:23–29)

*Not pictured

© Baker Publishing Group and Dr. James C. Martin. The British Museum.

	Artifact/Structure	Date	Description	Value
36	Khirbet el-Qom inscription	ca. 725 BC	In this artifact carved from a pillar in a burial cave, a protective hand hovers above the inscription, "Blessed be 'Uriyahu; he has been saved from his enemies by his Asherah."	This artifact illustrates the corrupted ideology espoused by some in Judah that linked the Lord with Asherah, a pagan goddess typically associated with Baal.
37*	Nimrud Tablet III	732 BC	Assyrian tablet celebrating the accomplishments of the Assyrian Tiglath-Pileser III in Syria and Palestine	This Assyrian royal document illustrates the role of Tiglath-Pileser III in the succession of Hoshea. It says that the Assyrian ruler removed King Pekah of Israel and put Hoshea on the throne in his place (2 Kings 15:30).
38	Siloam inscription	701 BC	Inscription found at the exit point of a water tunnel in Jerusalem that delivers water from the Gihon Spring to the Siloam Pool. It describes the way in which two excavating teams cutting through the City of David ridge from opposing sides met in the middle.	This inscription likely marks the tunnel built by King Hezekiah to provide water within Jerusalem to meet the needs of refugees fleeing there in advance of the Assyrian invasion of the promised land (2 Kings 20:20). It also provides details about the way in which this major public works project was accomplished.
39	Judean *lmlk* jar handles	ca. 705 BC	Seal impressions on ceramic containers that included the phrase "for the king," indicating that the contents of the vessel were designated for national service	Dating from the time of King Hezekiah, these containers were used to store food and wine in key Judean cities in advance of the military incursion of the Assyrian army under Sennacherib.
40	Broad wall	ca. 705 BC	Foundation courses of a very wide segment of Jerusalem's defensive wall located on the Western Hill of the capital city	The remains of this wall demonstrate that King Hezekiah expanded Jerusalem onto Jerusalem's Western Hill, an area known as the Second District (2 Kings 22:14 HCSB), in advance of the Assyrian invasion. The broad wall is mentioned in Nehemiah 3:8; 12:38.

*Not pictured

© Baker Publishing Group and Dr. James C. Martin. The British Museum.

	Artifact/Structure	Date	Description	Value
41	Lachish reliefs	701 BC	Stone panels commissioned by the Assyrian king Sennacherib and installed in the entrance hall to his throne room that boast about his defeat of the strongly fortified Judean city of Lachish	These panels offer a detailed illustration of Assyrian siege techniques and corroborate the great harm Sennacherib was doing to the fortified cities of Judah at the time of King Hezekiah (2 Kings 18:13–17).
42	Taylor Prism	700 BC	A six-sided, baked-clay column that contains the annals of the Assyrian king Sennacherib, including a record of his 701 BC campaign to the west	This artifact speaks of Sennacherib's attack on Judah, laying siege to forty-six of its fortified cities and barricading Hezekiah in Jerusalem "like a bird in a cage" (2 Kings 18:17–37).
43	Ketef Hinnom silver scrolls	ca. 600 BC	Small silver scrolls discovered in an Iron Age tomb in Jerusalem that are inscribed with the priestly blessing of Numbers 6:24–26	These scrolls are the most ancient artifacts discovered to date with a recognizable portion of the Bible written on them.
44	Lachish letters	587 BC	Potsherds that contain drafts of twenty-two letters composed by the Judean commander of Lachish during the Babylonian siege of his fort in southern Judah	These notes provide a firsthand report of how badly the war was going for Judah as Nebuchadnezzar was closing the noose around Jerusalem; only the forts at Lachish and Azekah were holding out (Jer. 34:7).
45*	Jehoiachin Rations Tablet	595–570 BC	Clay tablet from the palace at Babylon that lists defeated kings who were living in the palace of Nebuchadnezzar and receiving a ration of grain and oil	This table mentions Jehoiachin, king of Judah, corroborating his deportation and his changing circumstances following his exile to Babylon (2 Kings 25:27–30).

*Not pictured

	Artifact/Structure	Date	Description	Value
46	Babylonian Chronicle	597 BC	One of a series of tablets that record Babylonian court history, 605–595 BC. In connection with Nebuchadnezzar, we find the following: "(He) besieged the city of Judah . . . he seized the city and captured the king. He appointed there a king of his own choice."	This reference to the 597 BC siege of Jerusalem corroborates the capture and exile of King Jehoiachin and subsequent appointment of Judah's final king of the Old Testament era, Zedekiah (2 Kings 24:10–17).
47	Area G	586 BC	These homes in the administrative section of Jerusalem provide evidence of the fierce fighting and fires that destroyed Jerusalem following the Babylonian siege.	The damage of this area corroborates the description of Jerusalem's destruction by King Nebuchadnezzar of Babylon (2 Kings 25:8–12).
48	Cyrus Cylinder	ca. 535 BC	This cylinder inscription alludes to the public policy of Cyrus the Persian, who returned exiled peoples to their homelands along with stolen sacred objects and fostered the well-being of sacred centers throughout his empire.	Although Israel is not formally mentioned, this artifact corroborates the policies of Cyrus, who sponsored the return of Judah's exiles from Babylon and authorized the rebuilding of the temple in Jerusalem with royal assistance (Ezra 1).
49	Silver bowl of Artaxerxes I	400s BC	Silver bowl that functioned as a wine-drinking vessel and is inscribed with the name "Artaxerxes"	Nehemiah was among the court officials whose responsibility included bringing wine to King Artaxerxes I (Neh. 2:1), making this a vessel Nehemiah may have touched.
50	Dead Sea Scrolls	250 BC–AD 68	A collection of manuscripts most likely produced by the Essenes who worked at Qumran and then secured their sacred writings in the surrounding caves	This collection of manuscripts includes texts of the Old Testament in Hebrew that predate the earliest surviving complete manuscript of the Old Testament by one thousand years. The collection also includes commentaries that illustrate how some Jews were interpreting the Old Testament during the intertestamental period.

Noah's Ark

This multideck vessel was simply crafted. It was designed for survival rather than navigation. The ark was 450 feet long, 75 feet wide, and 45 feet tall. An 18-inch opening above the main roof provided access to light and fresh air.

Tabernacle

Israel had only one sanctuary, to remind them that they paid allegiance to only one God. The tabernacle was highly portable and had multiple zones, which imposed increasing restrictions on those approaching the inner-most chamber, the place where the Lord was present in a special way.

1 **Courtyard** (*Exod. 27:9–19; 38:9–20*). The tabernacle courtyard defined the sacred space within the Isra-elite camp. This is where the worshipers would meet the priests with their sacrifices. The courtyard was 150 feet long and 75 feet wide. It was bordered by a 7.5-foot-high set of white linen curtains suspended on posts and bars, which were secured by ropes and stakes.

2 **Altar of burnt offering** (*Exod. 27:1–8*). The altar of burnt offering is where daily sacrifices were made to the Lord. It was made of wooden panels overlaid in bronze and included four distinct horns on its four corners. It was 7.5 feet long, 7.5 feet wide, and 4.5 feet tall.

3 **Bronze basin** (*Exod. 30:17–21*). Aaron and his sons used this circular water container to wash their hands and feet prior to performing their official priestly duties.

4 **Tabernacle** (*Exod. 26:1–37; 36:8–38*). Multiple layers of material were draped over a wood-framed struc-ture to create the tabernacle proper (30 feet long and 15 feet wide), which was divided into two rooms: the holy place and the most holy place. The outer layers were weather resistant, while the interior layer provided color and design. Access to the interior of the tabernacle was denied to all but Israel's priests.

Dress of the High Priest

© Ritmeyer Archaeological Design

The high priest was the divinely appointed intermediary between the Lord and his people. His dress distinguished him from all others and was symbolic of his role (Exod. 28).

1 **Robe.** A woven blue robe with pomegranates and bells alternating on its hem was worn over a white linen tunic.
2 **Ephod and sash.** The ephod and sash were woven with blue, purple, and scarlet yarn that included thin gold threads, making it sparkle in the sunlight.
3 **Breastplate.** A woven breastplate, nine inches square, was made of the same material as the ephod. Twelve precious stones were set into the ephod, each inscribed with the name of one of Israel's twelve tribes. The breastplate formed a pouch in which the Urim and Thummim were kept and was attached to the sash and shoulder pieces by gold rings and chains.
4 **Shoulder pieces.** The shoulder pieces had onyx stones set in gold filigree. The names of six Israelite tribes were engraved on each onyx stone according to birth order.
5 **Gold plate.** A gold plate was inscribed with the words HOLY TO THE LORD and attached to a white linen turban.

Solomon's Temple

Solomon built a temple for the Lord in Jerusalem that had the same floor plan, worship furnishings, and rites as the earlier tabernacle (1 Kings 5–7). But while the tabernacle was a portable tent, the temple was a permanent stone structure (90 feet long and 30 feet wide).

1 **Altar of burnt offering** (30 feet long and wide, 15 feet tall). This great altar stood before the temple of Solomon and was the focal point of Israel's worship, since only the priests could enter the temple proper. It had a hollow center filled with stone and soil so that moisture and blood could drain away.

2 **Sea** (15 feet in diameter). The sea was set on the backs of twelve cast bulls.

3 **Cast bronze pillars** (each is more than 32 feet tall). The pillars are named Jakin ("he establishes") and Boaz ("in him strength").

4 **Table of the bread of the presence**

5 **Lampstands**

6 **Incense altar**

7 **Holy place**

8 **Holy of holies, or most holy place**

9 **Ark of the covenant**

10 **Store rooms**

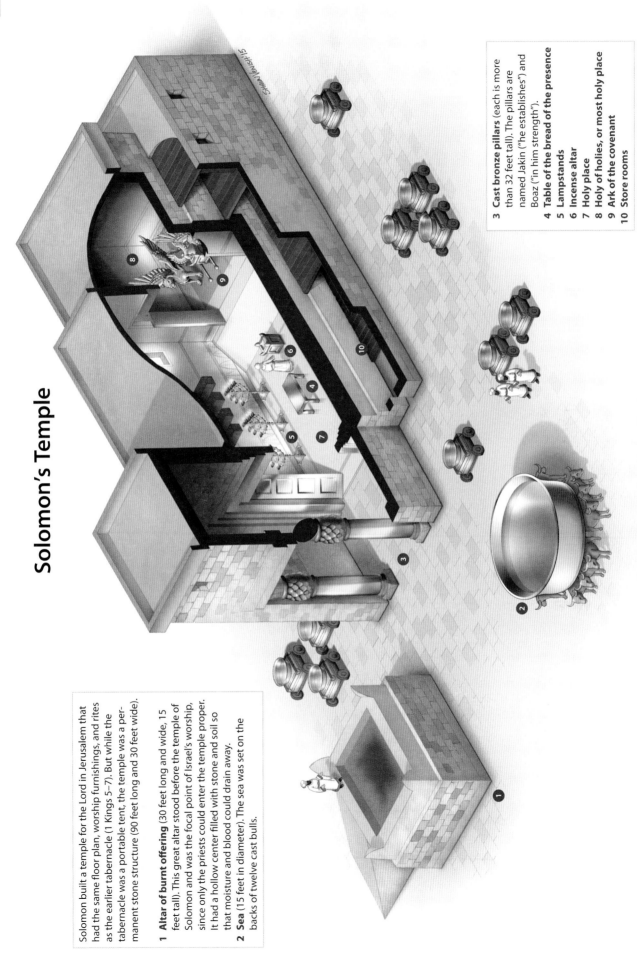

Worship Furniture

1 The lampstand *(Exod. 25:31–40; 27:20–21; Lev. 24:2–4)*. This golden lampstand held seven lamps, which the priests filled daily with special oil in order to provide continuous lighting within the holy place.

2 Table of the bread of the presence *(Exod. 25:23–30; Lev. 24:5–9)*. This wooden table was overlaid with gold and placed within the holy place. It held twelve loaves of bread, which were replaced each Sabbath—one loaf for each of Israel's tribes that lived and found meaning for life in the presence of the Lord.

3 Altar of incense *(Exod. 30:1–10, 34–38)*. This wooden altar, overlaid with gold, was placed within the holy place immediately in front of the curtain that hid the ark of the covenant from view. Each morning and evening the priests serviced this altar with incense, an aromatic made from a special recipe.

4 Ark of the covenant *(Exod. 25:10–22)*. This was the most sacred piece of worship furniture in Israel. It was a wooden box overlaid with gold, measuring 45 inches long by 27 inches wide and tall. The contents changed over time but included the two tablets of the law given to Moses, a jar with manna from Israel's wilderness sojourn, and the staff of Aaron that bloomed miraculously. The mercy seat covered the contents of the ark and included two cherubim. God was present in a special way above this ark, so no mortal except Israel's high priest could enter the holy of holies, where it was kept (Lev. 16:1–34).

Four-Room Israelite House

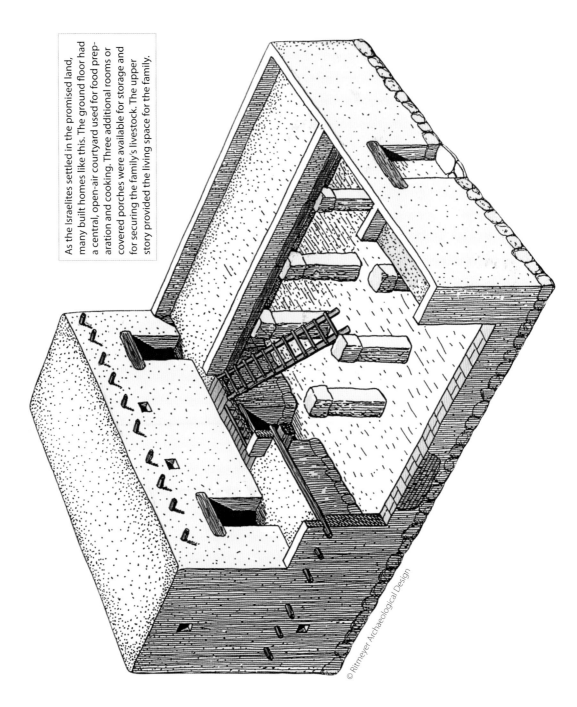

As the Israelites settled in the promised land, many built homes like this. The ground floor had a central, open-air courtyard used for food preparation and cooking. Three additional rooms or covered porches were available for storage and for securing the family's livestock. The upper story provided the living space for the family.

© Ritmeyer Archaeological Design

The Baker Book of Bible Charts, Maps, and Time Lines
© 2016 Baker Publishing Group. **Reproduction of this page is prohibited.**

Bedouin Tent

Early in the Old Testament era, the descendants of Abraham lived in mobile shelters. These tents were made from loosely woven panels of goat's hair, which swelled when wet to make the tent water resistant and relaxed when dry to allow air to circulate. Even after Israel had moved into permanent homes, tents, ropes, and stakes are mentioned in the Old Testament as metaphors (Isa. 33:20; 54:2).

Burial Practices

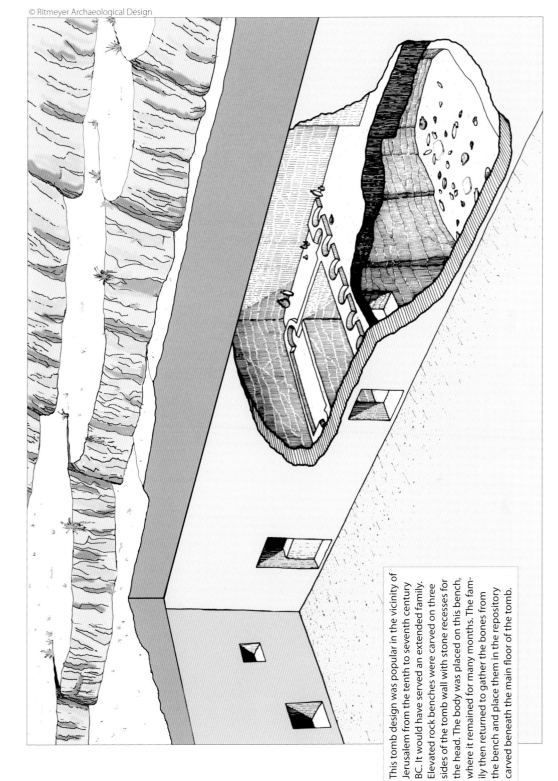

This tomb design was popular in the vicinity of Jerusalem from the tenth to seventh century BC. It would have served an extended family. Elevated rock benches were carved on three sides of the tomb wall with stone recesses for the head. The body was placed on this bench, where it remained for many months. The family then returned to gather the bones from the bench and place them in the repository carved beneath the main floor of the tomb.

City Defensive Systems

Old Testament cities were defended by multiple layers of protection designed to delay attackers, cause casualties, and plant seeds of discouragement.

1 **Entry ramp.** The entry ramp was oriented so that the approaching soldiers' right side—the side opposite from which most carried their shield—was exposed to attack.

2 **Revetment wall.** Cities were often protected by more than one wall. The lower, or revetment, wall often had a plastered mud-brick superstructure built on a field-stone foundation.

3 **Glacis.** The glacis was an artificial slope (30°–40° incline) established between the revetment wall and main defensive wall. This exposed killing zone was often covered with plaster, making it even harder for an attacker to cross.

4 **Main defensive wall.** The main defensive wall and its towers provided both a protective barrier and a firing platform that gave defenders an array of shooting angles.

5 **Gatehouse.** The city's main entry was secured not just by a swinging gate but by a gatehouse. This created a narrow, enclosed passageway into the city that was flanked by opposing guardrooms. The restricted entry narrowed the stream of attacking soldiers and provided cover for defenders, who could thrust spears into the attackers from the guardrooms.

Ancient Ships: Merchant and Military

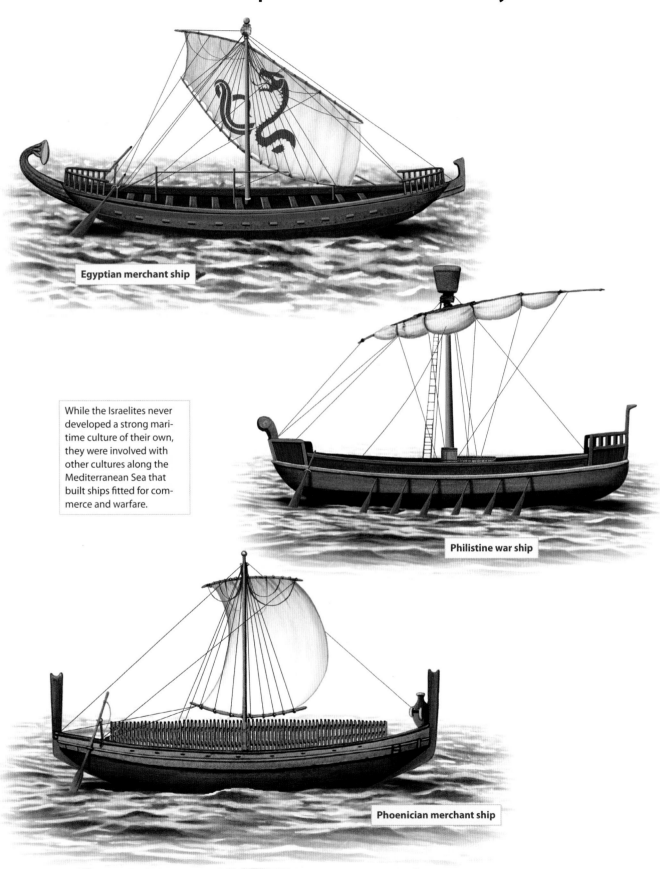

Egyptian merchant ship

While the Israelites never developed a strong maritime culture of their own, they were involved with other cultures along the Mediterranean Sea that built ships fitted for commerce and warfare.

Philistine war ship

Phoenician merchant ship

Musical Instruments

Hand drum (timbrel)

Cymbals

Lyre (harp or zither)

The Bible celebrates the use of music and mentions a variety of musical instruments. The most common are illustrated here.

Trumpet

Shofar (ram's horn)

Flute (double pipe)

Jerusalem of David

Following the civil war that occurred after the death of King Saul, David captured the city of Jebus and its water system. It was then developed into the capital of Israel that was known as the City of David or Jerusalem.

1 **Royal palace of David**
2 **Spring Tower**
3 **Pool Tower**
4 **Central Valley**
5 **Kidron Valley**
6 **Future site of the temple**

SHAUN VENISH '15

Jerusalem of Solomon

Solomon expanded Jerusalem to include the ridge immediately north of the City of David more than doubling the size of the capital city of Israel.

1 Royal palace of David
2 Spring Tower
3 Pool Tower
4 Palace complex of Solomon
5 Temple
6 Central Valley
7 Kidron Valley

Jerusalem of Hezekiah

Hezekiah expanded Jerusalem westward across the Central Valley to the sharply defined ridge above the Hinnom Valley.

1 Royal palace of David
2 Spring Tower
3 Pool Tower
4 Siloam Pool
5 Temple
6 Central Valley
7 Kidron Valley
8 Hinnom Valley

PART THREE

NEW TESTAMENT

New Testament Time Line

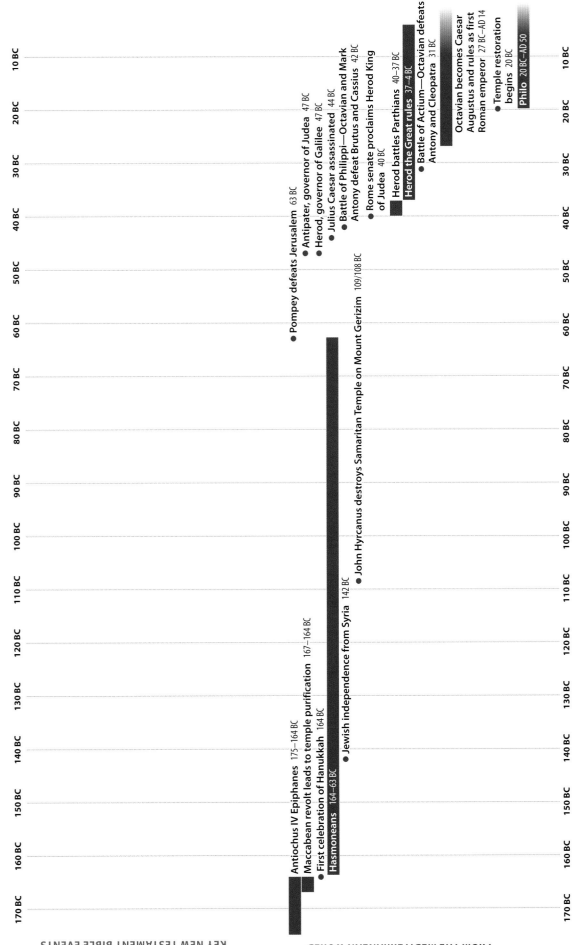

KEY NEW TESTAMENT BIBLE EVENTS

KEY PEOPLE/EVENTS FROM THE MEDITERRANEAN WORLD

170 BC   160 BC   150 BC   140 BC   130 BC   120 BC   110 BC   100 BC   90 BC   80 BC   70 BC   60 BC   50 BC   40 BC   30 BC   20 BC   10 BC

Antiochus IV Epiphanes 175–164 BC
Maccabean revolt leads to temple purification 167–164 BC
First celebration of Hanukkah 164 BC
Hasmoneans 164–63 BC
Jewish independence from Syria 142 BC
John Hyrcanus destroys Samaritan Temple on Mount Gerizim 109/108 BC

Pompey defeats Jerusalem 63 BC
Antipater, governor of Judea 47 BC
Herod, governor of Galilee 47 BC
Julius Caesar assassinated 44 BC
Battle of Philippi—Octavian and Mark Antony defeat Brutus and Cassius 42 BC
Rome senate proclaims Herod King of Judea 40 BC
Herod battles Parthians 40–37 BC
Herod the Great rules 37–4 BC
Battle of Actium—Octavian defeats Antony and Cleopatra 31 BC
Octavian becomes Caesar Augustus and rules as first Roman emperor 27 BC–AD 14
Temple restoration begins 20 BC
Philo 20 BC–AD 50

The Baker Book of Bible Charts, Maps, and Time Lines
© 2016 Baker Publishing Group. May be reproduced for classroom use only, not for resale.

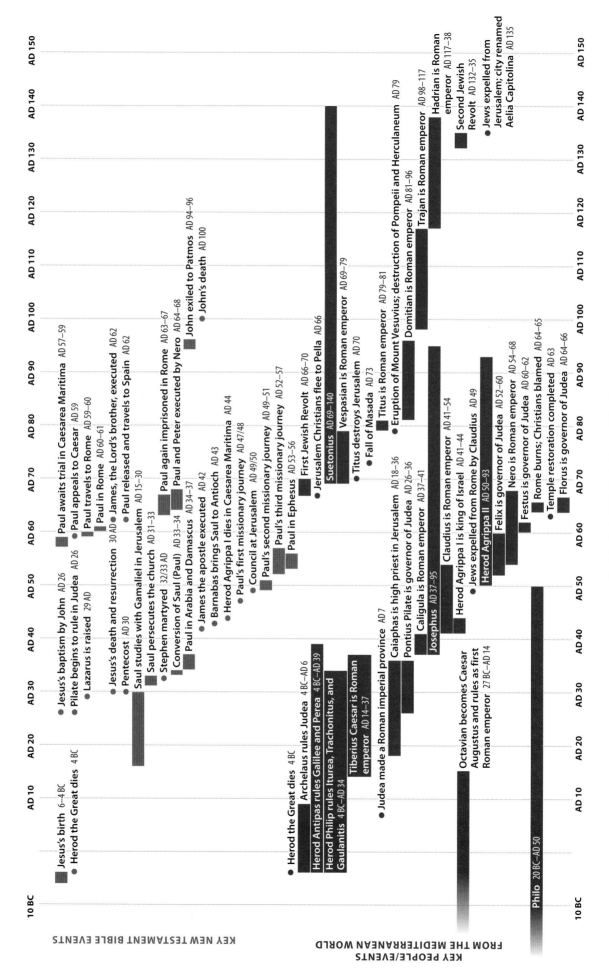

KEY NEW TESTAMENT BIBLE EVENTS

KEY PEOPLE/EVENTS
FROM THE MEDITERRANEAN WORLD

New Testament Israel

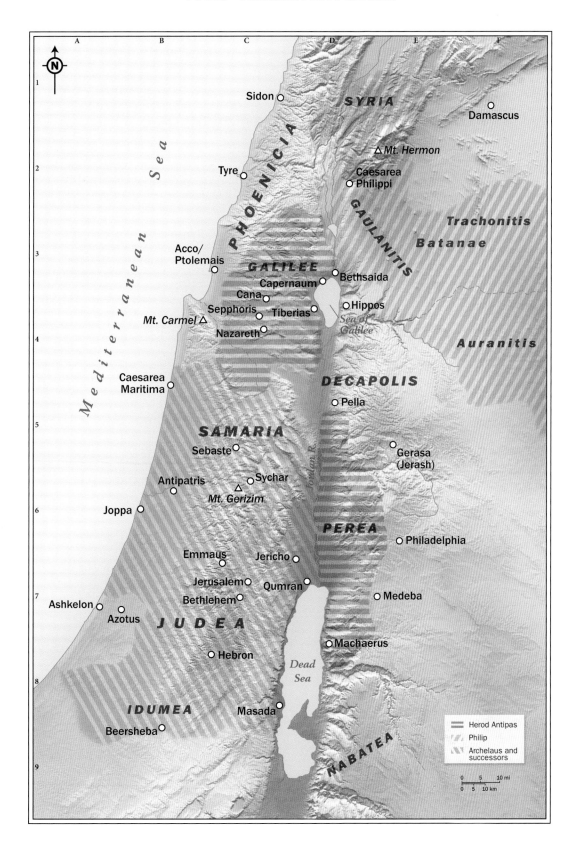

Sidon

SYRIA

Damascus

△ Mt. Hermon

Caesarea Philippi

Tyre

PHOENICIA

GAULANITIS

Trachonitis

Batanae

Acco/ Ptolemais

GALILEE

Bethsaida

Capernaum

Cana

Hippos

Sepphoris

Tiberias

Sea of Galilee

Mt. Carmel △

Nazareth

Auranitis

Mediterranean Sea

Caesarea Maritima

DECAPOLIS

Pella

SAMARIA

Sebaste

Gerasa (Jerash)

Antipatris

Sychar

△ Mt. Gerizim

Joppa

PEREA

Philadelphia

Emmaus

Jericho

Jerusalem

Qumran

Medeba

Bethlehem

Ashkelon

Azotus

JUDEA

Machaerus

Hebron

Dead Sea

IDUMEA

Masada

Beersheba

NABATEA

Jordan R.

Herod Antipas
Philip
Archelaus and successors

0   5   10 mi
0   5   10 km

Galilee in the Time of Jesus

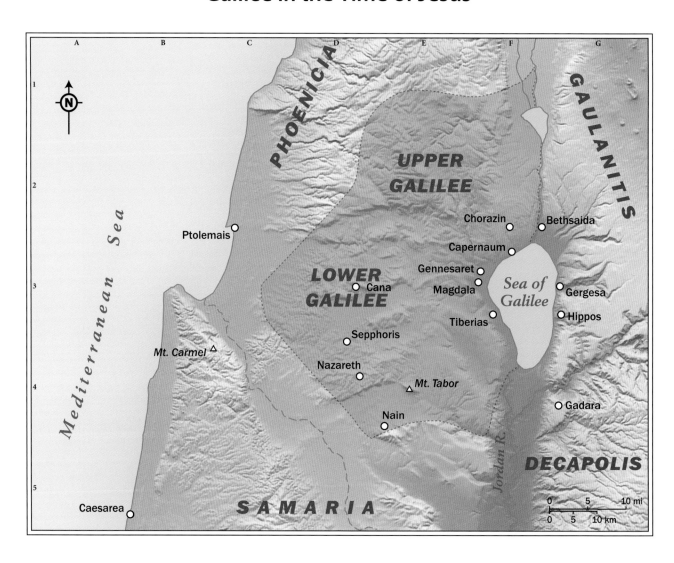

Galilee and Surrounding Regions
in the Time of Jesus

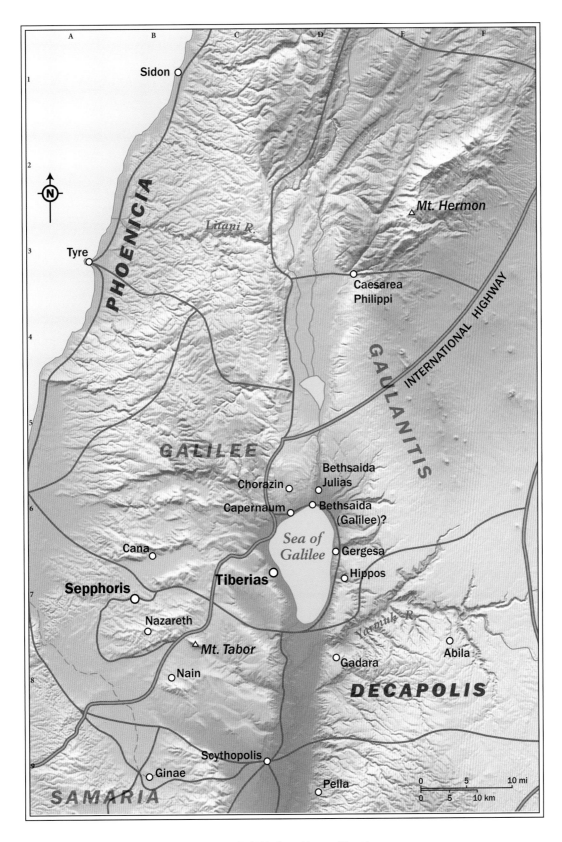

New Testament Jerusalem

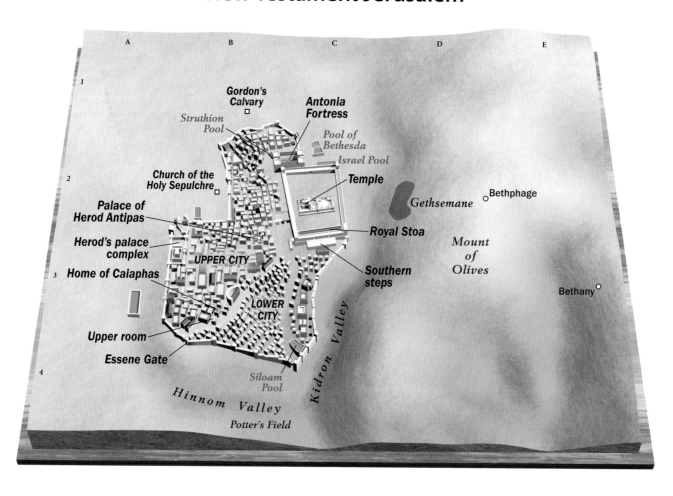

Early Travels of Philip, Peter, and Paul

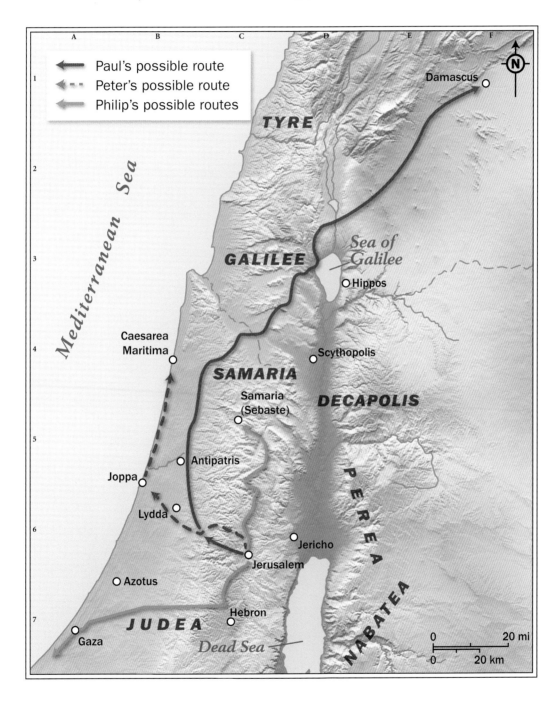

Paul's possible route
Peter's possible route
Philip's possible routes

Damascus

TYRE

GALILEE

Sea of Galilee

O Hippos

Caesarea Maritima

SAMARIA

Scythopolis

Samaria (Sebaste)

DECAPOLIS

Antipatris

Joppa

Lydda

Jericho

Jerusalem

PEREA

Azotus

Hebron

NABATEA

JUDEA

Gaza

Dead Sea

Mediterranean Sea

0   20 mi
0   20 km

N

Paul's First Missionary Journey

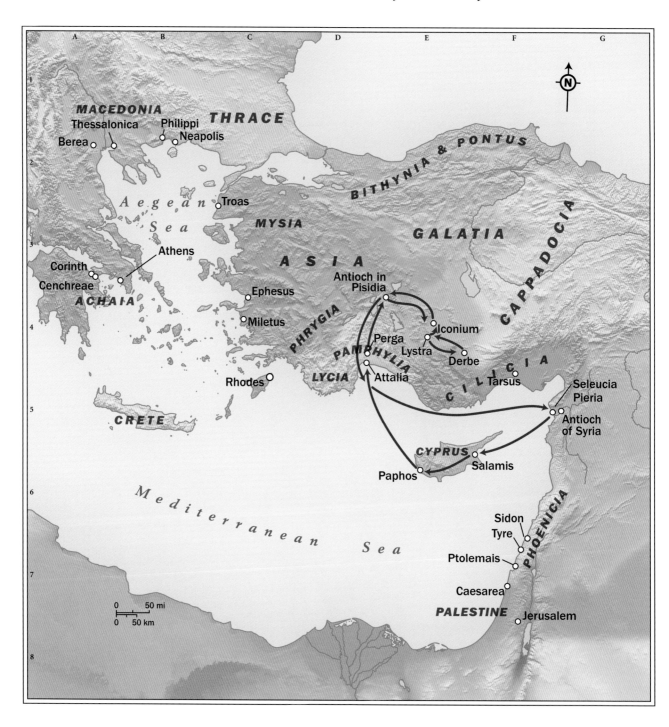

Paul's Second Missionary Journey

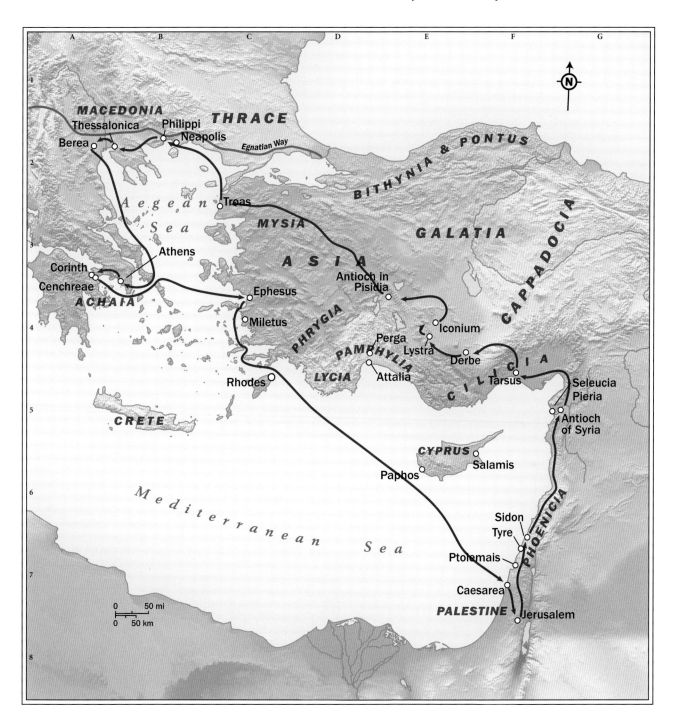

Paul's Third Missionary Journey

Paul Travels to Rome

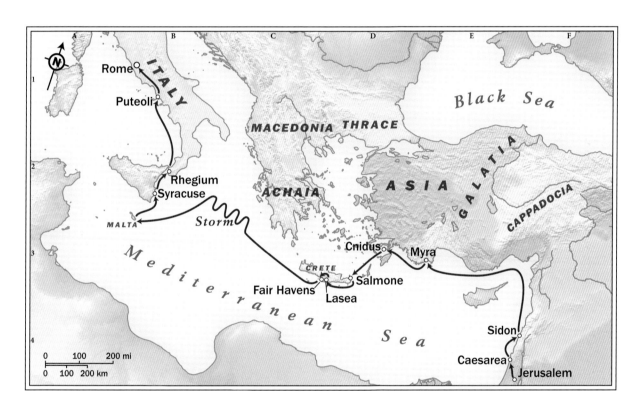

Seven Churches of Revelation

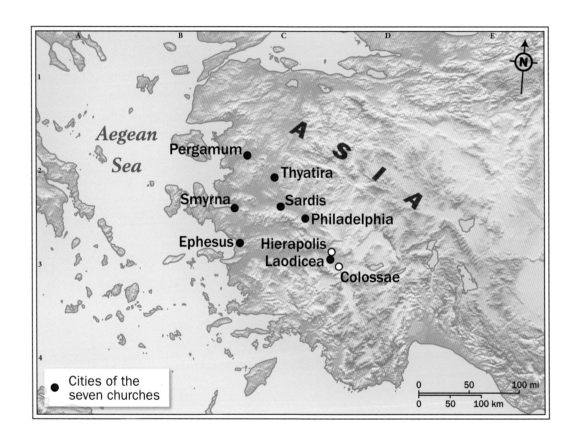

The Baker Book of Bible Charts, Maps, and Time Lines

Jewish Population Centers in the Roman World

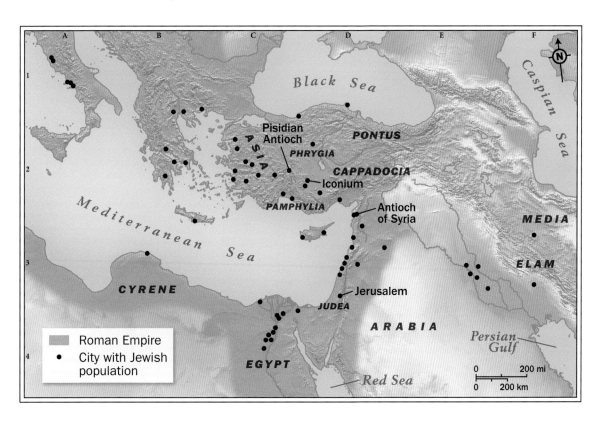

Key Quotations of the Old Testament in the New Testament

New Testament Reference	Topic	Pentateuch	Historical Books	Major Prophets	Minor Prophets	Poetry
Matthew 1:22–23	Immanuel			Isaiah 7:14		
Matthew 2:5–6	Bethlehem				Micah 5:2	
Matthew 2:17–18	Grief in Ramah			Jeremiah 31:15		
Matthew 3:3	Forerunner			Isaiah 40:3		
Matthew 4:4	Trust in the wilderness	Deuteronomy 8:3				
Matthew 4:7	Testing God	Deuteronomy 6:16				
Matthew 4:10	Obedient service to God	Deuteronomy 6:13				
Matthew 4:14–16	Messiah's geographical influence			Isaiah 9:1–2		
Matthew 8:17	Messiah's healing			Isaiah 53:4		
Matthew 11:10	Forerunner				Malachi 3:1	
Matthew 12:17–21	Messiah's qualities			Isaiah 42:1–4		
Matthew 13:14–15	Spiritual dullness			Isaiah 6:9–10		
Matthew 13:35	Use of parables					Psalm 78:2
Matthew 15:7–9	Empty worship			Isaiah 29:13		
Matthew 19:4–5	Marriage	Genesis 1:27; 2:24				
Matthew 21:4–5	Messiah's arrival in Zion				Zechariah 9:9	
Matthew 21:13	Temple contamination			Isaiah 56:7; Jeremiah 7:11		
Matthew 21:42	Cornerstone rejected					Psalm 118:22–23
Matthew 22:37–38	Greatest commandment	Leviticus 19:18; Deuteronomy 6:5				
Matthew 22:44	Messiah as the son of David					Psalm 110:1
Matthew 24:15	Abomination that causes desolation			Daniel 9:27; 11:31; 12:11		
Matthew 24:29	End times			Isaiah 13:10; 34:4		
Matthew 24:30	Son of Man			Daniel 7:13		
Matthew 26:31	Messiah abandoned				Zechariah 13:7	
Matthew 27:35	Cast lots for clothing					Psalm 22:18
Matthew 27:45–46	Forsaken by God					Psalm 22:1
Mark 1:2–3	Forerunner			Isaiah 40:3	Malachi 3:1	

The Baker Book of Bible Charts, Maps, and Time Lines

New Testament Reference	Topic	Pentateuch	Historical Books	Major Prophets	Minor Prophets	Poetry
Mark 7:6–7	Hypocrisy			Isaiah 29:13		
Mark 9:48	Hell			Isaiah 66:24		
Mark 10:6–8	Marriage	Genesis 1:27; 2:24				
Mark 11:17	Temple contamination			Isaiah 56:7; Jeremiah 7:11		
Mark 12:10–11	Cornerstone rejected					Psalm 118:22–23
Mark 12:29–31	Greatest commandment	Leviticus 19:18; Deuteronomy 6:4–5				
Mark 12:36	Messiah as the son of David					Psalm 110:1
Mark 13:14	Abomination that causes desolation			Daniel 9:27; 11:31; 12:11		
Mark 13:24–25	End times			Isaiah 13:10; 34:4		
Mark 13:26	Son of Man			Daniel 7:13		
Mark 14:27	Messiah abandoned				Zechariah 13:7	
Mark 15:34	Forsaken by God					Psalm 22:1
Luke 3:4–6	Forerunner			Isaiah 40:3–5		
Luke 4:4	Trust in the wilderness	Deuteronomy 8:3				
Luke 4:8	Obedient service to God	Deuteronomy 6:13				
Luke 4:12	Testing God	Deuteronomy 6:16				
Luke 4:18–19	Messiah's work			Isaiah 61:1–2		
Luke 7:27	Forerunner				Malachi 3:1	
Luke 8:10	Use of parables			Isaiah 6:9		
Luke 19:46	Temple contamination			Isaiah 56:7; Jeremiah 7:11		
Luke 20:17	Cornerstone rejected					Psalm 118:22
Luke 20:42–43	Messiah as son of David					Psalm 110:1
Luke 21:27	Son of Man			Daniel 7:13		
Luke 22:37	Messiah as criminal			Isaiah 53:12		
John 1:23	Forerunner			Isaiah 40:3		
John 6:31	Life-giving bread	Exodus 16:4				
John 6:45	Salvation from God			Isaiah 54:13		
John 12:15	Messiah's arrival in Zion				Zechariah 9:9	
John 12:38–40	Messiah's rejection			Isaiah 6:10; 53:1		

New Testament Reference	Topic	Pentateuch	Historical Books	Major Prophets	Minor Prophets	Poetry
John 13:18	Betrayal of the Messiah					Psalm 41:9
John 19:24	Messiah's clothing divided					Psalm 22:18
John 19:36	Messiah's bones unbroken					Psalm 34:20
John 19:37	Messiah pierced				Zechariah 12:10	
Acts 1:20	Replacing Judas					Psalms 69:25; 109:8
Acts 2:16–21	Arrival of the last days				Joel 2:28–32	
Acts 2:25–28	Messiah's body would not decompose					Psalm 16:8–11
Acts 2:34–35	Messiah as David's son					Psalm 110:1
Acts 3:22–23	Messiah as prophet	Deuteronomy 18:15, 18–19				
Acts 3:25	All people blessed through Abraham	Genesis 22:18; 26:4				
Acts 4:11	Rejected cornerstone					Psalm 118:22
Acts 4:25–26	Opposition to the Messiah					Psalm 2:1–2
Acts 7:3	Covenant with Abram	Genesis 12:1–3				
Acts 7:42–43	Past sins of Israel				Amos 5:25–27	
Acts 8:32–33	Messiah's suffering			Isaiah 53:7–8		
Acts 13:33	Jesus is God's son					Psalm 2:7
Acts 13:34–35	Messiah's body would not decompose			Isaiah 55:3		Psalm 16:10
Acts 13:47	Salvation for gentiles			Isaiah 49:6		
Acts 15:15–18	Salvation for gentiles				Amos 9:11–12	
Romans 1:17	Righteous live by faith				Habakkuk 2:4	
Romans 3:4	God's faithfulness					Psalm 51:4
Romans 3:10–18	No one is righteous			Isaiah 59:7–8		Psalms 5:9; 10:7; 14:1–3; 36:1; 53:1–3; 140:3; Ecclesiastes 7:20
Romans 4:3	Abraham righteous by faith	Genesis 15:6				
Romans 4:7–8	Righteousness through faith					Psalm 32:1–2
Romans 4:16–18	Righteousness through faith	Genesis 15:5; 17:5				
Romans 9:6–9	Israel more than Israel	Genesis 18:10, 14; 21:12				

New Testament Reference	Topic	Pentateuch	Historical Books	Major Prophets	Minor Prophets	Poetry
Romans 9:15	Election based on God's mercy	Exodus 33:19				
Romans 9:25–29	Mercy to the gentiles			Isaiah 1:9; 10:22–23	Hosea 1:10; 2:23	
Romans 9:33	Messiah as stumbling block			Isaiah 8:14; 28:16		
Romans 10:5–8	Righteousness by faith	Leviticus 18:5; Deuteronomy 30:13–14				
Romans 10:11–13	Righteousness by faith			Isaiah 28:16	Joel 2:32	
Romans 10:16–21	Israel's opportunity squandered	Deuteronomy 32:21		Isaiah 53:1; 65:1–2		Psalm 19:4
Romans 11:4	Remnant in Israel		1 Kings 19:18			
Romans 11:7–10	Risk of hardening one's heart	Deuteronomy 29:4		Isaiah 29:10		Psalm 69:22–23
Romans 11:26–27	All Israel saved			Isaiah 59:20–21		
Romans 12:19–20	Show mercy to your enemies	Deuteronomy 32:35				Proverbs 25:21–22
Romans 14:11	Final judgment			Isaiah 45:23		
Romans 15:9–12	Gentiles glorify God	Deuteronomy 32:43	2 Samuel 22:50	Isaiah 11:10; 52:15		Psalm 117:1
1 Corinthians 3:19–20	Wise fools					Job 5:13; Psalm 94:11
1 Corinthians 6:16	Marriage	Genesis 2:24				
1 Corinthians 9:9	Rights of an apostle	Deuteronomy 25:4				
1 Corinthians 15:45	Natural and spiritual bodies	Genesis 2:7				
1 Corinthians 15:54–55	Victory over death			Isaiah 25:8	Hosea 13:14	
2 Corinthians 6:2	Time of God's favor			Isaiah 49:8		
2 Corinthians 6:17–18	Not yoked with unbelievers			Isaiah 52:11		
2 Corinthians 8:15	Economic equality	Exodus 16:18				
2 Corinthians 10:17	Boast in the Lord			Jeremiah 9:24		
Galatians 3:6	Saved by faith	Genesis 15:6				
Galatians 3:8	Salvation of gentiles	Genesis 12:3; 18:18; 22:18				
Galatians 3:10	Curse on sinners	Deuteronomy 27:26				
Galatians 3:11	Righteous live by faith				Habakkuk 2:4	
Galatians 3:13	Curse of crucifixion	Deuteronomy 21:23				
Galatians 5:14	Love your neighbor as yourself	Leviticus 19:18				
Ephesians 4:26	Anger					Psalm 4:4
Ephesians 5:31	Marriage	Genesis 2:24				

The Baker Book of Bible Charts, Maps, and Time Lines

New Testament Reference	Topic	Pentateuch	Historical Books	Major Prophets	Minor Prophets	Poetry
Ephesians 6:3	Obedience owed parents	Deuteronomy 5:16				
1 Timothy 5:18	Compensation for church workers	Deuteronomy 24:5				
Hebrews 1:5–13	Superiority of Jesus's words	Deuteronomy 32:43	2 Samuel 7:14			Psalms 2:7; 45:6–7; 102:25–27; 110:1
Hebrews 2:11–12	Jesus's human nature					Psalm 22:22
Hebrews 3:7–15	Warning against unbelief					Psalm 95:7–11
Hebrews 4:4	Sabbath rest	Genesis 2:2				
Hebrews 5:5–6	Jesus as son of God and priest					Psalms 2:7; 110:4
Hebrews 7:17, 21	Jesus as priest					Psalm 110:4
Hebrews 8:8–12	New covenant			Jeremiah 31:31–34		
Hebrews 9:20	Relationship of blood and covenant	Exodus 24:8				
Hebrews 10:5–7	The sufficient sacrifice					Psalm 40:6–8
Hebrews 10:15–17	Jesus's sacrifice and the new covenant			Jeremiah 31:33–34		
Hebrews 10:37–38	Righteousness and faith				Habakkuk 2:3–4	
Hebrews 12:5–6	Endure hardship as discipline					Proverbs 3:11–12
Hebrews 13:5–6	Being content with God's provision	Deuteronomy 31:6				Psalm 118:6–7
James 2:8	Love of your neighbor	Leviticus 19:18				
James 2:23	Faith and righteousness	Genesis 15:6				
James 4:6	Humility					Proverbs 3:34
1 Peter 1:16	Holy living	Leviticus 19:2; 20:7				
1 Peter 1:24–25	Immortality for mortals			Isaiah 40:6–8		
1 Peter 2:6	Christ the cornerstone			Isaiah 28:16		
1 Peter 2:22	Righteous living			Isaiah 53:9		
1 Peter 3:10–12	Receiving God's blessing					Psalm 34:12–16
1 Peter 5:5	Humility					Proverbs 3:34
Revelation 1:13	Jesus the son of man			Daniel 7:13		
Revelation 2:27	Jesus's dominance					Psalm 2:9
Revelation 14:14	Jesus the son of man			Daniel 7:13		
Revelation 19:15	Jesus's dominance					Psalm 2:9

Key Old Testament Figures in the New Testament

Person	Key Scripture	Key Insights
Aaron	Hebrews 5:4; 7:11	Jesus was called by God to be the High Priest like Aaron was called by God to be high priest. Jesus, as a non-Levite, provided the perfection that the priestly descendants of Levi could not.
Abel	Matthew 23:35 (Luke 11:51); Hebrews 12:24	Jesus used Abel's death together with that of Zechariah (son of Jehoiada) in a merism intended to capture the full sweep of Old Testament history. Abel's blood, which cries out for retribution, contrasts with the blood of Jesus, which announces forgiveness.
Abraham	Matthew 1:1 (Luke 3:34); 3:9; 8:11; Luke 1:73; 3:8; John 8:39–40, 56–58; Acts 3:25; Romans 4:1–3, 12–13; 9:8; Galatians 3:6–9; Hebrews 11:8, 17, 19	As promised in the Old Testament, Jesus was a descendant of Abraham. The uniqueness of Jesus is highlighted by the fact that although he existed before Abraham was born, Jesus was a descendant of Abraham. Mention of Abraham is used as a symbol of the Old Testament covenant promises made to him. Being a physical descendant of Abraham does not guarantee eternal salvation when faith is lacking. Both Jews and gentiles who repent and produce fruits of faith will sit at the feast given by Abraham in the coming kingdom of God. Abraham was justified by faith; consequently all believers who are justified by faith are called "descendants of Abraham."
Adam	Romans 5:12–21; 1 Corinthians 15:22, 45; 1 Timothy 2:13–14	As Adam was the gateway for sin and death, so Jesus is the gateway to forgiveness and life. The creation order of Adam and Eve and the order in which they fell into sin are linked to instructions on worship.
Cain	1 John 3:12; Jude 1:11	The self-absorbed and loveless behavior of Cain is the foil of what it means to love and be loyal to the Lord.
David	Matthew 1:1; 9:27; 12:3–4 (Mark 2:25–26); 22:42–45 (Mark 12:35–37; Luke 20:41–44); John 7:42; Acts 2:25–31; Revelation 3:7; 5:5; 22:16	As promised in the Old Testament, Jesus was a descendant of David. The uniqueness of Jesus is highlighted by the fact that although he existed before David was born, Jesus was a descendant of David. David illustrated that "lawful" living that honors the ultimate law to love could mean breaking certain demands of the written law code. Jesus is affirmed as Messiah because he did not decompose in the grave as David had.

Person	Key Scripture	Key Insights
Elijah	Matthew 11:14; 17:10–12 (Mark 9:11–13); Luke 1:17; 4:25–26; 9:30–31; James 5:17	John the Baptist was the new Elijah who would introduce the coming of the Messiah. At Jesus's transfiguration, Elijah confirmed the correctness of Jesus's plan to suffer and die in Jerusalem. Elijah is used as an example of a prophet sent to bring God's Word to the gentiles. Elijah illustrates the power of a righteous person's prayer.
Elisha	Luke 4:27	Elisha is used as an example of a prophet sent to bring God's Word to the gentiles.
Eve	2 Corinthians 11:3; 1 Timothy 2:13–14	The creation order of Adam and Eve and the order in which they fell into sin are linked to instructions on worship. Satan's ability to deceive Eve illustrates our vulnerability to being deceived by false teaching.
Hagar	Galatians 4:24–25	As a slave, Hagar becomes a symbol of the Mosaic covenant, which binds sinners as slaves.
Isaac	Matthew 8:11; 22:32; Luke 13:28; Acts 7:32; Romans 9:7–8; Galatians 4:28	Mention of Isaac becomes symbolic of the Abrahamic covenant and salvation by divine promise. Isaac lives in heaven and welcomes gentiles, for they are heirs of God's promises along with the Jews.
Jacob	Matthew 1:16; 8:11; Luke 13:28; Acts 3:13; Romans 9:13	Jesus is connected to the nation of Israel by identifying him as a descendant of Jacob. Mention of Jacob becomes symbolic of the Abrahamic covenant and salvation by divine promise. Jacob lives in heaven and welcomes gentiles, for they are heirs of God's promises along with the Jews. Jacob is an example of God's merciful election.
Job	James 5:11	Job provides the example of faithful perseverance.
Jonah	Matthew 12:39–41 (Luke 11:29–32)	Jesus shared many similarities with Jonah (both were prophets, lived on the Nazareth Ridge, spent three days and nights in an undesirable place, and delivered God's Word to gentiles). Yet Jesus contrasts himself with Jonah as having so much more to offer.
Joshua	Hebrews 4:8	Because the "rest" Joshua delivered was incomplete, Jesus came to fulfill the Sabbath promise of rest.
Melchizedek	Hebrews 7	Jesus was a priest like Melchizedek, who was not a descendant of Levi and yet was appointed for special service as a priest.

Person	Key Scripture	Key Insights
Moses	Matthew 8:4; 19:8; Mark 10:3–4; Luke 9:30–31; 24:27, 44; John 5:45–46; Acts 3:32; Romans 10:5; 2 Corinthians 3:7–15; Hebrews 3:1–6	Moses became the symbol for Torah in general and the law code within it in particular. In Torah, Moses told the world to expect the coming of a greater prophet. At Jesus's transfiguration, Moses confirmed Jesus's identification as that prophet and the correctness of Jesus's plan to suffer and die in Jerusalem. As significant as Moses was, Jesus is worthy of greater honor than Moses. Paul compares his more desirable new covenant ministry to the ministry of Moses under the old covenant.
Noah	Matthew 24:27–38 (Luke 17:26–27); 2 Peter 2:5	The ordinariness of Noah's era leading to the great flood is likened to the ordinariness of the time leading up to Jesus's second coming. Noah illustrates God's willingness to spare the righteous on the day of judgment.
Queen of Sheba (Queen of the South)	Matthew 12:42 (Luke 11:31)	This gentile queen traveled a great distance to connect to the wisdom shared by Solomon. Her faithful pursuit of truth is contrasted with Jesus's detractors, who had someone greater than Solomon in their midst.
Rahab	Matthew 1:5; Hebrews 11:31; James 2:25	Rahab was a gentile who provides a righteous example of faith in action and who became a forbearer of Jesus.
Solomon	Matthew 6:29 (Luke 12:27); 12:42 (Luke 11:31)	The splendor of Solomon pales in comparison to the flowers of the field, which Jesus used as an example of God's willingness to care for those tempted to worry. The wisdom of Solomon pales in comparison to the teachings of Jesus.

Promises of Jesus Fulfilled prior to AD 100

Jesus's Promise	Reference	Promise Fulfilled	Reference
Andrew, the fisherman, would "fish for people."	Matthew 4:18–20; Mark 1:16–18	Andrew brought Peter to Jesus. Andrew brought gentile God-fearers to Jesus.	John 1:40–41; 12:21–22
Simon Peter, the fisherman, would "fish for people."	Matthew 4:18–20; Mark 1:16–18; Luke 5:10–11	Peter preached in Jerusalem on Pentecost. Peter preached in Samaria. Peter preached in Caesarea Maritima in the home of Cornelius. Peter wrote to believers in Asia Minor.	Acts 2:14–41; 8:14–25; 10:24–48; 1 Peter 1:1
The centurion's servant would be healed without Jesus going to his sickbed.	Matthew 8:8–13	The centurion's servant was healed.	Matthew 8:13
When the disciples were arrested, the Holy Spirit would provide the disciples with words to speak.	Matthew 10:17–20; Mark 13:11; Luke 12:11–12; 21:12–15	The Holy Spirit gave Peter words to speak when arrested by the Sanhedrin. The apostles knew what to say before the Sanhedrin.	Acts 4:8; 5:27–32
Peter would receive the authority to teach.	Matthew 16:19–20	Jesus gave Peter the authority to teach.	Matthew 28:18–20; John 21:15–18
Jesus announced that he would suffer, die, and rise from the dead in Jerusalem.	Matthew 16:21; 17:22; 20:17–19; Mark 8:31; 10:32–34; Luke 9:22; 18:31–33	Jesus suffered, died, and rose from the dead in Jerusalem.	Matthew 26–28; Mark 14–16; Luke 22–24; John 18–21
Some of the disciples would see the Son of Man coming into his kingdom before they died.	Matthew 16:28; Mark 9:1; Luke 9:27	Within days, Peter, James, and John saw Jesus transfigured before their eyes in heavenly glory.	Matthew 17:1–8; Mark 9:2–12; Luke 9:28–36
James would die as a martyr.	Matthew 20:21–23; Mark 10:35–39	James died a martyr.	Acts 12:1–2
The Jewish rejection of Jesus would create an opportunity for the gentiles to hear the gospel and be saved.	Matthew 21:42–43	When the Jews rejected the good news, the gospel was immediately taken to the gentiles.	Acts 9:15; 13:46; 18:6; 22:21

Jesus's Promise	Reference	Promise Fulfilled	Reference
Jerusalem's worship complex would be destroyed.	Matthew 24:2; Mark 13:2; Luke 21:6	Jerusalem's worship complex was destroyed by the Romans in AD 70.	Unrecorded
The gospel would be preached throughout the known world.	Matthew 24:14; Luke 24:47	The gospel message expanded from Jerusalem, to Judea, Samaria, and the ends of the earth.	The book of Acts as outlined in Acts 1:8
The disciples would abandon Jesus.	Matthew 26:31; Mark 14:27	The disciples abandoned Jesus.	Matthew 26:56; Mark 14:50
Jesus would meet the apostles in Galilee following his resurrection.	Matthew 26:32; Mark 14:28	Jesus met the apostles in Galilee following his resurrection.	Matthew 28:16; John 21:1
Peter would deny Jesus three times before the rooster crowed.	Matthew 26:34; Mark 14:30; Luke 22:34; John 13:38	Peter denied Jesus three times before the rooster crowed.	Matthew 26:69–75; Mark 14:66–72; Luke 22:54–62; John 18:15–18, 25–27
Jesus promised Jairus that his daughter would be raised to life.	Luke 8:50	Jesus raised Jairus's daughter from the dead.	Luke 8:55
Jesus promised the thief on the cross that he would enter paradise that very day.	Luke 23:43	The thief on the cross died and entered paradise that very day.	Unrecorded
Jesus promised that the Holy Spirit would come upon the disciples in Jerusalem.	Luke 24:49; John 14:16; 15:26; 16:7; Acts 1:5–8	The Holy Spirit came upon the apostles in Jerusalem.	Acts 2:1–4
Jesus announced that the temple (his body) would be destroyed and then restored on the third day.	John 2:19	Jesus rose from the dead on the third day.	Matthew 27; Mark 15; Luke 23; John 19
Jesus told the disciples and Martha that her brother would rise from the dead.	John 11:11, 23	Jesus raised Lazarus from the dead.	John 11:43–44
Jesus promised he would not leave the disciples as orphans.	John 14:18	Jesus appeared to the disciples after his resurrection.	John 20:19–31
Jesus told Peter that he would die as a martyr.	John 21:18–19	Peter died as a martyr.	Unrecorded

Jewish Sects and Jesus

Pharisees

Who were the Pharisees?

Ideological descendants of the Ḥassidim of the intertestamental period who fought to maintain their Jewish identity in the face of religious persecution.

A New Testament religious and political party that pursued, policed, and demanded a form of righteous living that conformed to their lofty standards.

Teachers of the common people, the rabbis, who led in the synagogues.

The authorized religious teachers who certified the next generation of authorized religious teachers.

What did the Pharisees believe?

That divine truth was provided in the written Word of the Old Testament as well as in the traditional oral interpretation and extensions of that Word, which they traced back to Moses (the oral law).

That righteous living was the highest virtue, with special emphasis placed on Sabbath observance.

That there was a spirit world filled with both angels and demons.

That the soul was immortal and that there would be a bodily resurrection.

That heaven was reserved for Torah-observing Jews and just a few Torah-observing gentiles.

How did the Pharisees and Jesus interact?

Pharisees like Nicodemus, Joseph of Arimathea, and Saul (Paul) came to believe in Jesus as the Messiah.

Generally Pharisees did not like

the way Jesus spent time with those regarded as public sinners, like tax collectors and prostitutes;

the more casual relationship Jesus appeared to have with Sabbath observance;

the fact that Jesus was not "authorized" to teach by any of their own authorized teachers.

Jesus criticized

their elevation of the oral law, making it the equivalent of divine law, particularly with regard to Sabbath observance;

the burden that the oral law placed on ordinary Israelites;

their prideful, self-aggrandizing behavior;

their failure to demonstrate love and mercy;

their attitude toward gentiles.

Sadducees

Who were the Sadducees?

Claimed to be descendants of Zadok, the high priest at the time of David and Solomon.

Distinguished from the ordinary priests, they were the aristocratic priests who lived in Jerusalem and formed a political party with well-to-do families.

Controlled the everyday affairs of the temple in Jerusalem.

Dominated the Jewish ruling council (Sanhedrin) during the time of the New Testament.

Established a working relationship with the occupying power of Rome by showing a willingness to compromise their Jewish identity and accept the ideology of the Roman world in exchange for the benefits it yielded.

What did the Sadducees believe?

That divine truth was derived only from the written Old Testament (the Torah or Pentateuch in particular) without recourse to the oral law.

That the fate of mortals resided in the choices they made rather than in divine providence.

That the real world did not include spiritual beings.

That there was no resurrection or life beyond death.

That material possession, power, and social prestige were the ultimate rewards in life and were to be pursued at all costs.

How did Jesus and the Sadducees interact?

The Sadducees saw Jesus as a threat to the status quo, which gave them power over the temple and thus the wealth and notoriety the temple could provide.

Jesus directly criticized

their failure to believe in life after death and the resurrection;

their infatuation with power, prestige, and wealth, not only when he spoke on these topics but also when he disrupted the buying and selling in the temple markets.

Zealots

Who were the Zealots?

A less-well-defined Jewish movement that opposed Rome's occupation of the promised land and all those who collaborated with Rome.

What did the Zealots believe?

That there could be no peace with the Romans who occupied their land.

That Rome's occupation was not a call to repent but a call to revolt.

That the payment of Roman taxes was a sign of disloyalty to the Almighty.

That being a righteous, Torah-observing Jew meant to reject all things Roman.

That national liberty for Israel was the chief goal of living.

How did the Zealots and Jesus interact?

The Zealots would not have liked

Jesus's failure to use his power and influence in support of national liberation;

Jesus's relationship with tax collectors in general and Matthew in particular;

Jesus's kindly treatment of centurions and the inclusion of gentiles in the kingdom of God;

Jesus's directive to pay the taxes to Caesar that belonged to him;

Jesus's call to love one's enemies and pray for them.

Direct encounters with the Zealots are not mentioned in the gospels as such, but Jesus counted Simon the Zealot among his disciples (Luke 6:15).

Essenes

Who were the Essenes?

A religious movement within Judaism scattered about Israel, including places like Jerusalem and Qumran.

A group that abhorred the way in which the temple in Jerusalem was being operated.

A somewhat ascetic group that directed its energies toward prayer, communal support, ritual purity, and waiting for the end of time.

A group that paid particular attention to the life of the mind, giving attention to the copying, study, and interpretation of Scripture.

What did the Essenes believe?

That God was sovereign.

That mortals were created with an immortal soul.

That communal living prevented the unhealthy formation of a class-oriented society.

That personal wealth was a risk, so goods were held communally, used for the common good, and used to help those in need.

That the duty of mortals was to live a righteous life, including a strict observance of the Sabbath.

How did the Essenes and Jesus interact?

There is no direct mention of Jesus interacting with a member of an Essene community, but given their presence in the places he taught, they likely heard him.

The Essenes would have liked

Jesus's call to abandon the world to follow him;

Jesus's criticism of the aristocratic priests;

Jesus's warning about infatuation with wealth;

Jesus's teaching on the immortality of mortals;

Jesus's emphasis on prayer;

Jesus's attention to the Word of God;

Jesus's call for care of the needy;

Jesus's eschatological focus on the kingdom of God to come.

Monetary System of the New Testament

Gold Coins

Coin/Unit	Value	Reference
Aureus	25 days of common labor 25 sheep	Likely the coin behind the reference to "gold" in Matthew 10:9

Silver Coins

Coin/Unit	Value	Reference
Greek drachma Roman denarius	1 day of common labor 1 sheep	The agreed-upon wage in the parable of the workers in the vineyard (Matt. 20:1–16) The coin used to pay the Roman poll tax and so used in Jesus's response to the question on paying taxes to Caesar (Matt. 22:15–21) Estimated two hundred denarii needed to purchase food for feeding the crowd in the feeding of the five thousand (Mark 6:30–44) Jesus was anointed with three hundred denarii worth of perfume at Bethany (Mark 14:5) One of the ten coins lost and then found in the parable of the lost coin (Luke 15:8–10)
Didrachm (two drachma)	2 denarii 2 days of common labor 2 sheep	The amount a Jew needed to pay the annual temple tax (Matt. 17:24)
Greek stater Tyrian shekel	4 drachma 4 days of common labor 4 sheep	Due to its higher silver content, the Tyrian shekel was the coin required for payments made at the temple in Jerusalem, precipitating a need for money changers (Matt. 17:27; 21:12–15). Judas was given thirty such coins for betraying Jesus (Matt. 26:15).
Mina	100 days of common labor 100 sheep	A man of noble birth gave one mina to each of ten servants with the expectation they would use it to earn more in the parable of the ten minas (Luke 19:11–27)
Talent	6,000 days or 16 years of common labor 6,000 sheep	A man gave five, two, and one talent(s) to three servants with the expectation they would use it to earn more in the parable of the talents (Matt. 25:14–30). A forgiven debt of ten thousand talents did not incite merciful treatment of the one who owed the debtor far less in the parable of the unmerciful servant (Matt. 18:21–35) .

Bronze Coins

Coin/Unit	Value	Reference
Assarion (pl. asses)	$1/16$ of a day of common labor 16 needed to purchase a sheep 2 needed to purchase dinner at an inn	The heavenly Father is attentive to the well-being of every sparrow, even though two of them can be purchased for as little as one assarion (Matt. 10:29; Luke 12:6).
Quadrans or kodrantes	¼ of an assarion $1/64$ of a day of common labor 64 needed to purchase a sheep	Jesus urged the settling of legal matters prior to going to court to avoid prison time that would not expire until paying the last kodrantes (Matt. 5:26).
Lepton	The least valued coin ½ of a quadrans $1/128$ of a day of common labor 128 needed to purchase a sheep	Jesus celebrated the gift of the widow that consisted of two such coins (Mark 12:42; Luke 21:2). Jesus urged the settling of legal matters prior to going to court to avoid prison time that would not expire until paying the last lepton (Luke 12:59).

Greco-Roman Religious World

Greco-Roman Religious Worldview

Phenomena observed in nature and other realities of the human experience were assigned to the actions and influence of unseen deities.

The wide range of natural phenomena and otherwise unexplained human experiences required a full pantheon of deities, each responsible for specific areas of influence.

The Romans used the framework of the Greek pantheon to develop their system for explaining the world, often giving the Greek deities Roman names.

Prayer, sacrifice, and a full year of festivals were used to gain the cooperation of these deities and to influence their behavior.

Because the influence of these deities was felt in both personal and public life, religion and politics were intimately joined.

When the emperor was conceived to operate with a divine spirit within him, it was a short step to the practice called emperor worship. While only Caligula (AD 37–41) and Domitian (AD 81–96) insisted on being worshiped prior to their deaths, the offering of worship to the emperor was occasionally demanded of those whose loyalty to Rome was suspect.

Greco-Roman Deities and the New Testament

Deity	Area of Influence	New Testament Connection
Ares or Mars	The god of thunder who was responsible for strength and courage in war and who ironically was responsible for civil order.	In Athens, Paul spoke at the Areopagus (hill of Ares) about the "unknown God" (Acts 17:22–23).
Artemis or Diana	The goddess of the moon who influenced hunting and wild animals. At Ephesus she was worshiped as the mother goddess who provided fertility and nurture.	Paul's preaching so disrupted the financially profitable worship of Artemis at her temple in Ephesus that a riot broke out (Acts 19:23–41).
Dike (Justice)	The goddess who personified justice and sought to restore balance in the face of unfairness, punishing the wrongdoer and rewarding the virtuous.	After Paul survived a shipwreck and while he warmed himself by the fire, a snake fastened itself to his hand. The locals assumed this was an act of Justice repaying Paul for some unjust act he had committed (Acts 28:4).
Hermes or Mercury	This son of Zeus was the god who championed eloquence and persuasion. Depicted with winged feet and a traveler's cap with wide brim, he oversaw the well-being of roads, travel, and messengers.	In Lystra, the locals called Paul Hermes because he was the chief speaker (Acts 14:12).
Zeus or Jupiter	Often pictured with a lightning bolt in hand, he was regarded as god of sky and weather. More important, this deity was the king of the gods and also happened to be the patron deity of Lystra.	In Lystra, the locals called Barnabas Zeus (Acts 14:12).
Pan or Fanus	Half man and half goat, Pan was the god of shepherds and nature.	A Pan grotto was located at the city of Caesarea Philippi.
Caesar Augustus	Although he did not solicit public worship, he allowed temples to be built in his honor.	Herod the Great built temples for Augustus at Samaria, Caesarea Philippi, and Caesarea Maritima.

Rome and Its Provinces

Distinctions between Senatorial and Imperial Provinces

	Senatorial Provinces	Imperial Provinces
Ultimate Authority	Governors answered to the Senate	Governors answered to the Roman emperor
Characteristics	Closer to Rome More Roman citizens Long-held territory Less prone to revolt	More distant from Rome Fewer Roman citizens Newly acquired territory More prone to revolt
Rulers	Proconsul (seasoned senator from the senatorial ranks appointed as governor) or propraetor (seasoned administrator from the equestrian ranks appointed as governor)	Legates (governor of senatorial rank where Roman troops were more prevalent), prefect/procurator (imperial administrators of equestrian rank who had gained the confidence of the emperor), or client king (territories ruled by local royals who had gained the confidence of the emperor)
Military Presence	Roman legions	Mix of Roman troops and locally recruited auxiliary soldiers trained by Rome and led by Roman commanders

Life for the Provincials

Provinces were governed for the benefit of Rome and the provincial governor rather than for the benefit of the residents.

The chief responsibilities of provincial governors were collecting tax revenue and maintaining peace.

Provincial governors ruled with near-absolute power, establishing public policy, leading the police force, and serving as the court of law.

Provincial governors sought to consolidate their power by handing out favors and by making local alliances.

The provincial residents were taxed in order to pay the salaries of those who governed their province and for supporting the lifestyle of the leaders in Rome.

Provincial residents faced a revolving door of expectations given that governors changed frequently and quickly changed public policy.

Provincial residents had limited rights and could not expect justice to be distributed equally.

The recourse to abuses was limited. Provincial residents could appeal to the emperor and Roman senate in the case of extreme abuses. However, Roman citizens within the provinces had the right to appeal personal legal cases to the emperor.

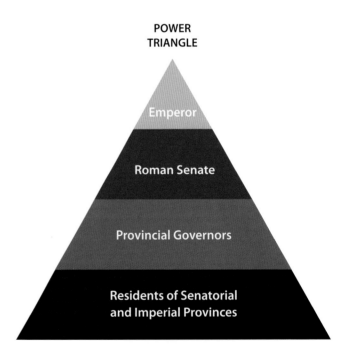

POWER TRIANGLE

Emperor

Roman Senate

Provincial Governors

Residents of Senatorial and Imperial Provinces

Roman Emperors and the New Testament

Emperor	Dates	Christian or Jewish Connection
Caesar Augustus (Octavian)*	27 BC–AD 14	He issued a census order that moved Mary and Joseph from Nazareth to Bethlehem for Jesus's birth (Luke 2:1). Herod the Great built temples in honor of Augustus at Caesarea Maritima, Caesarea Philippi, and Sebaste.
Tiberius Caesar*	AD 14–37	He ruled the Roman Empire during the majority of Jesus's life. He appointed Pilate as prefect of Judea in AD 26 (Luke 3:1).
Caligula	AD 37–41	Caligula saw himself as a deity and ordered his own image installed in synagogues and at the temple in Jerusalem, with the vision of turning it into an imperial worship site. He died before accomplishing the latter.
Claudius*	AD 41–54	He appointed Herod Agrippa I as ruler of Judea and Galilee (AD 41). He managed a Roman world devastated by a severe famine foretold by Agabus (Acts 11:28). Claudius issued an order expelling all Jews from Rome in AD 49, an order that swept up Christians as well, including Aquila and Priscilla (Acts 18:2).
Nero	AD 54–68	Paul, who had been arrested and held in Caesarea Maritima, sought to have his case heard before this emperor and was likely released in AD 62 (Acts 25:11; 28:19). When Rome burned in AD 64, Christians became the scapegoats, providing the context for the martyrdom of Peter and Paul. The first Jewish revolt started in AD 66. Masada was seized by the Jewish *sicarii*.
Galba	AD 68	Jewish losses continued to mount, and the Roman general Vespasian encircled Jerusalem in AD 68.
Otho	AD 69	Jerusalem was under siege.
Vitellius	AD 69	Jerusalem was under siege.
Vespasian	AD 69–79	Jerusalem fell and the temple complex was destroyed by the Roman general Titus in AD 70. The stunning loss of the temple precipitated a time of reassessment of what it meant to be Jewish. Masada fell in AD 73. Quiet returned to the Holy Land, allowing Christians to regroup.
Titus	AD 79–81	Quiet conditions continued in the Holy Land.
Domitian	AD 81–96	He insisted on the title *Dominus et Deus*, identifying himself as "Lord and God." He used sacrifice to the image of the emperor as a test of loyalty. These demands of the imperial cult brought on the persecution of Christians addressed in the hope-filled book of Revelation.

*Denotes formal mention in the New Testament

Roman Prefects and the New Testament

Prefect	Dates	New Testament Connection
Coponius	AD 6–9	Replaced Herod's incompetent son, Archelaus, who had been named ethnarch of Judea and Samaria His revised tax system fueled the flames of a Jewish independence movement that simmered and grew until the time of the first Jewish revolt sixty years later.
Marcus Ambivius	AD 9–12	
Annius Rufus	AD 12–15	
Valerius Gratus	AD 15–26	
Pontius Pilate*	AD 26–36	Attempted to install images of the emperor in Jerusalem Confiscated temple funds to build a new aqueduct Described by Philo as inflexible, inhumane, merciless, corrupt, cruel, and prone to order executions without trial, all of which added to his political vulnerability Presided over the civil trial of Jesus and his state-ordered execution (Matt. 27:2, 19; Mark 15:1; Luke 3:1; 23:1)
Marcellus	AD 36–37	
Marullus	AD 37–41	
Herod Agrippa I, client king of Judea and Galilee	*AD 41–44*	*As a friend of Emperor Claudius, he negotiated improved civil rights for the Jews.* *Persecuted Christians in Jerusalem and paid the price for his actions (Acts 12:1, 19–24)*
Cuspius Fadus	AD 44–46	Responsible for beheading Theudas (Acts 5:36)
Tiberius Alexander	AD 46–48	Alexandrian Jew who had repudiated the Jewish faith Time of famine foreseen by Agabus (Acts 11:28–30)
Cumanus	AD 48–52	Period with multiple episodes of violence When a Roman soldier exposed himself in view of those worshiping at the temple, a riot ensued that ended with the death of thousands of Passover pilgrims.

Break in sequence

Prefect	Dates	New Testament Connection
Antonius Felix*	AD 52–60	Married to Drusilla, a Jewish princess and the sister of Herod Agrippa I Actively sought and executed Jewish revolutionaries, leading to greater activity by the Jewish *sicarii* Presided over the trial of Paul at Caesarea Maritima and held him there for two years as a favor to Jews who opposed Paul's teaching (Acts 23:25–24:27)
Porcius Festus*	AD 60–62	Judea was ripe for revolt as Claudius reversed the grant of civil rights he earlier extended to the Jews. Inherited the case of Paul from his predecessor When Festus sought to do the Jews a favor by transferring Paul back to Jerusalem, Paul quickly appealed for his case to be adjudicated before the emperor in Rome (Acts 24:24–26:32).
Albinus	AD 62–64	Renovation of the temple completed, leading to unemployment for eighteen thousand workers Increased taxes, used extortion, and actively repressed the *sicarii* Judean society became increasingly violent and unstable.
Gessius Florus	AD 64–66	Time of great civil disorder, extortion, and violence that animated all-out revolt against Rome
First Jewish revolt (Break in sequence)	*AD 66–70*	*As war broke out, many Christians in Jerusalem fled to Pella.* *Jewish resisters seized Masada.*
Lucilius Bassus	AD 71–73	Tasked with bringing an end to the Jewish revolt following the AD 70 fall of Jerusalem Oversaw the sieges of Herodium, Machaerus, and Masada
Flavius Silva	AD 73–81	Masada fell. Military colony set up at Emmaus with eight hundred soldiers

*Denotes formal mention in the New Testament

Herodian Kings and the New Testament

King	Dates	Family Data	Area Ruled	New Testament Connection
Herod the Great	37–4 BC	Son of Antipater	King of Judea, then all of Palestine	Named king of Judea in 40 BC by the Roman senate Defeated opposition in Judea and achieved throne by 37 BC Directed the renovation of the temple in Jerusalem Ruled when John the Baptist and Jesus were born (Luke 1:5) Received the wise men and sought to execute the Christ child in Bethlehem, forcing Mary, Joseph, and Jesus to flee to Egypt (Matt. 2:1–19)
Archelaus	4 BC–AD 6	Son of Herod the Great	Ethnarch of Judea, Samaria, and Idumea	The incompetent and cruel ruler who caused Mary, Joseph, and Jesus to divert from Judea and settle in Nazareth of Galilee when they returned from Egypt (Matt. 2:22–23)
Herod Antipas	4 BC–AD 39	Son of Herod the Great	Tetrarch of Galilee and Perea	Rebuilt Sepphoris as the capital of Galilee and then built a new capital on the virgin site of Tiberias Ruled as John the Baptist preached in the wilderness (Luke 3:1) Arrested and executed John the Baptist (Matt. 14:1–12; Mark 6:14–29; Luke 3:19) Used as a threat by Pharisees seeking to manipulate Jesus's itinerary (Luke 13:31–33) Interrogated Jesus in Jerusalem prior to his execution (Luke 23:7–12)
Herod Philip	4 BC–AD 34	Son of Herod the Great	Tetrarch of Iturea, Gaulanitis, and Traconitis	Rebuilt Paneas and named it Caesarea Philippi Received only incidental mention (Luke 3:1)
Herod Agrippa I	AD 41–44	Grandson of Herod the Great	King of Judea and then added Galilee and Perea	As a friend of Emperor Claudius, he negotiated improved civil rights for the Jews. As a defender of the Pharisees, he persecuted Christians in Jerusalem (Acts 12:1). Executed the apostle James, brother of John (Acts 12:2) Arrested Peter (Acts 12:3–4) Struck down by the Lord for taking divine honor (Acts 12:19–24)
Herod Agrippa II	AD 48–100	Great-grandson of Herod the Great	Initially control of the temple in Jerusalem before adding Iturea, Gaulanitis, Trachonitis, and the Decapolis	Observed the growing social and economic tensions leading to the first Jewish revolt and destruction of the temple in Jerusalem Listened to Paul present his case in Caesarea Maritima during Paul's trial before the Roman prefect Festus (Acts 25:13–26:32)

Genealogies of Jesus

Genealogies in the Bible

Definition

A genealogy is a selected and often stylized list of names indicating individuals who have a family relationship to one another as reckoned through one's father's side of the family, which marked one's legal ancestry.

Functions

Prominent people needed to demonstrate that they had a worthy family heritage because personal identity and character were intimately bound to family heritage.

Individuals who wished to qualify for certain social roles had to demonstrate that they possessed the family heritage to qualify for those roles (examples include Israelite kings and high priests; Exod. 28:1; Deut. 17:14–15).

To qualify as the Messiah, the candidate had to be a descendant of Abram (Gen. 12:1–3), Isaac (Gen. 21:12), Jacob (Gen. 28:3–4), Judah (Gen. 49:10), and David (2 Sam. 7:11–16).

Genealogy of Jesus in Matthew (1:1–17)

Characteristics

Placed at the very beginning of Matthew.

Traces the genealogy of Jesus from Abraham through Joseph, the husband of Mary.

Moves forward in time.

Organized in three groups of fourteen. This may be employing the number of "completeness" (seven) by doubling it to make the groups of fourteen, or this may be a *gematria*, a literary device in which a number is derived from the value of Hebrew consonants. In this case, the consonants in David's Hebrew name (D-V-D) add up to fourteen (D/4 + V/6 + D/4 = 14), hence emphasizing David's place in the genealogy.

Includes four women, all of whom are gentile.

Functions

Demonstrates that the plan of salvation evolves over thousands of years, negotiating complexity and challenges along the way.

Demonstrates that the plan of salvation includes gentiles by including four gentiles in Jesus's genealogy.

Demonstrates that Jesus qualifies as the promised Messiah because his genealogy reckoned through his legal father, Joseph, includes the necessary individuals from the past.

Follows the line of descent via David's son Solomon, emphasizing Jesus's royal heritage and accounting for the differences with Luke's genealogy.

Genealogy of Jesus in Luke (3:23–27)

Characteristics

Placed between Luke's account of Jesus's baptism and temptation.

Traces the genealogy of Jesus from Adam through Joseph, the husband of Mary.

Moves backward in time.

Its seventy-seven names are organized into groups of seven, each of which concludes with a prominent figure. This may be a literary device that uses the connotation of "completeness" associated with the number seven.

Functions

Demonstrates that the plan of salvation evolves over thousands of years, negotiating complexity and challenges along the way.

Demonstrates that the plan of salvation includes gentiles by starting with Adam.

Demonstrates that Jesus qualifies as the promised Messiah because his genealogy reckoned through his legal father, Joseph, includes the necessary individuals from the past.

Follows the biological line of descent through David's son Nathan, accounting for the differences with Matthew's genealogy.

Gospel Harmony

	Matthew	Mark	Luke	John
Introductory material				
Preface			1:1–4	
Prologue—Word became Flesh				1:1–18
Genealogies	1:1–17		3:23–37	
Birth and early years of Jesus				
Birth of John the Baptist foretold			1:5–25	
Birth of Jesus foretold to Mary			1:26–38	
Mary visits Elizabeth			1:39–56	
Birth and early life of John the Baptist			1:57–80	
Birth of Jesus foretold to Joseph	1:18–25			
Birth of Jesus			2:1–20	
Jesus presented in the temple			2:21–40	
Visit of the Magi	2:1–12			
Flight of the holy family to Egypt	2:13–23			
Jesus in the temple at age twelve			2:41–52	
John prepares the way	3:1–12	1:1–8	3:1–18	1:19–28
Baptism and early ministry of Jesus				
Baptism of Jesus	3:13–17	1:9–11	3:21–23	1:29–34
Temptations of Jesus	4:1–11	1:12–13	4:1–13	
Jesus begins to gather disciples				1:35–51
Wedding at Cana				2:1–11
Jesus and Nicodemus				3:1–21
John the Baptist's testimony about Jesus				3:22–36
Jesus heals the son of a royal official				4:43–54
Jesus heals at the Bethesda pools in Jerusalem and calls upon the testimony of his Father				5:1–47
Jesus in Galilee				
Strategic move to Capernaum	4:12–17			
Jesus gathers the twelve disciples	4:18–22; 9:9–13; 10:2–4	1:16–20; 2:13–17; 3:13–19	5:1–11, 27–32; 6:12–16	
Teaching and healing in Capernaum	8:14–17	1:21–34	4:31–41	
Jesus in the synagogues of Galilee	4:23–24	1:35–39; 3:7–12	4:42–44	
Sermon on the Mount	5:1–7:29		6:20–49	

	Matthew	Mark	Luke	John
Healing of a man with leprosy	8:1–4	1:40–45	5:12–16	
Healing of the centurion's servant	8:5–13		7:1–10	
Cost of following Jesus	8:18–22		9:57–62	
Authority demonstrated in the healing of a paralyzed man	9:1–8	2:1–12	5:17–26	
Question on fasting	9:14–17	2:18–22	5:33–39	
Raising Jairus's daughter	9:18–26	5:21–43	8:40–56	
Disabled and demon possessed healed	9:27–34			
Jesus sends out the twelve disciples	9:35–11:1	6:6–13	9:1–6	
Jesus and John the Baptist	11:2–19		7:18–35	
Rest for the weary	11:25–30			
Woe to the cities of opportunity	11:20–24		10:13–15	
Anointed by a sinful woman in Capernaum			7:36–50	
Lord of the Sabbath	12:1–14	2:23–3:6	6:1–11	
Jesus the Servant in Isaiah 42	12:15–21			
Jesus and Beelzebub	12:22–37	3:20–30	11:17–22	
Sign of Jonah	12:38–45		11:24–32	
Jesus's mother and brothers	12:46–50	3:31–35	8:19–21	
Parables of Jesus	13:1–52	4:1–34	8:4–18	
Rejection in Nazareth	13:53–58	6:1–6	4:14–30	
Arrest and execution of John the Baptist	14:1–12	6:14–29	3:19–20	
Feeding of the five thousand	14:13–21	6:30–44	9:10–17	6:1–15
Jesus walks on water	14:22–36	6:45–56		6:16–24
Bread of life and response				6:25–71
Lesson on ritual purity	15:1–20	7:1–23		
Healing of the blind man at Bethsaida		8:22–26		
Temple tax paid	17:24–27			
Entry into and leadership in God's kingdom	18:1–9	9:33–37	9:46–48	
Parable of the lost sheep	18:10–14		15:1–7	
Lessons on forgiveness	18:15–35			
Accept all who are for us		9:38–41	9:49–50	
Managing and defeating sin		9:42–50		
Lesson on divorce	19:1–12	10:1–12		
Jesus on Herod and Jerusalem			14:31–35	
Children in the kingdom	19:13–15	10:13–16	18:15–17	
Lesson on wealth and the kingdom	19:16–30	10:17–31	18:18–30	

	Matthew	Mark	Luke	John
Parable of the workers in the vineyard	20:1–16			
Jesus again announces his coming death	20:17–19	10:32–34	18:31–33	
Mother's request for James and John	20:20–28	10:35–45		
Jesus beyond Galilee				
Widow's son at Nain			7:11–17	
Jesus and the Samaritan woman				4:1–42
Stilling the storm and the healing of demon possessed in the Decapolis	8:23–34	4:35–5:20	8:22–39	
Healings in Phoenicia	15:21–28	7:24–37		
Feeding of the four thousand in the Decapolis	15:29–39	8:1–13		
Lesson taught by the feeding of the four thousand and five thousand	16:1–12	8:14–21		
Peter's great confession near Caesarea Philippi	16:13–20	8:27–30	9:18–20	
Jesus announces his coming death	16:21–28	8:31–9:1	9:21–27	
Transfiguration	17:1–13	9:2–13	9:28–36	
Boy with demon healed	17:14–23	9:14–32	9:37–45	
Jesus in Judea				
Jesus and the Feast of Tabernacles				7:1–52
Woman caught in adultery				8:1–11
Jesus affirms his identity				8:12–59
Blind man healed at the Siloam pool				9:1–41
Jesus the good shepherd				10:1–21
Jesus at the Feast of Dedication				10:22–42
Parable of the good Samaritan			10:25–37	
Jesus, Mary, Martha, and the one thing needful			10:38–42	
Prayer			11:1–13	
Jesus and Beelzebub			11:14–28	
Sign of Jonah	12:38–45		11:29–32	
Lessons from the lamp			11:33–36	
Warnings about the Jewish religious leaders			11:37–12:12	
Parable of the rich fool			12:13–21	
Discussion about worry			12:22–34	
Jesus's second coming			12:35–59	
Parable of the fig tree			13:1–9	
Healing a disabled woman on Sabbath			13:10–17	

	Matthew	Mark	Luke	John
Travels to and from Jerusalem				
Samaritan opposition			9:51–56	
Jesus sends out the seventy-two			10:1–24	
Wide and narrow roads			13:22–30	
Lessons on obedience and humility			14:1–14	
Cost of being a disciple			14:25–34	
Parables about lost things			15:1–32	
Story about the shrewd manager			16:1–15	
Rich man and poor Lazarus			16:19–31	
Raising of Lazarus				11:1–54
Ten healed of leprosy			17:11–19	
Jesus's second coming			17:20–37	
Parable of the persistent widow			18:1–8	
Story of the Pharisee and the tax collector			18:9–14	
Healing of blind Bartimaeus	20:29–34	10:46–52	18:35–43	
Jesus and Zacchaeus			19:1–10	
Parable of the ten minas			19:11–27	
Jesus's final days in Jerusalem				
Jesus's triumphal entry	21:1–11	11:1–11	19:28–44	12:12–19
Temple cleansing	21:12–17	11:12–19	19:45–48	2:13–16
Withered fig tree	21:18–22	11:20–26		
Jesus's authority questioned	21:23–27	11:27–33	20:1–8	
Parable of the two sons	21:28–32			
Parable of the tenants	21:33–46	12:1–12	20:9–19	
Jesus announces his impending death				12:20–36
Continued unbelief in Jerusalem				12:37–50
Parable of the wedding banquet	22:1–14		14:15–24	
Taxes to Caesar	22:15–22	12:13–17	20:20–26	
Marriage at the resurrection	22:23–33	12:18–27	20:27–40	
The greatest commandment	22:34–40	12:28–34		
Jesus as the Son of God	22:41–46	12:35–37	20:41–44	
Woes pronounced on Jewish leaders	23:1–39	12:38–40	20:45–47	
The poor widow's gift		12:41–44	21:1–4	
Signs and time of end times	24:1–51	13:1–37	21:5–38	
Parable of the ten virgins	25:1–13			

	Matthew	Mark	Luke	John
Parable of the talents	25:14–30			
Fate of the sheep and the goats	25:31–46			
Plotting against Jesus	26:1–5	14:1–2	22:1–2	
Jesus anointed by Mary	26:6–13	14:3–9		12:1–11
Judas agrees to betray Jesus	26:14–16	14:10–11	22:3–6	
Passover preparation	26:17–19	14:12–17	22:7–13	
Jesus anticipates Judas's betrayal	26:20–25	14:18–21	22:21–23	13:18–30
Rank in God's kingdom			22:24–30	
Jesus washes the disciples' feet				13:1–20
Passover becomes Lord's Supper	26:26–30	14:22–26	22:14–20	
Jesus anticipates Peter's denial	26:31–35	14:27–31	22:31–34	13:31–38
Jesus comforts the disciples				14:1–16:33
Jesus prays for himself and the church				17:1–26
Struggle in Gethsemane	26:36–46	14:32–42	22:39–46	18:1
Jesus is arrested	26:47–56	14:43–52	22:47–53	18:2–27
Jesus before the Sanhedrin	26:57–68	14:53–65		18:12–14, 19–24
Peter's denial	26:69–75	14:66–72	22:54–62	18:15–18, 25–27
Death of Judas	27:1–10			
Jesus before Pilate	27:11–31	15:1–20	22:63–23:25	18:28–19:16
Jesus is crucified	27:32–56	15:21–41	23:26–49	19:16–37
Jesus is buried, and the guard is set	27:57–66	15:42–47	23:50–56	19:38–42
Jesus's resurrection, appearances, and ascension				
Resurrection	28:1–15	16:1–8	24:1–12	20:1–9
Jesus and Mary Magdalene		16:9–11		20:10–18
Jesus with the Emmaus disciples		16:12–13	24:13–35	
Jesus appears to the Ten			24:36–48	20:19–23
Jesus appears to the Eleven		16:14		20:24–31
Jesus in Galilee	28:16–20	16:15–18		21:1–23
Jesus's ascension		16:19–20	24:50–52	

The Apostles

The apostles were all personal students of Jesus, sharing varying degrees of public and private time with him. They were specifically selected as eyewitnesses of what Jesus had said and done, particularly with regard to his resurrection, so that they could provide firsthand accounts about Jesus to the world (Acts 1:8, 21–22).

Key passages that identify the fourteen men (including Matthias and Saul/Paul) given this honor include Matthew 10:2–4; Mark 3:14–19; Luke 6:13–16; Acts 1:13–14, 26; 9:1–16; and Galatians 1:1, 11–17.

Name	Home	Key Insights	Key Scriptures
Simon/Peter, son of Jonah (John)	Bethsaida in Galilee	Brother of Andrew Fisherman who partnered with James and John Passionate and outspoken One of three in Jesus's inner circle Verbally acknowledged Jesus as the Messiah Denied Jesus three times but later was restored to service by Jesus Key spokesperson at Pentecost Fostered a change in Jewish attitude toward gentiles His sermons or recollections provided John Mark with the information shaped into the Gospel of Mark Author of 1–2 Peter Likely died as a martyr in Rome	Matthew 4:18–20; 16:16–23; 26:33–35, 69–75; John 21:15–23; Acts 2:14–40; 10:1–11:18
Andrew, son of Jonah (John)	Bethsaida in Galilee	Brother of Peter who brought Peter to Jesus Fisherman Identified the boy with five loaves and two small fish during the feeding of the five thousand Told Jesus about Greek pilgrims to Jerusalem who wanted to meet him	Matthew 4:18–20; John 1:40–42; 6:8; 12:20–22
James, son of Zebedee	Galilee	Brother of John Fisherman who partnered with Peter One of the "Sons of Thunder" One of three in Jesus's inner circle Presumed his rank merited sitting at Jesus's right or left hand Martyred by Herod Agrippa I	Matthew 4:21–22; Mark 3:17; 10:35–41; Acts 12:2
John, son of Zebedee	Galilee	Brother of James Fisherman who partnered with Peter One of the "Sons of Thunder" One of three in Jesus's inner circle Presumed his rank merited sitting at Jesus's right or left hand Disciple "whom Jesus loved" Connected to the inner circle of the high priest in Jerusalem Directed to care for Jesus's mother at Calvary Leader of the Christian movement in Jerusalem following Pentecost Exiled to Patmos, where he received the vision that became the book of Revelation Author of the Gospel of John and 1–3 John	Matthew 4:21–22; Mark 3:17; 10:35–41; John 18:15 ; 19:26–27; Acts 3:1–4:30; Revelation 1:1–9

Name	Home	Key Insights	Key Scriptures
Philip	Bethsaida in Galilee	Told Nathanael about Jesus Gave voice to the obvious lack of food preceding the miraculous feeding of the five thousand Approached by Greek pilgrims to Jerusalem who wanted to meet Jesus Asked to see the Father	John 1:43–48; 6:5–7; 12:20–22
Bartholomew/ Nathanael	Cana in Galilee	Jesus knew he was sitting under a fig tree when Philip told him about Jesus. Called Jesus "the Son of God and King of Israel"	John 1:43–51; 21:2
Thomas/Didymus	Galilee	A twin Asked to be shown "the way" Wanted tangible evidence of Jesus's resurrection and doubted until he received it	John 11:16; 14:5; 20:24–29
Matthew, son of Alphaeus/ Levi	Capernaum in Galilee	Former tax collector Invited other "sinners" to have dinner with Jesus Author of the Gospel of Matthew	Matthew 9:9–13; Mark 2:14
James, son of Alphaeus	Galilee	Possibly the brother of Matthew Among the least known of the apostles	Mentioned only in the lists of disciples
Thaddaeus/Judas, son of James	Galilee	Among the least known of the apostles Asked Jesus why he had not revealed himself more broadly as the Messiah	John 14:22
Simon the Zealot	Galilee	Among the least known of the apostles Zealot	Mentioned only in the lists of disciples
Judas	Kerioth in Judea	Only non-Galilean among the twelve apostles Treasurer and thief Betrayed Jesus with a kiss in exchange for thirty silver coins Attempted to undo the betrayal by returning the money Filled with remorse, he took his own life	Matthew 26:14–16, 47–49; 27:3–10; John 6:70–71; 12:4–6; 13:2, 27; Acts 1:18–20
Matthias	Unknown	Selected by the Holy Spirit to replace Judas	Acts 1:26
Saul/Paul	Tarsus in Cilicia	A Roman citizen A Pharisee devoted to ending the perceived heresy about Jesus held by followers of "the Way" Converted on the road to Damascus by an appearance of the risen Jesus Became the missionary to the gentiles Became the most prominent author of the New Testament	Acts 9:1–31; Galatians 1:11–17

Sermons and Discourses of Jesus

Scripture	Audience	Location	Theme or Topic
Matthew 5–7; Luke 6:17–49	Disciples and a gathering crowd	Mount Arbel	Sermon on the mount/plain Advanced theological instruction particularly directed to the Twelve in advance of being sent out
Matthew 10:5–42	Twelve disciples	Galilee	Instructions on where to go, what to do, what to say, and what to expect as the disciples were sent out to Israelite villages to speak about the coming of God's kingdom
Matthew 11:2–29; Luke 7:18–35	John's disciples and a gathering crowd of Israelites	Galilee	The identity of John the Baptist as the promised forerunner, the identity of Jesus as the promised Messiah, and the enduring "rest" he brings
Matthew 12:22–45; Mark 3:22–30	Pharisees	Galilee	Jesus's relationship to demons is contrasted with the demonic nature of the Pharisees' words, actions, and thoughts.
Matthew 13:1–52; Mark 4:1–34; Luke 8:4–18	Gathering crowd	Shoreline of the Sea of Galilee	Set of parables using agricultural, household, and fishing imagery to teach about the kingdom of heaven
Matthew 15:1–20; Mark 7:1–23	Pharisees and teachers of the law, a gathering crowd, and eventually the disciples alone	Galilee	The worship life of the Jewish religious leaders is criticized as Jesus clarifies what it means to be ritually clean. This prepares the disciples to meet and interact with gentiles as they travel into gentile regions.
Matthew 18:1–35	Twelve disciples	Galilee	A discussion of how God looks at sinners is coupled with a discussion of how forgiven sinners are asked to look on those who have sinned against them.
Matthew 19:16–20:16; Mark 10:17–31	Wealthy young man and the disciples	Judea	Entry into the kingdom of God and what to expect as a worker in that kingdom
Matthew 23:1–39	Jewish crowd and the twelve disciples	Jerusalem	Denunciation of the Jewish religious leaders whose lives did not live up to the demands of their teaching
Matthew 24–25; Mark 13:1–37; Luke 21:5–36	Twelve disciples	Mount of Olives	Signs that will mark the coming of the last days and strategies to prepare for the coming day of judgment

Scripture	Audience	Location	Theme or Topic
Luke 4:16–30	Synagogue worshipers	Nazareth	Jesus identifies himself as the Messiah whose love and forgiveness extends to gentiles.
Luke 10:1–24	Seventy-two disciples	Judea	Words of direction and encouragement to the seventy-two who were sent into the villages of Judea are joined to words that celebrate the accomplishments of their time in those villages.
Luke 11:1–13	Twelve disciples	Judea	Instruction on prayer
Luke 11:37–54	Pharisees	Judea	Denunciation of the attitudes and behaviors of the Pharisees and teachers of the law
Luke 15	Mixed crowd of public sinners and religious leaders	Unknown	Parables on the "lost that were found" demonstrate the pervasiveness of God's grace.
Luke 16	Twelve disciples	Unknown	Discussion about the use of and risks associated with wealth
John 3:1–21	Nicodemus	Judea	Discussion of forgiveness and entry into the kingdom of God
John 5:19–47	Crowd opposed to Jesus	Judea	Testimony that supports Jesus's divine origins
John 6:25–59	Crowd	Capernaum in Galilee	Jesus as the bread of life
John 10:1–18	Crowd	Jerusalem	Jesus as the good shepherd
John 14–17	Twelve disciples	Jerusalem	Final words of encouragement, comfort, and direction for the disciples Jesus is about to leave

Jesus's "I Am" Declarations

I Am

The expression "I am" falls from Jesus's lips with stunning frequency in the Gospel of John; it provides a quiet but powerful link to his divine nature.

When Jesus uses the phrase "I am" to define his identity, he is mirroring the language that God used when identifying himself for Moses. When Moses asked God to reveal his name, the Lord replied, "I AM" (Exod. 3:14).

Each reference below is to a phrase in which John uses the Greek expression *egō eimi* or *eimi*.

John 4:26	*I am* the one speaking to you.
John 6:35	*I am* the bread of life.
John 6:41	*I am* the bread that came down from heaven.
John 6:48	*I am* the bread of life.
John 6:51	*I am* the living bread that came down from heaven.
John 8:12	*I am* the light of the world.
John 8:18	*I am* the one who gives witness about myself.
John 8:24	If you do not believe that *I am* the one . . .
John 8:58	Before Abraham was born, *I am*!
John 9:5	*I am* the light of the world.
John 10:7	*I am* the gate for the sheep.
John 10:9	*I am* the gate.
John 10:11	*I am* the good shepherd.
John 10:14	*I am* the good shepherd.
John 10:36	*I am* God's Son.
John 11:25	*I am* the resurrection and the life.
John 13:19	*I am* who *I am*.
John 14:6	*I am* the way and the truth and the life.
John 15:1	*I am* the true vine.
John 15:5	*I am* the vine.
John 18:8	*I am* he.
John 18:37	*I am* a king.

Miracles of Jesus

Miracle	Scripture	Location	Larger Outcome (If Stated)
Changed water into wine at a wedding	John 2:1–11	Cana	His disciples believed in him.
Healed a royal official's son	John 4:46–54	Cana/Capernaum	Royal official's entire household came to faith.
Provided a miraculous catch of fish	Luke 5:1–11	Sea of Galilee	Peter, James, and John became disciples of Jesus.
Healed many	Matthew 4:23–25	Galilee	People flocked to Jesus from Syria, Galilee, the Decapolis, Jerusalem, and Judea.
Healed a man with leprosy	Matthew 8:1–4; Mark 1:40–44; Luke 5:12–14	Galilee	Increasing crowds compelled Jesus to pursue quiet time outside the villages in lonely places.
Healed a centurion's servant	Matthew 8:5–13; Luke 7:1–10	Capernaum	The gentile centurion was held up as an example of faith.
Healed Peter's mother-in-law	Matthew 8:14–15; Mark 1:29–31; Luke 4:38–39	Capernaum	She began to wait on Jesus.
Drove out spirits and healed the sick	Matthew 8:16–17; Mark 1:32–34; Luke 4:40–41	Capernaum	Prophecy about the Messiah given by Isaiah was fulfilled.
Calmed a windstorm	Matthew 8:23–27; Mark 4:35–41; Luke 8:22–25	Sea of Galilee	The disciples asked who Jesus might be.
Healed the demon possessed by sending their demons into a herd of pigs	Matthew 8:28–34; Mark 5:1–20; Luke 8:26–39	Gadara	One man freed from the demons spread news about Jesus throughout the Decapolis.
Healed a paralyzed man	Matthew 9:1–8; Mark 2:1–12; Luke 5:17–26	Capernaum	The crowed praised God, recognizing Jesus had special authority.
Healed a woman subject to bleeding for twelve years	Matthew 9:20–22; Mark 5:25–34; Luke 8:43–48	Capernaum	
Raised Jairus's deceased daughter	Matthew 9:18–19, 23–26; Mark 5:22–24, 35–43; Luke 8:41–42, 49–56	Capernaum	News about Jesus spread throughout the region.
Healed two blind men	Matthew 9:27–31	Galilee	News about Jesus spread throughout the region.
Healed demon-possessed man unable to talk	Matthew 9:32–34	Galilee	The crowd was amazed, but the Pharisees claimed Jesus had used demons to do the miracle.
Healed a man with a shriveled hand	Matthew 12:9–14; Mark 3:1–6; Luke 6:6–11	Galilee	Pharisees and Herodians plotted to kill Jesus.
Healed a man who was blind and unable to speak	Matthew 12:22; Luke 11:14	Galilee	People inquired about the source of his power.
Fed five thousand households	Matthew 14:15–21; Mark 6:35–44; Luke 9:10–17; John 6:5–15	Remote place near Bethsaida	Many recognized Jesus as the prophet and attempted to make him their king by force.
Walked on water and enabled Peter to walk on water during a windstorm	Matthew 14:22–33; Mark 6:45–52; John 6:16–21	Sea of Galilee	The disciples acknowledged Jesus was the Son of God.

Miracle	Scripture	Location	Larger Outcome (If Stated)
Healed a Greek woman's daughter	Matthew 15:21–28; Mark 7:24–30	Vicinity of Tyre	
Fed four thousand households	Matthew 15:32–39; Mark 8:1–9, 14–21	Decapolis	Demonstrated the inclusive nature of Jesus's kingdom by providing a miracle for gentiles in parallel to the miracle provided for Jews. See Matthew 16:5–12.
Healed a boy prone to seizures	Matthew 17:14–20; Mark 9:14–29; Luke 9:37–43	Near Mount Hermon	Demonstrated the disciples' need to mature their faith and knowledge
Provided a four-drachma coin from the mouth of a fish	Matthew 17:24–27	Capernaum	Peter paid the temple tax for himself and Jesus.
Healed two blind men, including Bartimaeus	Matthew 20:29–34; Mark 10:46–52; Luke 18:35–43	Jericho	The healed men followed Jesus and joined the crowd in praising God.
Caused a fig tree to wither	Matthew 21:18–22; Mark 11:12–14, 20–25	Mount of Olives	Prompted a discussion on faith and the power of prayer
Healed a man possessed by a demon	Mark 1:21–27; Luke 4:33–36	Capernaum	The word spread throughout Galilee that Jesus was one who taught with authority.
Healed a man unable to hear or speak clearly	Mark 7:31–37	Decapolis	People were amazed and began sharing the news about Jesus.
Healed a blind man	Mark 8:22–26	Bethsaida	
Raised the deceased son of a widow	Luke 7:11–17	Nain	The crowd acknowledged Jesus as a great prophet; word about him spread all the way to Judea.
Healed a woman disabled for eighteen years	Luke 13:10–17	Judea	Jesus's opponents were humiliated.
Healed a man with abnormal swelling	Luke 14:1–6	Judea	Demonstrated that it was appropriate to heal on the Sabbath
Healed ten lepers	Luke 17:11–19	Border of Samaria and Galilee	Highlighted the thankful response of the Samaritan who had been healed
Healed a man who had been disabled for thirty-eight years	John 5:1–15	Bethesda pools in Jerusalem	Demonstrated that it was appropriate to heal on the Sabbath
Healed a man who had been born blind	John 9:1–41	Pool of Siloam in Jerusalem	The Pharisees were forced to discuss the source of Jesus's power.
Raised deceased Lazarus	John 11:1–54	Bethany	Many near Jerusalem put their faith in Jesus, which propelled the Jewish leaders to seek Jesus's execution, causing him to withdraw to Ephraim.
Healed the severed ear of Malchus	Luke 22:49–51; John 18:10	Gethsemane in Jerusalem	
Provided a miraculous catch of fish	John 21:1–14	Sea of Galilee	Jesus confirmed once again that he had risen from the dead.

Parables and Extended Illustrations of Jesus

Parable/Illustration	Scripture	Key Concept
The speck of sawdust and the plank	Matthew 7:3–5; Luke 6:41–42	Christians are called to reflect on their own faults before attempting to correct the faults they see in others.
The good and bad fruit	Matthew 7:16–20; Luke 6:43–45	A person's outward actions and words will be consistent with the spiritual status of their heart.
The wise and foolish builders	Matthew 7:24–27; Luke 6:47–49	A secure foundation for life is built not just on hearing God's Word but in putting those words into action.
The old/new wineskins	Matthew 9:16–17	The coming of God's kingdom cannot be fully housed within the thought world of Old Testament revelation.
The sower	Matthew 13:1–23; Mark 4:2–20; Luke 8:5–15	The message of Jesus will encounter a variety of responses. There are reasons why those who hear that message may fail to sustain a relationship with it.
The weeds	Matthew 13:24–30	Christians are called to spread the Word but defer final evaluation of those who hear it until judgment day.
The mustard seed and yeast	Matthew 13:31–33; Mark 4:30–32; Luke 13:18–21	The humble beginnings of the kingdom of God will mature into something much larger and more pervasive than expected.
The hidden treasure and the pearl	Matthew 13:44–46	The kingdom of heaven is fantastically valuable, so no effort should be spared in acquiring it.
The net	Matthew 13:47–50	Christians are invited to use the Word to gather broadly and leave the separating of the wicked from the righteous to the angels on judgment day.
The lost sheep	Matthew 18:12–14; Luke 15:3–7	The Father feels a personal passion to save every sinner. The repentance of just one sinner fills heaven with celebration.
The unmerciful servant	Matthew 18:21–35	Christians are called to forgive others with the same depth and sincerity that the Father has shown in forgiving them.
The workers in the vineyard	Matthew 20:1–16	Position and reward in the kingdom of heaven are determined by the gracious will of the heavenly Father.
The two sons	Matthew 21:28–32	The Father's good pleasure is reserved for those who hear and do what he asks of them.
The tenants	Matthew 21:33–46; Mark 12:1–12; Luke 20:9–19	The sustained rejection of the prophets and Jesus, God's Son, will result in loss of privileged status in the kingdom.
The wedding banquet	Matthew 22:1–14	Many will do the unthinkable and reject the invitation to join the kingdom of heaven.
The wise and wicked servants	Matthew 24:45–51	Jesus calls Christians to be wise and faithful in caring for the basic needs of others as they await his second coming.

Parable/Illustration	Scripture	Key Concept
The ten virgins	Matthew 25:1–13	Jesus calls Christians to be prepared at all times for his second coming because the precise time of his return is not known.
The talents	Matthew 25:14–30	It is not how much God gives us but how we use what God has given us that matters as we await his second coming.
The growing seed	Mark 4:26–29	The kingdom of heaven grows in unexpected and mysterious ways.
The canceled debt	Luke 7:41–43	The thankfulness and appreciation of the forgiven sinner are proportionate to the amount of sin that was forgiven.
The good Samaritan	Luke 10:25–37	Believers are encouraged to extend love and kindness beyond the restrictive social boundaries we are prone to draw.
The persistent friend	Luke 11:5–8	Jesus encourages Christians to pray with a bold persistence for the things we need.
The rich fool	Luke 12:16–21	Jesus warns against growing personal wealth at the expense of becoming rich toward God.
The barren fig tree	Luke 13:6–9	The season of God's presence on earth in Christ is limited, so there is an urgent need to respond.
The great banquet	Luke 14:15–24	Many will do the unthinkable and reject the invitation to join the kingdom of heaven.
The tower and the war	Luke 14:28–33	Those who commit to God's kingdom must do so only after carefully considering the cost ahead of time.
Lost coin	Luke 15:8–10	A single penitent sinner fills heaven with celebration.
Lost son	Luke 15:11–32	The Father's love for sinners extends beyond their rejection as he awaits the return of those who repent. He expects all believers to join him in celebrating the return of such sinners.
The shrewd manager	Luke 16:1–9	The best use of position and wealth is to advance the kingdom of God and so gain appreciative friends who will welcome our arrival in heaven.
The rich man and poor Lazarus	Luke 16:19–31	The Word of God is the only, as well as the sufficient, means for sinners to find forgiveness and eternal life.
The unworthy servant	Luke 17:7–10	When we work in God's kingdom, we should do so as servants who are simply fulfilling our necessary duties.
The persistent widow	Luke 18:1–8	Jesus encourages believers to pray with persistence even when it appears to be getting nowhere, because justice will be done at the time of Jesus's second coming.
The Pharisee and the tax collector	Luke 18:9–14	The humble and penitent will be lifted up while the proud and impenitent will be brought low.
The ten minas	Luke 19:11–27	Jesus's second coming will not come at once, but when it does, he expects that believers will have used their wealth and abilities wisely.

Palm Sunday to Easter Sunday

Day	Scripture	Events
Palm Sunday / Sunday of Triumphal Entry	Matthew 21:1–11 Mark 11:1–11 Luke 19:28–40 John 12:12–19	Jesus leaves Bethany and climbs over the Mount of Olives on his way to Jerusalem. Jesus rides a donkey into Bethphage (the perceived city limits of Jerusalem) and so fulfills Zechariah 9:9. Jesus is celebrated with coronation language as he rides the donkey down the Mount of Olives. Jesus returns to Bethany for the night.
Monday	Matthew 21:12–22 Mark 11:12–19 Luke 19:41–48	Jesus leaves Bethany and climbs over the Mount of Olives on his way to Jerusalem. On the Mount of Olives Jesus causes a fig tree to wither and employs the view of the Herodium to speak about the power of faith and prayer. Jesus weeps over the fate of Jerusalem. Jesus overturns the tables in the temple markets. After a time teaching in the temple complex, Jesus returns to Bethany for the night.
Tuesday	Matthew 21:23–26:5 Mark 11:20–14:2 Luke 20:1–21:38	Jesus leaves Bethany and climbs over the Mount of Olives on his way to Jerusalem. The message associated with the withered fig tree is reasserted as they pass it. Jesus teaches in the temple courts and participates in sharp exchanges with the Jewish religious leaders, prompting them to plot Jesus's execution. On the way back to Bethany, while crossing the Mount of Olives, Jesus speaks about the fate of Jerusalem and end times.
Wednesday	Matthew 26:14–16 Mark 14:10–11 Luke 22:1–6	Judas makes an agreement with the Jewish leaders to betray Jesus.
Thursday	Matthew 26:17–56 Mark 14:12–52 Luke 22:7–53 John 13:1–18:11	The upper room is secured and used for the Passover meal, which Jesus transforms into the initiation of the Lord's Supper. Jesus washes the disciples' feet. Jesus comforts the disciples and prays for himself, the disciples, and the church. Jesus and the disciples move to the garden of Gethsemane on the Mount of Olives, where Jesus struggles in prayer. Judas betrays Jesus, who is arrested and held by the Sanhedrin. The disciples scatter and flee.

Day	Scripture	Events
Good Friday (Shabbat begins at sunset)	Matthew 26:57–27:65 Mark 14:53–15:47 Luke 22:54–23:56 John 18:12–19:42	Peter denies Jesus three times. The Sanhedrin finds Jesus guilty of blasphemy. The Sanhedrin delivers Jesus to Pilate, charging that he is guilty of crimes against the Roman state. Pilate sends Jesus to Herod Antipas, ruler in Galilee, who questions him and then returns him to Pilate. Although Jesus is not charged with a capital crime, Pilate orders his execution. Jesus is taken to the Antonia Fortress, where he is mocked by the Roman soldiers and severely beaten in advance of his crucifixion. Jesus is taken to Calvary and crucified at 9:00 a.m. An unnatural darkness persists from noon until 3:00 p.m. Jesus surrenders his life. Joseph of Arimathea and Nicodemus secure custody of Jesus's body and bury him in a new tomb with the help of women who had come with Jesus from Galilee. The tomb is sealed, and guards are put in place after sunset.
Saturday		Jesus's body remains in the tomb.
Easter Sunday	Matthew 28:1–15 Mark 16:1–14 Luke 24:1–43 John 20:1–25	The tomb is opened to reveal Jesus has risen. A stream of visitors comes to the empty tomb and receives assurance that Jesus has risen. Jesus spends time with two disciples on the road to Emmaus. Jesus appears to the disciples in the upper room.

The Location of Jesus's Death and Resurrection

Garden Tomb (Gordon's Calvary, Gordon's Tomb)

History

8th–7th century BC	A tomb was excavated into the Garden Tomb hill that follows the pattern of tombs in this era.
4th–6th century AD	Byzantine Christians refashioned the burial site by cutting sarcophagi into the earlier rock benches and by carving crosses into the stone walls of the tomb.
1883	The site was first identified as the location of Jesus's death and resurrection by the British general Charles Gordon.
1894–present	The site was purchased by the Garden Tomb Association and developed into a peaceful garden and worship site.

Historical, Cultural, and Archaeological Observations

The site is located outside the first-century city walls of Jerusalem, a necessary reality for a Jewish cemetery and the language of Hebrews 13:12.

The site is located along a well-traveled road, the kind of public site favored for Roman crucifixions.

The site is located near the city (John 19:20).

The profile of the hill has recesses that resemble the facial features of a skull (John 19:17). However, the intention of the phrase "place of the skull" may be to describe a place of death or execution rather than the appearance of the site.

Neither the design of this tomb nor those nearby are from the first century AD, in contrast to the Gospel's statement that Jesus was buried in a "new tomb in which no one had ever been laid" (Matt. 27:60; John 19:41).

It seems unlikely that Byzantine Christians would have dramatically changed the site as they did if they had identified the site with the tomb of Jesus.

It seems unlikely that a spot of such significance would have gone unremembered and unmentioned in the historical record from the first century until the nineteenth century.

Church of the Holy Sepulchre (Church of the Resurrection)

History

AD 30	An abandoned rock quarry had become a cemetery for Jerusalem.
AD 66	Jewish Christians who left Jerusalem for Pella carried the memory of the site's location with them, bringing it back to Jerusalem when they returned by the close of the first century.
AD 135	Jewish Christians were driven from the city by Hadrian, but gentile Christians who remained maintained the memory of the site. Hadrian reconfigured the site, making it a pagan sanctuary.
ca. AD 300	Eusebius indicated the memory of the site had been preserved in the general area occupied by the sanctuary of Hadrian.
AD 312	The Roman emperor Constantine converted to Christianity and sent his mother, Helena, to Jerusalem, where the location of Jesus's resurrection had ironically been preserved by a pagan sanctuary.
AD 326–35	Helena removed the pagan platform and built and dedicated a church over the place of the crucifixion. Soon after, she placed a rotunda around the spot she believed was Jesus's tomb.
AD 614	This worship center was badly damaged by the Persians.
AD 1009	Systematic destruction of the sanctuary by Fatimid caliph Hakim
AD 1048	Modest rebuilding of the sanctuary
1099	Crusaders found the modest sanctuary and began major renovations.
1099–pesent	Despite the damage of fires and earthquakes, major segments of the Crusader church and some elements of the earlier Byzantine church can be seen in the current structure.

Historical, Cultural, and Archaeological Observations

The site is located near the city (John 19:20).

The site is located outside the first-century city walls of Jerusalem, a necessary reality for a Jewish cemetery and the language of Hebrews 13:12.

The site is near the Gennath Gate and roads leading west from the city, the kind of public site favored for Roman crucifixions.

Tombs of first-century design can be found at this location.

An unbroken memory linking this site to the crucifixion and resurrection of Jesus extends from the present back to the first century.

Key Sermons and Speeches in Acts

Acts	Speaker	Location	Audience	Key Content
2:14–39	Peter	Jerusalem	God-fearing Jews from throughout the world who have come to worship at the temple	Links the miracle of Pentecost to Joel 2:28–32 Links Jesus's resurrection to Psalm 16:8–11 Links Jesus's ascension to Psalm 110:1 Calls Israel to repent, believe, and be baptized
3:11–26	Peter	Jerusalem	Jewish worshipers at Solomon's Colonnade in the temple complex	Pointing to healing of the disabled beggar, asserts he speaks for Jesus, the glorified Messiah Calls Israel to repent and grasp the Old Testament promises to which they are heirs and that will bless them with forgiveness
4:8–12	Peter	Jerusalem	Jewish rulers, elders, and teachers of the law	Links the healing of the disabled beggar to the risen Christ, whom the Jewish leaders had rejected Asserts salvation is possible through Jesus alone
7:2–53	Stephen	Jerusalem	Jewish elders and teachers of the law, including Saul	Provides a review of Israel's history highlighting God's grace and faithfulness Contrasts this with Israel's persistent rejection of divine messengers, which continues into the present moment
10:34–43	Peter	Caesarea Maritima	Gentiles gathered in the home of Cornelius	Affirms that God's acceptance and forgiveness extends to people of all nations
11:4–17	Peter	Jerusalem	Jewish believers concerned that Peter had been with gentiles	Recounts the vision that urged him to stop viewing gentiles as unworthy of the gospel Confirms gentile inclusion by noting that these gentiles had the same Spirit-filled conversion experience as Jews
13:16–41	Paul	Pisidian Antioch	Jews and gentile God-fearers gathered in the synagogue	Recounts key elements of Jewish history that culminate in the coming of Jesus, the Messiah, whose identity was confirmed when he rose from the dead Invites them to believe and find forgiveness in Jesus
15:7–11	Peter	Jerusalem	Jewish believers who assumed gentiles had to obey the law of Moses	Asserts that God has provided the same signs of conversion and acceptance for both Jews and gentiles Emphasizes salvation by grace alone apart from obedience to the law of Moses

Acts	Speaker	Location	Audience	Key Content
15:13–21	James	Jerusalem	Jewish believers who assumed gentiles had to obey the law of Moses	Avoids any demands on gentiles that would make it difficult for them to turn to God Urges several lifestyle concessions from gentiles that would make it easier for Jews to turn to Jesus
17:22–31	Paul	Athens	Meeting of the Areopagus	God, the autonomous and powerful Creator who is unknown to them, wishes to make himself known in advance of their being judged by the one whom he raised from the dead.
20:18–35	Paul	Miletus	Elders from the church at Ephesus	Words of encouragement and direction for elders who must carry on the church's work replicating the tireless passion, courage, honesty, and humility of Paul, whom they will not see again
22:1–21	Paul	Jerusalem	Angry Jewish crowd gathered before the Antonia Fortress	Recounts his life's story as a zealous Jew leading to his conversion on the road to Damascus and his call to speak to all on behalf of Jesus, including the gentiles
24:10–21	Paul	Caesarea Maritima	The Roman governor Felix	Refutes the charges that he has violated Roman law either by stirring up dissension against Rome or by being the leader of a religious sect Rome had not approved
26:1–23	Paul	Caesarea Maritima	Herod Agrippa II, Bernice, the Roman governor Festus, and other high-ranking officers and leaders	Recounts his life's story as a zealous Jew leading to his vision on the road to Damascus, which changed his attitude toward Jesus and his life's mission Demonstrates that his testimony about the risen Jesus and the forgiveness he brings flows from expectations created in the Old Testament

Paul's Ministry and Letters

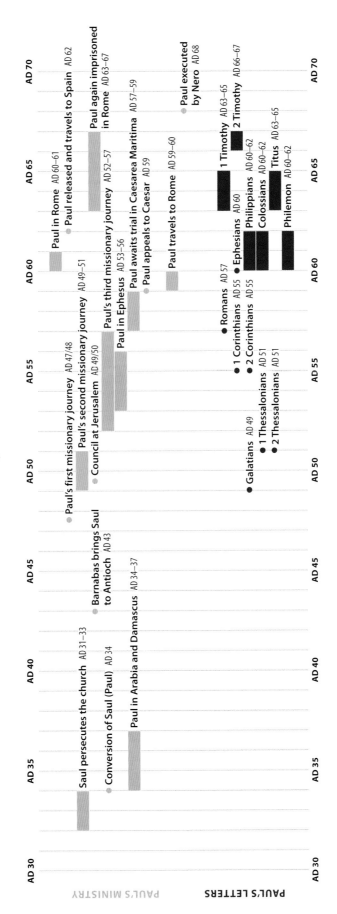

PAUL'S MINISTRY

Saul persecutes the church AD 31–33
Conversion of Saul (Paul) AD 34
Paul in Arabia and Damascus AD 34–37
Barnabas brings Saul to Antioch AD 43
Paul's first missionary journey AD 47/48
Paul's second missionary journey AD 49–51
Council at Jerusalem AD 49/50
Paul's third missionary journey AD 52–57
Paul in Ephesus AD 53–56
Paul awaits trial in Caesarea Maritima AD 57–59
Paul appeals to Caesar AD 59
Paul travels to Rome AD 59–60
Paul in Rome AD 60–61
Paul released and travels to Spain AD 62
Paul again imprisoned in Rome AD 63–67
Paul executed by Nero AD 68

PAUL'S LETTERS

Galatians AD 49
1 Thessalonians AD 51
2 Thessalonians AD 51
1 Corinthians AD 55
2 Corinthians AD 55
Romans AD 57
Ephesians AD 60
Philippians AD 60–62
Colossians AD 60–62
Philemon AD 60–62
1 Timothy AD 63–65
Titus AD 63–65
2 Timothy AD 66–67

AD 30 AD 35 AD 40 AD 45 AD 50 AD 55 AD 60 AD 65 AD 70

Spiritual Gifts

Each Christian is given a unique gift or collection of gifts that, when properly used, will foster the well-being of the Christian church as it moves forward to the time of Jesus's second coming.

	Romans 12:6–8	1 Corinthians 12:4–11	1 Corinthians 12:28–30	Ephesians 4:11	1 Peter 4:9–11
Prophecy	•	•	•	•	
Service	•				
Teaching	•		•	•	
Encouraging	•				
Giving	•				
Leading	•				
Mercy	•				
Wisdom		•			
Knowledge		•			
Faith		•			
Healing		•	•		
Miraculous powers		•	•		
Distinguishing spirits		•			
Speaking in tongues		•	•		
Interpreting tongues		•	•		
Apostle			•	•	
Helping			•		
Guidance			•		
Evangelist				•	
Pastor				•	
Hospitality					•
Serving					•
Speaking					•

Reading the Book of Revelation

	Amillennial	Premillennial	Postmillennial
General	Emphasizes the real past history from which the book grows with greater attention to the way it anticipates challenges that will come to the church prior to Jesus's second coming	Generally reads Revelation as a book about the future events that the church will meet as this world's history comes to a close	Emphasizes the real past history from which the book grows with greater emphasis on the way it anticipates the improvements that the preaching of the gospel will bring on earth
Seven Churches of Revelation 1–3	Real churches in Asia Minor in need of correction and encouragement and whose circumstances are reflected in the church throughout its history	Real churches in Asia Minor in need of correction and encouragement and whose circumstances are reflected in the church throughout its history	Real churches in Asia Minor in need of correction and encouragement and whose circumstances are reflected in the church throughout its history
Language of Revelation 4–19	Vivid, symbolic images that illustrate the challenges the church had met and would meet, culminating in the rescue Jesus will provide Emphasizes that multiple sets of visions may be used to represent the same challenge and remedy	Vivid, symbolic images that illustrate the challenges that lay ahead for the church and the rescue that Jesus will provide	Vivid, symbolic images that illustrate the challenges the church had met and would meet Emphasizes the optimism of an improving world as the gospel message is accepted by more and more people
"Millennium" of Revelation 20:1–4	A symbolic period of time that stretches from Jesus's first to his second coming that consists of many challenges en route to an eternal kingdom	A literal period of abundance and well-being that starts suddenly and is realized when Christ returns to physically rule with his people on earth (Dispensational Christians see a special role for the Jewish people during this time of Christ's rule.)	A symbolic period of time that stretches from Jesus's first to second coming during which the gospel gradually expands on earth to shape the ideal world
"Great Tribulation" of Revelation 7:14	The persecution of Christians at the time Revelation was written, which exemplifies the persecution of Christians to come	A limited time of extreme violence coming in the future May be preceded by a "rapture" during which believers will be extracted from the earth	The persecution of Christians at the time Revelation was written, with particular emphasis on how this correlates with persecutions to come
"Armageddon" of Revelation 16:16	Symbolic battle meant to emphasize the fierceness of the opposition that the church will meet between Jesus's first and second coming	Literal battle that may occur in the Jezreel Valley near Megiddo Will end the great tribulation and usher in the millennium	Symbolic battle meant to emphasize the power of God's Word in defeating the fierce opposition met by the church between Jesus's first and second coming
"Resurrections" of Revelation 20:4–6	The first resurrection is the conversion of a believer, and the second resurrection is their physical resurrection from the dead.	The first resurrection is a physical resurrection of believers that starts the millennium, and the second is the resurrection of nonbelievers at the end of the millennium.	The first resurrection is the conversion of a believer, and the second resurrection is their physical resurrection from the dead.

Archaeology of the New Testament

	Artifact/Structure	Date	Description	Value
1	Madaba Map	6th century AD	Mosaic map of the biblical world found on part of the floor of St. George's Church in Madaba, Jordan	Although only one-third of the map survives, it is the oldest Bible map found to date and tells us where Byzantine Christians believed Bible places were located. The map includes a particularly detailed presentation of Jerusalem.
2	Homes of Nazareth	1st century AD	Beneath the modern Church of the Annunciation in Nazareth, we find caves that were enlarged to form the interior room of first-century homes that had masonry facades.	Aids in defining the size and nature of Nazareth at the time Mary, Joseph, and Jesus lived there (Matt. 2:23). It was a small agricultural village with a population of about three hundred people.
3	Church of the Nativity	4th to 6th century AD	Byzantine church located in Bethlehem. Very early church traditions indicate that this church was built around the cave/animal shelter in which Mary gave birth to Jesus.	Supports this location as the one in which Jesus was born in Bethlehem and offers insight into the type of animal shelter that hosted his birth (Luke 2:1–20)
4	Herod the Great's tomb	1st century BC	Foundation of the seven-story structure that served as the tomb of Herod the Great at the Herodium	Herod was the Roman-appointed king of Judea who felt so threatened by the birth of the king of the Jews that he ordered the killing of all boys two years of age and under in Bethlehem. This caused Mary, Joseph, and Jesus to flee to Egypt (Matt. 2:1–18).

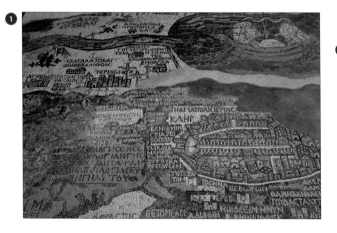

Artifact/Structure	Date	Description	Value
5 Temple Mount retaining wall	1st century BC to 1st century AD	Western segment of the retaining wall that supported the sprawling platform on which the Herodian temple complex was built	Marks the location of the New Testament temple complex in Jerusalem, which became the setting for many New Testament events
6 *Mikveh*	1st century AD	This *mikveh*, or Jewish traditional bath station, was used by Jewish worshipers who would undergo a ritual bath before going up to the temple. The stairs to the pool were often divided so that entry and exit would be made on opposing sides of the stairs.	This *mikveh* was one of many located in a building at the main entrance to the temple complex. It would have been used by many of the individuals we meet in the New Testament, including Mary, Jesus's mother, Jesus, and Paul.
7 Southern Steps	1st century AD	These steps were the main public entry into the temple complex and also were used as an outdoor classroom by the rabbis when teaching their students.	As the main entry to the temple, these steps were walked by many of the individuals we meet in the New Testament and may have been the location at which Jesus pursued answers to his questions when he was twelve years old (Luke 2:46–50).
8 Stone storage jars	1st century AD	Limestone, lathe-turned jars that were used by Jewish families during certain cleansing rituals. According to later Jewish tradition, the stone did not transfer ritual impurity like a ceramic vessel that could absorb and hold impurity.	These jars provide examples of the large, open-mouthed storage jars that held the water Jesus used to perform his first miracle, changing water into wine at Cana (John 2:1–11).

© Baker Publishing Group and Dr. James C. Martin. The British Museum.

	Artifact/Structure	Date	Description	Value
9	Synagogue at Capernaum	1st century AD	The lighter-toned limestone synagogue of a later era stands above the black, basalt foundation of the earlier synagogue that served Capernaum during Jesus's time.	The headquarters of Jesus's ministry in Galilee was in Capernaum. He taught and healed in this synagogue (Mark 1:21–28).
10	Peter's home at Capernaum	1st century AD	An *insula* home foundation surrounded by Byzantine church structures that identify the home as that of Peter	The home in which Peter, and likely Jesus, stayed during evenings in Capernaum (Matt. 8:14; Mark 1:29; Luke 4:38)
11	Galilee boat	1st century AD	Hull and structure of a preserved first-century fishing boat discovered near Ginosar on the western shore of the Sea of Galilee	Represents the size and design of the fishing boats that were used on the Sea of Galilee during the time of Jesus and are mentioned in the Gospels (Matt. 8:24; 13:2; 14:13, 22, 29)
12	Seat of Moses	3rd to 4th century AD	Basalt chair discovered within the synagogue at Korazin on which the authorized Jewish teacher sat to interpret and apply God's Word	The type of seat that Jesus mentioned in Matthew 23:2 when criticizing the teachers of the law and Pharisees who "sit in Moses's seat." Note that Jesus "sat down to teach" (Luke 4:20) in the synagogue at Nazareth.

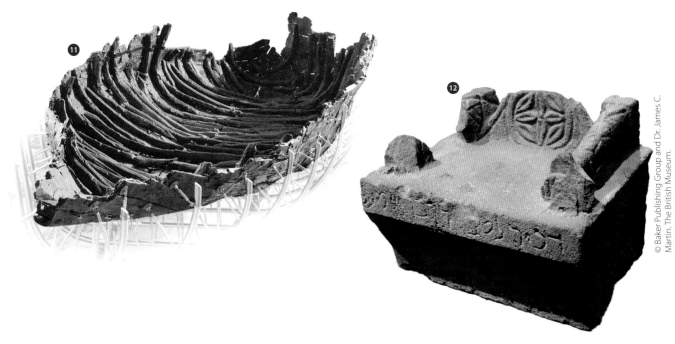

© Baker Publishing Group and Dr. James C. Martin. The British Museum.

	Artifact/Structure	Date	Description	Value
13	Synagogue at Gamla	1st century AD	The foundation and floor structure of a synagogue building that was destroyed before AD 70	This building preserves a Galilean-style Jewish synagogue like those in which Jesus spoke as he traveled about the northern portion of the promised land (Matt. 4:23; Mark 1:39).
14	Jacob's Well at Sychar	1st century AD	A well located near the first-century village of Sychar that was estimated to be 240 feet deep in the seventh century AD. As early as AD 333, an early Christian pilgrim identified this well with the one mentioned in John 4:12. By late in the fourth century AD, a church had been built over the well.	Likely the deep well where Jesus met and spoke with the Samaritan woman who had come to Jacob's well in order to draw water (John 4:1–26)
15	Pagan sacred area at Caesarea Philippi	1st century BC to 1st century AD	At the base of a surreal-looking cliff, we find a sacred area that at the time of Jesus included a temple built for Augustus and a sanctuary for Pan.	Jesus took the disciples to this region in order to have a conversation about his identity. It is where Peter identified Jesus as "the Christ, the Son of the living God" (Matt. 16:13–20).
16	Church at Kursi	6th century AD	Byzantine church and monastery complex built to remember the exorcism of demons known as the miracle of the swine, and also to recall Jesus's feeding of the four thousand	Marks the Decapolis area in which Jesus healed the demon possessed and fed four thousand (Mark 5:1–20; 7:31; 8:1–13)

	Artifact/Structure	Date	Description	Value
17	Pools of Bethesda	8th century BC to 1st century AD	A pair of large water reservoirs (215 feet by 160 feet and 175 feet by 130 feet) north of the temple complex in Jerusalem that captured and held run-off water from the Beth Zeta Valley	The location at which Jesus healed a disabled man who had been waiting by the pools. He had hoped to be healed when he entered the water at the moment it was miraculously stirred (John 5:3–9).
18	Siloam Pool (Shiloah Pool)	8th century BC to 1st century AD	A dam and water reservoir complex that held water at the southern end of Jerusalem's central valley near the exit point of Hezekiah's tunnel. Stairs surrounded the pool and were used to access the water.	The pool to which Jesus sent the man born blind to complete his healing (John 9:1–7)
19	Tomb of Lazarus	Earliest mention early 4th century AD by Eusebius	An eight-foot-square burial chamber in the village of New Testament Bethany that tradition identifies as the tomb of Lazarus	Possible location for the raising of Lazarus, the event that animated the Jewish leaders in Jerusalem to more urgently seek Jesus's execution (John 11:38–53)
20	*Judaea capta* coin	AD 69–79	This Roman sestertius was a coin minted by Vespasian to celebrate Rome's suppression of the First Jewish Revolt (AD 66–70). It mockingly employed a palm tree, the Jewish symbol of freedom.	The connection between the palm tree and Jewish freedom explains the crowd's use of palm branches on Palm Sunday (the Sunday of Triumphal Entry) as they celebrated Jesus's arrival in Jerusalem (John 12:13).

	Artifact/Structure	Date	Description	Value
21	Temple-complex rubble	AD 70	Stones that had composed the buildings and parapet of the temple complex in Jerusalem. They were broken apart and pushed from the Temple Mount by the Romans at the close of the First Jewish Revolt (AD 66–70).	The reality that Jesus anticipated for the temple complex when he observed that "not one stone here will be left on another; every one will be thrown down" (Matt. 24:2)
22	Aristocratic homes on Jerusalem's Western Hill	1st century AD	Foundations, floors, and contents of large, opulent homes built in the Upper City of Jerusalem that were likely used by the aristocratic Sadducees	These homes and their furnishings give us a look into the lives of the aristocratic Sadducees, whom we find in conflict with Jesus and the apostles in Jerusalem (Matt. 22:23–24; Acts 5:17).
23	Tyrian shekel	1st century AD	Due to its consistently high silver content, the Tyrian shekel was the coin that the Jewish leaders required for payment of religious taxes and for purchases made in the temple market of Jerusalem.	The required use of this coin precipitated the need for money changers at the temple in Jerusalem (Matt. 21:12–15). Because it was the coinage favored by the Jewish religious leaders, it is likely that thirty such coins were given in payment to Judas in order to purchase the betrayal of Jesus (Matt. 27:3–10).
24	Upper room	4th century AD	Upper room of Holy Zion Church, which was built by Byzantine Christians and later restored by the Crusaders. The church was built over the footprint of the Church of the Apostles (AD 73), a church established by Jewish believers in Jesus returning from Pella.	This "upper room" of the Crusader church in Jerusalem likely occupies the space of the upper room associated with the home in which Jesus arranged Passover the night before his death (Mark 14:15), where Jesus appeared to the disciples following his resurrection (Luke 24:33–43), and possibly where Pentecost began (Acts 2:1).

	Artifact/Structure	Date	Description	Value
25	Mount Zion steps	1st century AD	A set of stairs on the compound of St. Peter Gallicantu Church, which connects the top of Mount Zion with the bottom of the Hinnom Valley in Jerusalem	The stairs that Jesus likely descended after leaving the upper room when traveling with the disciples to the garden of Gethsemane. Following his arrest, the return trip to his hearings with Annas and Caiaphas would have been via the same steps.
26	Gethsemane	4th century AD	The modern Church of All Nations is built upon the footprint of an earlier Byzantine church, which Christians of that era used to mark the garden of Gethsemane, and the great stone on which Jesus struggled in prayer.	Marks the general area in which Jesus struggled in prayer the evening before his death on the cross (Matt. 26:36; Mark 14:32; Luke 22:39; John 18:1)
27	"Place of trumpeting" inscription	1st century AD	Inscription placed on a portion of the stone parapet that surrounded the Temple Mount complex in Jerusalem. It reads "To the place of trumpeting," indicating that it was the location where the priest would stand to sound the signaling trumpet.	Jewish traditional writings refer to the sounding of the trumpet at the temple as "cock crow." This may be the sound to which Jesus refers when he tells Peter that before "the rooster crows," he would deny Jesus three times (Matt. 26:34, 75).
28	Caiaphas ossuary	1st century AD	An elaborately decorated ossuary discovered in Jerusalem that was inscribed with the name "Joseph son of Caiaphas"	Caiaphas was high priest in Jerusalem AD 18–36. He is identified as the one before whom Jesus stood for a religious trial in the hours before his death (Matt. 26:3, 57).

© Baker Publishing Group and Dr. James C. Martin. The British Museum.

© Baker Publishing Group and Dr. James C. Martin. The British Museum.

	Artifact/Structure	Date	Description	Value
29	Pilate inscription	1st century AD	The name of Pontius Pilate is included in this dedicatory inscription associated with a Tiberium, likely a temple built in Caesarea Maritima that honored Emperor Tiberius.	Pilate was the Roman governor (procurator) of Judea AD 26–36. He is the Roman official who heard the case against Jesus, pronounced him innocent, and then ordered his execution (Matt. 27:2, 13, 17, 19, 22–26).
30	Herod's palace in Jerusalem	1st century BC to 1st century AD	A luxury palace built by Herod the Great in Jerusalem that was later used by the Roman governors as their chief residence when they were in the city on business. The Hippicus Tower foundation from the palace is pictured.	The trial of Jesus before Pilate likely occurred within the compound of this palace that included the "Stone Pavement" (John 19:13).
31	Crucified man's heel	1st century AD	Heel bone recovered from the ossuary of Yehohanan, son of Hagkol of Jerusalem. The iron nail embedded within the heel bone indicates that he was crucified.	Illustrates the type of nail and method that the Romans likely used to attach the condemned, like Jesus, to the cross (John 20:25; Acts 2:23; Col. 2:14)
32	Church of the Holy Sepulchre	4th century AD	The contemporary Church of the Holy Sepulchre (Church of the Resurrection) is built over the area that Byzantine Christians believed was the spot of Jesus's crucifixion and resurrection.	Adds to the historical continuity and physical evidence that identifies the area of this church as the authentic place of Jesus's crucifixion and resurrection (John 19:17–20)

© Baker Publishing Group and Dr. James C. Martin. The British Museum.

© Baker Publishing Group and Dr. James C. Martin. The British Museum.

	Artifact/Structure	Date	Description	Value
33	Jewish tomb	1st century AD	A first-century, *kochim*-style limestone tomb with a rolling stone door. Within the Jewish culture from 20 BC to AD 70, the *kochim*-style tomb was the style typically used for the family tomb.	Surviving first-century tombs around Jerusalem illustrate how Jesus's tomb would have looked and provide the setting against which to read the details of his burial and resurrection (John 19:41–20:1).
34*	Nazareth decree	Mid-1st century AD	Marble slab that contains a decree of Emperor Claudius apparently directed toward Jewish burials. It demands that graves remain undisturbed, blocking stones sealed, and bodies intact. Offenders will face the death penalty.	This may be an imperial response to the disturbance in Rome associated with a man named "Chrestus." The extreme penalty associated with disturbing a grave diminishes the credibility of the story circulated about the disciples coming during the night and stealing Jesus's body while the guards slept (Matt. 28:13).
35	Arch of Titus	ca. AD 81	A victory arch erected at the Forum of Rome to commemorate the defeat of Jerusalem by Titus at the close of the first Jewish revolt. The arch contains a relief depicting various worship items, including a menorah carried from the temple by Roman soldiers (AD 71).	The reality that Jesus anticipated for the temple complex in Jerusalem during his end-times discourse (Matt. 24:2, 15–21)
36	Sergius Paulus inscription	1st century AD	An inscription found near Pisidian Antioch that contains the name Sergius Paulus	Sergius Paulus was a Roman proconsul at Paphos on the island of Cyprus who sent for Paul and became a believer (Acts 13:6–12). Following his time on Cyprus, Paul traveled to Pisidian Antioch. This artifact supports the notion that Sergius Paulus's extended family had large estates near Pisidian Antioch and may explain why Paul visited this area after leaving Cyprus (Acts 13:13–14).
37	Egnatian Way	2nd century BC into the 5th century AD	Segment of the Egnatian Way near Philippi, which connected Rome (via the Adriatic Sea) with Byzantium	Paul would likely have used this road segment as he traveled from Neapolis to Philippi and on to Thessalonica (Acts 16:11–17:9).

*Not pictured

	Artifact/Structure	Date	Description	Value
38	Paul's Philippian jail	5th century AD	Stone crypt near the forum of Philippi that the Byzantine Christians identified as the jail in which Paul and Silas were held	Possibly the jail that held Paul and Silas and in which their jailer came to know Jesus as his Savior (Acts 16:22–34)
39*	Politarch inscription	2nd century AD	An inscription on an arch that spanned the Egnatian Way on the west side of Thessalonica that uses the Greek term *politarch*	During Paul and Silas's time in Thessalonica, they were dragged before city officials whom Luke identifies as *politarchs* (Acts 17:6, 8; NIV translates as "city officials").
40	Mars Hill	1st century AD	Prominent rock outcropping within ancient Athens identified with the first-century meeting place of the Areopagus (hill of Ares/Mars)	During Paul's time in Athens, he used their so-called Unknown God as a starting point for speaking about Jesus before a meeting of the Council of the Areopagus (Acts 17:19–34).
41	Bema at Corinth	AD 25–50	The bema (Latin, *rostra*), or elevated speaker's platform, at Corinth from which public announcements were made and where citizens met with public officials to adjudicate legal cases	When Paul was charged with a crime in Corinth, he was likely taken to this bema to appear before the proconsul Gallio (Acts 18:12–17).
42	Gallio inscription	AD 52	A badly broken inscription commissioned by the emperor Claudius and discovered at Delphi that mentions "Gallio, my friend, and the proconsul (of Achaia)"	Paul was summoned to a legal hearing before "Gallio, proconsul of Achaia" during his time in Corinth (Acts 18:12). This inscription plays a critical role in establishing the time line for Paul's ministry.

*Not pictured

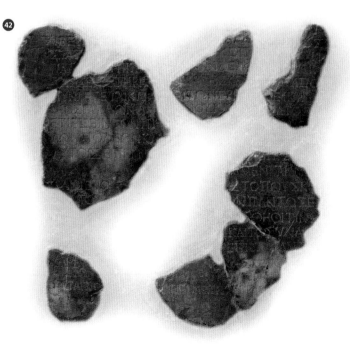

	Artifact/Structure	Date	Description	Value
43	Temple of Artemis at Ephesus	6th century BC	Although little has survived, the temple of Artemis at Ephesus was considered one of the seven wonders of the ancient world. This massive structure was 60 feet in height and distinguished by its 127 Ionic columns.	When Paul spoke about there being only one true God, it caused a riot led by many who were intimately linked theologically and economically to the worship of Artemis in the city of Ephesus (Acts 19:23–41).
44	Theater at Ephesus	3rd century BC to 5th century AD	The theater at Ephesus went through many building and renovation phases during its long history. Reaching nearly 100 feet in height, it could accommodate 25,000 people on its three levels.	Paul's preaching in Ephesus led to the seizing of his traveling companion, Aristarchus. The rampaging crowd rushed him into the theater, seeking action against him (Acts 19:28–29).
45	Statue of Artemis	1st century AD	This first-century statue depicts Artemis of Ephesus. She was the goddess of hunting, wilderness, and wild animals.	When Paul's preaching offended the adherents of Artemis at Ephesus, a riot broke out in that city (Acts 19:28–34).
46	Herod's palace at Caesarea Maritima	Est. 22 BC	The palace of Herod the Great built in the lavish port city of Caesarea Maritima	Roman governors like Pilate, Felix, and Festus used this as their primary residence when they were assigned to Israel. Paul was kept under guard at this palace during his two-year stay in this city (Acts 23:35).

	Artifact/Structure	Date	Description	Value
47	Mamertine prison in Rome	Built in the 7th century BC	Subterranean, two-story structure located on the northeast side of the Capitoline Hill adjacent to the Roman Forum to hold those awaiting trial before the emperor	Structure that tradition has linked with the detention of Peter and particularly of Paul. It illustrates the conditions of Paul's detention as he awaited trial prior to his execution (2 Tim. 1:16; 2:9; 4:6–8).
48	Erastus inscription	ca. AD 50	A reassembled stone inscription from Corinth that contains the name "Erastus" and that identifies him as an *aidele*, a city business manager or treasurer	Likely the name of the important civic official in Corinth who became a Christian and is identified by name in Romans 16:23, a letter written from Corinth. He also may be acknowledged in 2 Timothy 4:20 and Acts 19:22.
49	Temple warning inscription	1st century AD	A warning sign associated with a partition wall erected on the Temple Mount in Jerusalem to divide the area where gentiles were allowed (Court of the Gentiles) from those reserved exclusively for those of Jewish descent	Illustrates the cultural separation between Jews and gentiles that was the norm in Israel as the early church worked to bring the gospel to both. This may be the image Paul has in mind when he speaks of Jesus removing "the barrier, the dividing wall of hostility" between Jews and gentiles in Ephesians 2:14.
50	Imperial cult temple at Pergamum	1st–2nd century AD	Ruins of the temple built for the worship of Emperor Trajan at Pergamum, the official hub of the imperial cult in Asia Minor	Roman emperors either quietly allowed or aggressively demanded their recognition as divine beings during the first three centuries AD. During this time, imperial cult worship facilities spread throughout the Roman world, including Greece, Asia Minor, and even Israel. Direct reference to Christianity's clash with this cult may be found in Revelation 2:13; 13:14–15.

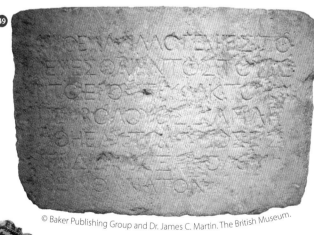

© Baker Publishing Group and Dr. James C. Martin. The British Museum.

Judean Home (Cave)

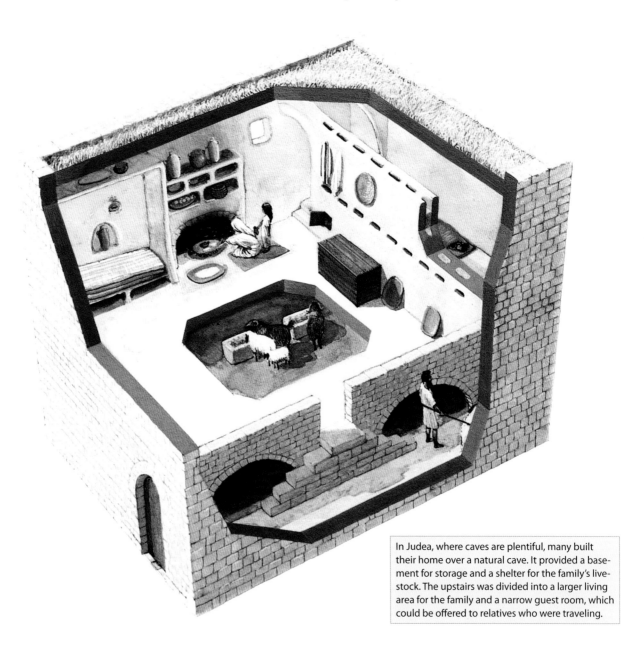

In Judea, where caves are plentiful, many built their home over a natural cave. It provided a basement for storage and a shelter for the family's livestock. The upstairs was divided into a larger living area for the family and a narrow guest room, which could be offered to relatives who were traveling.

Insula Home Complex

In the area around the Sea of Galilee, extended families built their living compounds around an open-air courtyard called an *insula* (Latin for island). The courtyard provided a place in which the extended family could interact, accomplish household tasks, and keep their livestock at night. Each nuclear family had a small, private room on the perimeter of the courtyard to which they could retreat in the evening.

Capernaum

The town of Capernaum on the Sea of Galilee became both the home of Jesus and the base for his ministry in Galilee. It provided Jesus with access to the fishing boats he used to travel the lakeshore and was the location of the synagogue in which he frequently taught and healed.

Synagogue

The synagogue was the largest public building in many Jewish towns. It was a place for prayer, education, and communal worship, as well as the site for other civic gatherings formerly associated with the city gate.

1 *Mikveh.* This pool was used for ritual purification prior to worship.

2 **Entry.** The synagogue entry faced Jerusalem.

3 **Chamber.** The Old Testament scrolls were kept here.

4 **Speaking platform.** The Old Testament scrolls were read from this platform.

5 **Steps.** The steps were used for public seating.

Fishing Techniques

The **cast net** was a hand-thrown net used to fish the shallow water near shore. It was round, eighteen to twenty-five feet in diameter, with stone weights attached to the perimeter. The fisherman would twirl the net overhead, using centrifugal force to open the net to its full diameter, and then throw it over a shoal of fish, trapping them beneath it.

The **drag net** was rectangular in shape, one thousand feet long and twelve feet high. It was used to fish the shallows. Floats were attached to the top of the net and weights were attached to the base so that this net would stand vertically in the water. It was deployed by the combined efforts of a crew in a boat and on shore. The boat crew began by pulling the net to its full length perpendicular to the shoreline. Then the boat turned parallel to the shore, and both crews dragged this vertical curtain through the water, driving fish ahead of it. Eventually the boat arched back to the shore, corralling the fish, which were harvested when the net was pulled on shore.

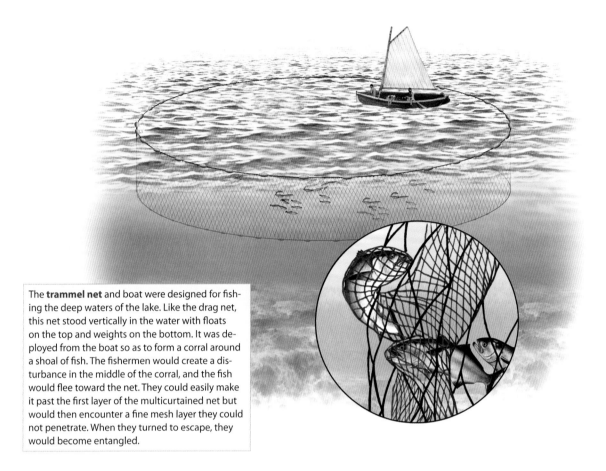

The **trammel net** and boat were designed for fishing the deep waters of the lake. Like the drag net, this net stood vertically in the water with floats on the top and weights on the bottom. It was deployed from the boat so as to form a corral around a shoal of fish. The fishermen would create a disturbance in the middle of the corral, and the fish would flee toward the net. They could easily make it past the first layer of the multicurtained net but would then encounter a fine mesh layer they could not penetrate. When they turned to escape, they would become entangled.

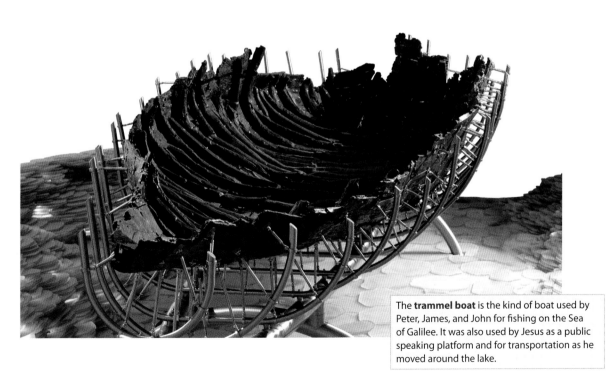

The **trammel boat** is the kind of boat used by Peter, James, and John for fishing on the Sea of Galilee. It was also used by Jesus as a public speaking platform and for transportation as he moved around the lake.

Mikveh

The law code of the Old Testament required God's chosen people to remain ritually clean. One of the ways ritual purity was restored when lost was through washing with water. In urban settings, this need was met by a *mikveh*, a small pool fed by a natural water source. It was deep enough for its users to immerse themselves.

Triclinium Table

On Maundy Thursday, Jesus and the disciples likely reclined around a low table like this in the upper room. Each took a position around the table that related to the social role they played during the meal and to their social status among those dining together.

Crucifixion Methods

The Romans reserved crucifixion for robbers, deserters, and political insurrectionists.

The **flagellum** consisted of a wooden handle with leather straps tied into knots, which were imbedded with bone and sharp metal bits. Repeated lashing with this device prior to the actual crucifixion left the condemned incapable of resisting what was to come.

During the **crucifixion**, the condemned person was attached to a tree or set of wooden posts using either ropes, nails, or a combination of both. A variety of postures were used, but each one extended the arms at or above head level. The Gospels do not reveal the method used for Jesus's crucifixion, but the earliest Christian reports indicate Jesus was crucified on a t-shaped cross.

Kochim Tomb

When Joseph of Arimathea offered his tomb for the burial of Jesus, it was likely a *kochim*-style tomb. The main room of the tomb had a bench around its perimeter, which was to prepare the body before placing it in one of the smaller *kochim* (niches). In twelve to eighteen months, the family would return to the tomb, gather the remains from the *koch*, and place them in a limestone box called an ossuary.

Herod's Temple Complex

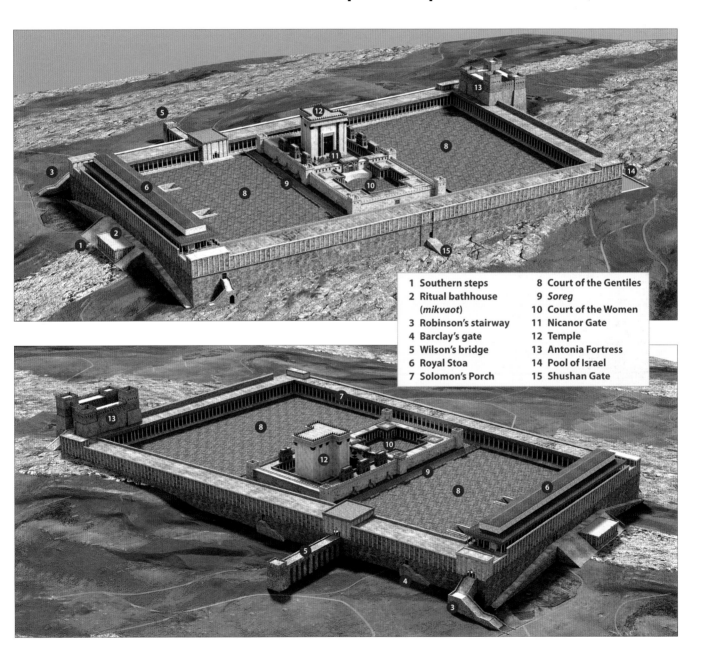

1	Southern steps	8	Court of the Gentiles
2	Ritual bathhouse (*mikvaot*)	9	*Soreg*
		10	Court of the Women
3	Robinson's stairway	11	Nicanor Gate
4	Barclay's gate	12	Temple
5	Wilson's bridge	13	Antonia Fortress
6	Royal Stoa	14	Pool of Israel
7	Solomon's Porch	15	Shushan Gate

New Testament Temple Design

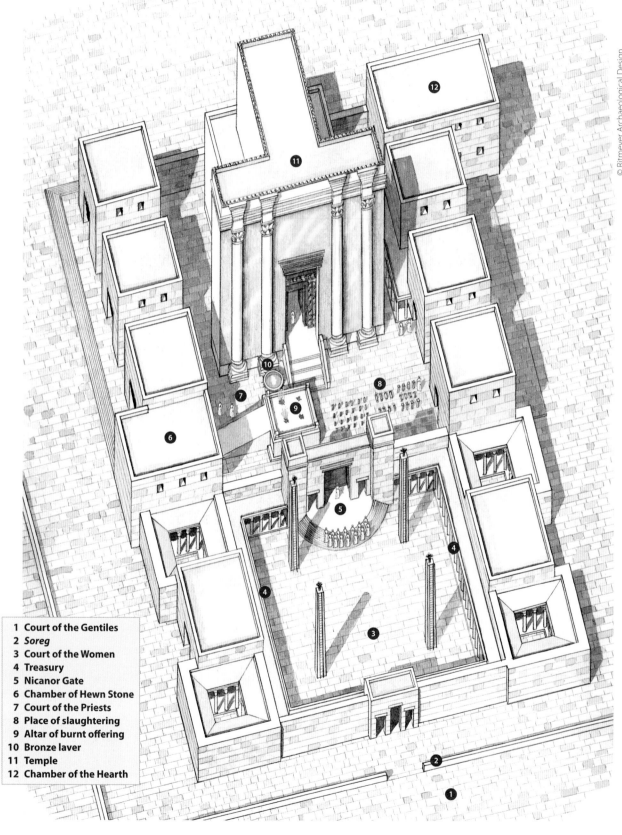

1 **Court of the Gentiles**
2 *Soreg*
3 **Court of the Women**
4 **Treasury**
5 **Nicanor Gate**
6 **Chamber of Hewn Stone**
7 **Court of the Priests**
8 **Place of slaughtering**
9 **Altar of burnt offering**
10 **Bronze laver**
11 **Temple**
12 **Chamber of the Hearth**

© Ritmeyer Archaeological Design

Jerusalem at the Time of the New Testament

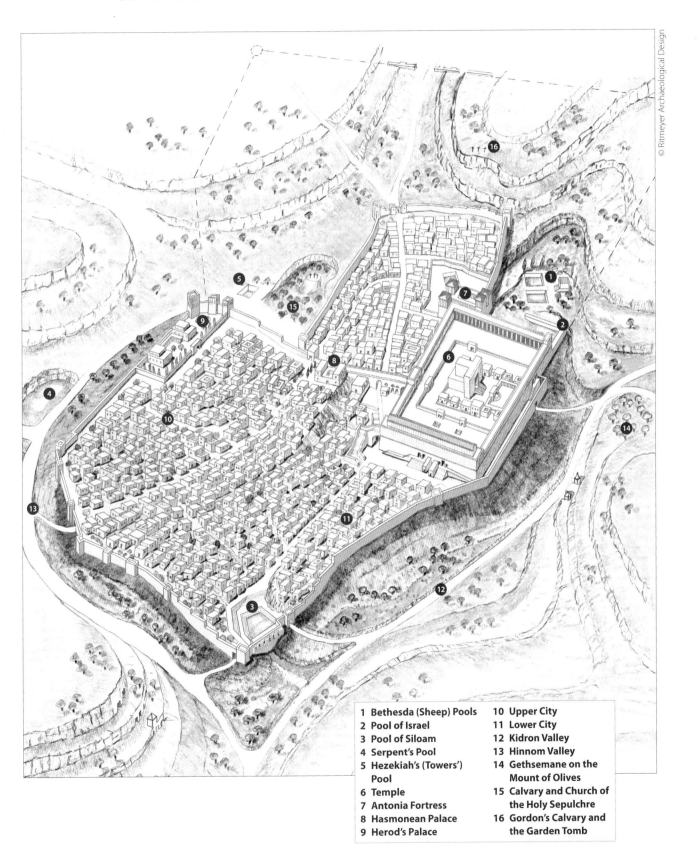

© Ritmeyer Archaeological Design

1	Bethesda (Sheep) Pools	10	Upper City
2	Pool of Israel	11	Lower City
3	Pool of Siloam	12	Kidron Valley
4	Serpent's Pool	13	Hinnom Valley
5	Hezekiah's (Towers') Pool	14	Gethsemane on the Mount of Olives
6	Temple	15	Calvary and Church of the Holy Sepulchre
7	Antonia Fortress	16	Gordon's Calvary and the Garden Tomb
8	Hasmonean Palace		
9	Herod's Palace		

Jesus in Jerusalem

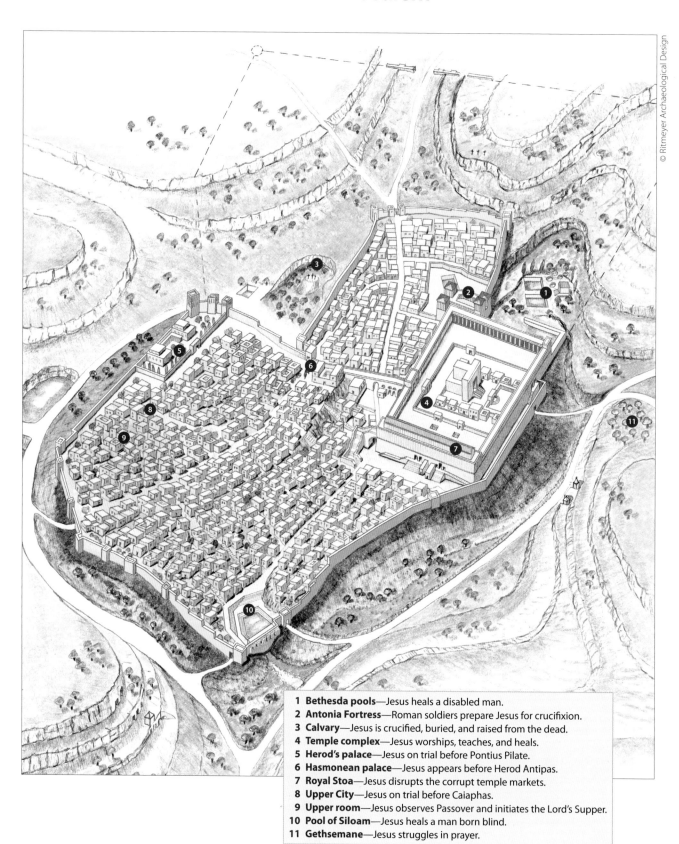

© Ritmeyer Archaeological Design

1 **Bethesda pools**—Jesus heals a disabled man.
2 **Antonia Fortress**—Roman soldiers prepare Jesus for crucifixion.
3 **Calvary**—Jesus is crucified, buried, and raised from the dead.
4 **Temple complex**—Jesus worships, teaches, and heals.
5 **Herod's palace**—Jesus on trial before Pontius Pilate.
6 **Hasmonean palace**—Jesus appears before Herod Antipas.
7 **Royal Stoa**—Jesus disrupts the corrupt temple markets.
8 **Upper City**—Jesus on trial before Caiaphas.
9 **Upper room**—Jesus observes Passover and initiates the Lord's Supper.
10 **Pool of Siloam**—Jesus heals a man born blind.
11 **Gethsemane**—Jesus struggles in prayer.

Caesarea Maritima Palace and Harbor

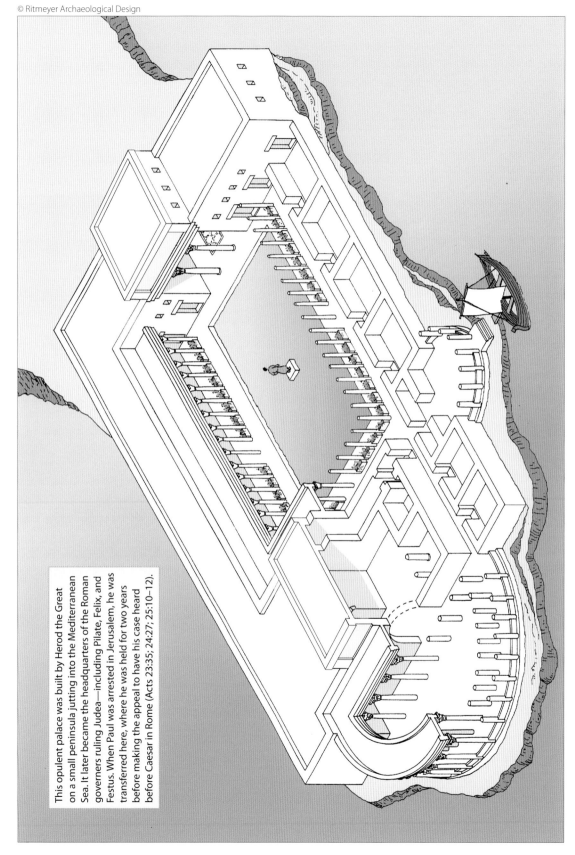

This opulent palace was built by Herod the Great on a small peninsula jutting into the Mediterranean Sea. It later became the headquarters of the Roman governers ruling Judea—including Pilate, Felix, and Festus. When Paul was arrested in Jerusalem, he was transferred here, where he was held for two years before making the appeal to have his case heard before Caesar in Rome (Acts 23:35; 24:27; 25:10–12).

The Baker Book of Bible Charts, Maps, and Time Lines
© 2016 Baker Publishing Group. **Reproduction of this page is prohibited.**

Temple of Artemis at Ephesus

© meunierd / Shutterstock.com

Paul spent many months preaching the gospel in Ephesus. Among the challenges he faced was that posed by the worship of Artemis (Acts 19) and the visual impact of her temple. It is listed among the seven wonders of the ancient world. The temple was designed to impress by both its size (377 feet by 180 feet) and design (127 columns, each 62 feet tall). This photo depicts a replica of the temple.

Index to Maps

The Baker Book of Bible Charts, Maps, and Time Lines

Bring the Bible to life with these
full-color resources

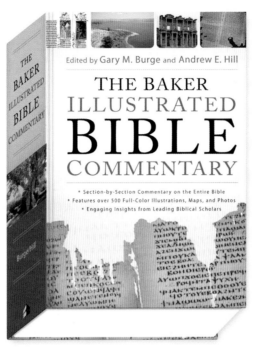

Edited by Gary M. Burge and Andrew E. Hill

THE BAKER
ILLUSTRATED
BIBLE
COMMENTARY

• Section-by-Section Commentary on the Entire Bible
• Features over 500 Full-Color Illustrations, Maps, and Photos
• Engaging Insights from Leading Biblical Scholars

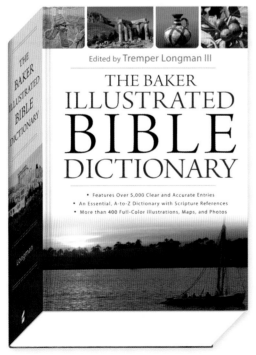

Edited by Tremper Longman III

THE BAKER
ILLUSTRATED
BIBLE
DICTIONARY

• Features Over 5,000 Clear and Accurate Entries
• An Essential, A-to-Z Dictionary with Scripture References
• More than 400 Full-Color Illustrations, Maps, and Photos

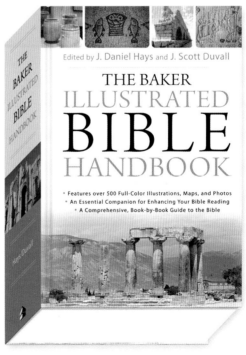

Edited by J. Daniel Hays and J. Scott Duvall

THE BAKER
ILLUSTRATED
BIBLE
HANDBOOK

• Features over 500 Full-Color Illustrations, Maps, and Photos
• An Essential Companion for Enhancing Your Bible Reading
• A Comprehensive, Book-by-Book Guide to the Bible

Discover what life was like
in Bible times

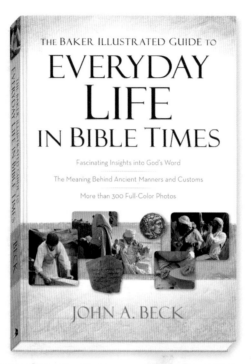
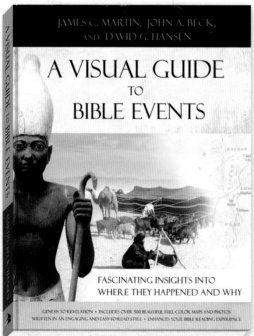
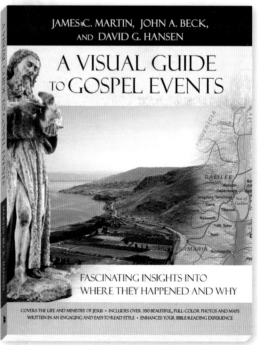